George G. Djolov

The Economics
of Competition
The Race to Monopoly

More pre-publication
REVIEWS, COMMENTARIES, EVALUATIONS . . .

"The theory and policy of competition has always been one of the core topics in economics, and thus it obviously has a long and rich history. No wonder, then, that it is taken for granted that it is perfectly known what economic giants such as Cournot, Bertrand, or Von Stackelberg have contributed to the theory of competition with their seminal works. However, in this book, George Djolov convincingly shows how the prevailing textbook orthodoxy has moved away from exact interpretation of what the great thinkers had actually said, and how they have been misinterpreted, occasionally in some important aspects. Carefully reading and analyzing the original path-breaking works from the past and combining their proper meaning with recent developments, Djolov opens a new perspective at the very nature of competition as we are currently facing it in the global, knowledge-based economy. Djolov claims that, in fact, disequilibrium prevails and price is not determined by marginal cost in this competition, in which the bottom line is freedom of entry, a different concept from standard notions or barriers to entry.

This book is more than a courageous challenge to the mainstream economic routine, it actually represents an important advance in the analysis and understanding of competition. It has the potential to make many popular textbooks obsolete and to become a standard reference in the field. Written in a clear and accessible style, this book simply must be read by everyone—students, scholars, and businessmen alike."

Dr. Bojan Pretnar
*Professor ordinarius,
Ljubljana University;
Deputy Director for Policy Development,
Office for Strategic Planning
and Policy Development,
World Intellectual Property
Organization (WIPO),
Geneva, Switzerland*

Best Business Books®
An Imprint of The Haworth Press, Inc.
New York • London • Oxford

The Economics of Competition

The Race to Monopoly

BEST BUSINESS BOOKS®
Robert E. Stevens, PhD
David L. Loudon, PhD
Editors in Chief

Doing Business in Mexico: A Practical Guide by Gus Gordon and Thurmon Williams

Employee Assistance Programs in Mananged Care by Norman Winegar

Marketing Your Business: A Guide to Developing a Strategic Marketing Plan by Ronald A. Nykiel

Customer Advisory Boards: A Strategic Tool for Customer Relationship Building by Tony Carter

Fundamentals of Business Marketing Research by David A. Reid and Richard E. Plank

Marketing Management: Text and Cases by David L. Loudon, Robert E. Stevens, and Bruce Wrenn

Selling in the New World of Business by Bob Kimball and Jerold "Buck" Hall

Many Thin Companies: The Change in Customer Dealings and Managers Since September 11, 2001 by Tony Carter

The Book on Management by Bob Kimball

The Concise Encyclopedia of Advertising by Kenneth E. Clow and Donald Baack

Application Service Providers in Business by Luisa Focacci, Robert J. Mockler, and Marc E. Gartenfeld

The Concise Handbook of Management: A Practitioner's Approach by Jonathan T. Scott

The Marketing Research Guide, Second Edition by Robert E. Stevens, Bruce Wrenn, Philip K. Sherwood, and Morris E. Ruddick

Marketing Planning Guide, Third Edition by Robert E. Stevens, David L. Loudon, Bruce Wrenn, and Phylis Mansfield

Concise Encyclopedia of Church and Religious Organization Marketing by Robert E. Stevens, David L. Loudon, Bruce Wrenn, and Henry Cole

Market Opportunity Analysis: Text and Cases by Robert E. Stevens, Philip K. Sherwood, J. Paul Dunn, and David L. Loudon

The Economics of Competition: The Race to Monopoly by George G. Djolov

Concise Encyclopedia of Real Estate Business Terms by Bill Roark and Ryan Roark

Marketing Research: Text and Cases, Second Edition by Bruce Wrenn, Robert Stevens, and David Loudon

Concise Encyclopedia of Investing by Darren W. Oglesby

The Economics
of Competition
The Race to Monopoly

George G. Djolov

Best Business Books®
An Imprint of The Haworth Press, Inc.
New York • London • Oxford

For more information on this book or to order, visit
http://www.haworthpress.com/store/product.asp?sku=5505

or call 1-800-HAWORTH (800-429-6784) in the United States and Canada
or (607) 722-5857 outside the United States and Canada

or contact orders@HaworthPress.com

Published by

Best Business Books®, an imprint of The Haworth Press, Inc., 10 Alice Street, Binghamton, NY 13904-1580.

PUBLISHER'S NOTE
The development, preparation, and publication of this work has been undertaken with great care. However, the Publisher, employees, editors, and agents of The Haworth Press are not responsible for any errors contained herein or for consequences that may ensue from use of materials or information contained in this work. The Haworth Press is committed to the dissemination of ideas and information according to the highest standards of intellectual freedom and the free exchange of ideas. Statements made and opinions expressed in this publication do not necessarily reflect the views of the Publisher, Directors, management, or staff of The Haworth Press, Inc., or an endorsement by them.

Cover design by Marylouise E. Doyle.

Library of Congress Cataloging-in-Publication Data

Djolov, George.
    The economics of competition : the race to monopoly / George G. Djolov.
        p. cm.
    Includes bibliographical references and index.
    ISBN-13: 978-0-7890-2788-7 (hard : alk. paper)
    ISBN-10: 0-7890-2788-7 (hard : alk. paper)
    ISBN-13: 978-0-7890-2789-4 (soft : alk. paper)
    ISBN-10: 0-7890-2789-5 (soft : alk. paper)
    1. Competition. 2. Monopolies. 3. Competition—Mathematical models. 4. Industrial policy.
5. Pharmaceutical industry—South Africa—Case studies. I. Title.

    HD41.D56 2006
    338.6′048—dc22   2005024029

To Hilary, with love.

ABOUT THE AUTHOR

George G. Djolov, MCom, is the Executive Chief Economist of the federation of South Africa's chambers of commerce and industry, CHAMSA in Johannesburg, South Africa. He was formerly the Chief Economist of the Pharmaceutical Manufacturers' Association of South Africa, the body representing local and multinational ethical drug companies in South Africa. Mr. Djolov has published in several journals, including the *Journal of World Intellectual Property, Economic Affairs, Estudios de Economia,* the *South African Journal of Economic and Management Sciences,* and the *South African Medical Journal.* He is a member of the Eastern Economic Association and the Economic Society of South Africa. His areas of interest include the economics of competition, monopoly power, international trade, political economy, public policy, and regulation.

CONTENTS

Foreword

George Djolov has written a unique text; because of this characteristic the book merits a wide readership. Djolov is dissatisfied with the conventional paradigm from which much of modern industrial organization springs. Nagging doubts about the validity of the structure: conduct: performance model of industrial economics are not, of course, new. However, such reservations have too often been regarded as the thoughts of the maverick. For example, Schumpeter's chapters on the monopoly problem in *Capitalism, Socialism, and Democracy* made a disappointingly small impact on professional thinking. Although the book itself was widely acclaimed, this was not for its understanding of innovative competition and its linkages with so-called monopoly, but rather for its gloomy predictions about the future of the market economy.

Yet unless one understands that innovation and "monopoly" are intertwined, then antimonopoly regulation could stifle innovation, and Schumpeter's pessimistic forecasts could become self-fulfilling.

Djolov's intention is that we avoid this pitfall. As an economist with a strong background in industry he explains the weaknesses of the perfect competition model as a policy guide. Competition is not the "end state" of the mathematical theorist, it is a process, which to be fully understood requires a renaissance of Schumpeter.

Djolov uses some little-publicized comparative statics theory to amplify this point and then, for emphasis, he turns to an empirical case study of the pharmaceutical industry in South Africa.

Few industries are more dependent on innovation (or its lack) for the success (or failure) of existing or new-entrant firms. Few industries are subject to so many regulations—whether they be antitrust laws, safety and efficacy requirements, price controls, restrictions on consumer choice, or complex intellectual property rules. In few countries have these regulations been more stringently or overtly imposed on the industry than in South Africa. Djolov aims to convince us that the industry is indeed "competitive" in the true sense. He believes

doi:10.1300/5505_a

market failures are rare and "government failures" are much more common and more damaging. Regulators have incentives to be seen "doing something." The holding down of prices, the withholding of products from the market, and the weakening of patent protection are examples. What is not seen (as a consequence of such actions) is the research activity that is foregone as a result of artificially depressed prices and profits. What is also not visible, at least at first, is the withdrawal of investment. In addition, although new products withheld from the market on grounds of safety may save one life, what is not known are the positive benefits which are thereby lost to consumers who might not have been at risk from side-effect dangers but who are deprived of the opportunity to use improved therapies.

In short, failure to properly understand competition may provide us with regulations that lower today's expenditures on living, but do so at the expense of tomorrow's better life.

Professor W. Duncan Reekie
University of the Witwatersrand
Johannesburg, South Africa

Preface

The need for a book such as this seems, to me, to be twofold. First, the pedagogical need for a coherent description of the competitive process, one that plugs in time and knowledge as integral parts of rivalry in the marketplace. Such a description should be scrupulously scientific, but it should also be adapted to the understanding, interests, and experience of people outside of the profession of economics.

The text offered here attempts to do just this, revealing to the reader all those complex relationships that make up the ordered whole of competition in economics, while at the same time kindling an interest in pursuing the topic in greater depth and detail.

The second need arises from the general condition of our age, and specifically the popular understanding in economics of competition and its role in economic activity. To my mind, there is an urgent need to present to readers within the profession, as well as students and those in affiliated and applied fields—such as policymakers and business people—a sort of accounting of economic theories of competition; to examine and weigh with care the intellectual heritage that has come down to us and to bring it to bear upon its foundations.

It is not uncommon to find economists concerned with competition taking refuge in increasingly complex models that emphasize the end state of competitive equilibrium, namely "perfect competition"—while interest in the disequilibrium adjustments that lead up to such a state wanes.

Models that ought to inform us of their own descriptive merit on competition do not, unless explicable in terms of perfect competition. Such is the faith placed in the Cournot, Bertrand, and Stackelberg models of oligopolistic or monopolistic competition. Yet the way they are used and understood today bears little relation to the original models developed by our economic forefathers. The book attempts to provide insight into this "layering process," by means of which such

doi:10.1300/5505_b

questionable orthodoxy is established, by drawing attention to their explication in the original texts.

The emphasis on the equilibrium state of "perfect competition" leads inevitably to a search for "imperfections" and "failures" in markets. It is a short step from here to proposals for government action to correct and even preempt such failures. Indeed, since all real-world markets appear imperfect by the perfectly competitive yardstick, the scope for government intervention seems virtually unlimited. It would be unstoppable were it not for mounting criticisms of the market-failure approach to policymaking. Some have arisen from within the economics mainstream—for instance, the Lipsey-Lancaster second-best critique of piecemeal tinkering with markets.

Correction of presumed market failure by government ways and means is itself grounded in the utopian idea that the cost of government intervention is so insignificant as to warrant no concern. However, the Buchanan-Tullock public choice legion of economics and the Stigler-Peltzman-Becker theories of regulation and political influence have shattered this notion. As Niskanen's *Bureaucracy and Representative Government* reminds us, people in the state sector are neither omniscient nor altruistic but just like other people. Consequently, government fails too, and it cannot be reasonably assumed that state action to remedy market failures will necessarily be beneficial.

The Coase-Alchian-Demsetz rekindling of the importance of ownership points to the competitive solution being found in the property rights of individuals, namely in their exclusive right to use their resources as they see fit. That dominion over what is theirs leads property owners to take full account of all the benefits and costs of employing those resources in a particular manner. In short, efficient outcomes stem from the legislatively uninterrupted creation and flow of entitlements as determined by the market relations buyers and sellers give rise to. This is where competition comes in.

Competition is not a state but a process, taking place over time. The long-run equilibrium of perfect competition, embodied in the famous formula that price equals marginal cost, is not an appropriate policy tool to which all markets should be forced to succumb. Such a result does not represent competition at all but an end state in which competition has been exhausted. Under "perfect" competition, the market is at rest—frozen at a point in time.

The actual nature of competition is in direct contrast to this—the essence of competition in practice is dynamic *disequilibrium,* characterized by continuous change. Rivalry in the marketplace involves searching for, discovering, and exploiting profit opportunities that have not previously been secured. In a nutshell, discovery is at the center of the competitive process. As Ludwig Lachmann (1959, pp. 67-73) wrote in an article in *Metroeconomica:*

> Time and Knowledge belong together. The creative acts of the mind need not be reflected in changing preferences, but they cannot but be reflected in acts grasping experience and constituting objects of knowledge and plans of action. All such acts bear the stamp of the individuality of the actor. . . . Economic change is linked to change in knowledge, and future knowledge cannot be gained before its time. Knowledge is generated by the spontaneous acts of the mind. . . . As soon as we permit time to elapse we must permit knowledge to change, and knowledge cannot be regarded as a function of anything else.

So knowledge is not perfect. Our present knowledge, to be revised later as experience accrues, is not only the basis of any plan of action we may contemplate but also a source of superior future knowledge. The corollary of this is that knowledge is naturally dispersed and is uncovered only by those in competition to find better ways of satisfying consumers.

In reality, as Schumpeter reminds us in *Capitalism, Socialism, and Democracy,* firms and/or entrepreneurs—the originators of economic progress—compete in ways that enable them to erect downward-sloping demand curves for their products, i.e., firms create monopoly power. Firms or entrepreneurs achieve this by making themselves the only producer or supplier of their product(s). This encompasses elements of branding, quality, and in general amounts to producing something that is downright unique and no rival has or can match. All of these invite in their precincts both promotional and research and development activities, and they jointly form part of the rivalry arsenal of competitors that produces product differentiation between them. It is also what gives them the impetus to vie on the premise of price if any of them are to encourage consumer demand to their advantage.

However, for the economist stuck in the modalities of perfect competition or the regulator consumed with using it under the besiege of Hayek's fatal conceit, product differentiation, absolute cost advantages, and economies of scale can and do turn into barriers to entry and impediments to market contestability.

In a free market, as is to be expected from what the name denotes in its direct meaning, freedom of entry cannot be foreclosed. Barriers to competition—observed in society as being denied the experience of a beneficial trading outcome—are thus a feature of government *diktat,* for the competitive process does not produce enduring monopolies.

What theory tells us in that regard is reflected in practice. To highlight this, together with the practical examples included in the book, attention is also paid to the statutory experience of competition (antitrust) laws in the United States, the European Union, the Organisation for Economic Co-operation and Development (OECD) countries, and South Africa, in view of the similarity with which the legislation of these very different countries treats monopoly and market power.

The overwhelming conclusion that comes to the fore from this investigation is that, despite the best intentions of regulators—giving them the benefit of the doubt—antitrust laws become obstacles to market processes rather than defenses against the emergence of monopoly. They have more to do with impeding than aiding the competitive process, cultivating fertile ground for Krueger's syndrome, i.e. rent-seeking. Indeed, it is not uncommon to find competition laws imposing regulations on some businesses that blatantly enhance or protect the profits of others.

One of the remedies for the ailing health of the competition statutes might be to slough off contemporary orthodox competition and monopoly theory, namely the perfect competition model, as an informative standard to policymaking, but the evidence offered by texts such as Dominick Armentano's *Antitrust and Monopoly* and Robert Bork's *The Antitrust Paradox* is stronger for their repeal.

Monopoly unsupported by government regulation and government barriers to entry is not an impediment to competition—indeed, the competitive process itself literally takes care of that, not necessarily immediately but certainly and spontaneously!

The book, quite unlike experimental economics, demonstrates this dictum by opting for a live "laboratory," namely the marketplace—specifically the pharmaceutical market in South Africa. In their joint

2002 report *WTO Agreements and Public Health,* the Geneva-based World Trade Organization (WTO) and World Health Organization (WHO) inform us that the market has attracted much global attention following a four-year court case between thirty-nine of the largest multinational pharmaceutical companies and the South African government on the issue of access to drugs. In spite of the international attention received, the market has hitherto not been the subject of formally extensive or exclusive coverage, and *The Race to Monopoly* seeks to ameliorate this by documenting it properly—in the process demonstrating the aforementioned proposition that monopoly is self-limiting within the context of unrestricted competition.

A number of factors make the South African pharmaceutical industry an ideal subject for this purpose. First, the market has the distinctive feature—along with only a few others in the world—of being relatively free in the economic sense of the word, i.e., pricing freedom exists, also covering new product introductions. From a public policy perspective—with the notable exception of the United States—it appears the international norm leans in the opposite direction. Reflecting on the price-control policies of pharmaceuticals in fifty-six countries, the United Nations Industrial Development Organization articulated in its 1992 report *The World's Pharmaceutical Industries* that "almost all governments regulate product prices, though a few choose to limit profits or to influence prices through more indirect means" (p. 141).

Second, the dualistic nature of the market—divided into a private and public sector—serving different income groups, affords the opportunity to observe how pricing freedom allows manufacturers to instinctively price discriminate in markets with differing price sensitivities, pricing at a lower level in the more price-sensitive state sector—to the benefit of all. The sector of the market that is able to pay has access to the latest innovative treatments, while the poor gain access to products they would not otherwise be able to afford. Producers reap greater profits, affording the means and incentive to engage in further research and development in order to develop tomorrow's products more quickly. A portion of these additional profits comes from the more affluent members of society, who are most able to purchase innovations (as indicated by their willingness to pay) and thereby subsidize the lower price for the less-well-off members.

Third, the South African market satisfies the prerequisite for innovation. Innovative activity is a sine qua non in the pharmaceutical industry. In 1981 the OECD observed in its report *Multinational Enterprises, Governments and Technology* that South Africa, along with the United Kingdom and Scandinavian countries "are the locations of choice" for the clinical research activities of the multinational pharmaceutical industry.

Taking cognizance of the breadth and depth of the book, it is intended to serve as principle or supporting text for anyone wishing to acquire or broaden their knowledge and understanding of the economics of competition. In that sense its immediate audience comprises scholars and practitioners of competition (antitrust) law, microeconomics, industrial economics, industrial organization, managerial economics, and marketing strategy. That said, works such as Paul Krugman's *Industrial Organisation and International Trade* (in Schmalensee and Willig [1989] and Maurice Obstfeld and Kenneth Rogoff's Exchange Rate Dynamics Redux [1995]) show that monopolistic/oligopolistic competition is increasingly making inroads in international economics.

Thus, this text may also be useful for scholars and practitioners pursuing this approach to the traditional domain of macroeconomics. Finally, the book should strike a chord with both beginners and experts in public health wishing to acquaint themselves with the South African pharmaceutical industry, given its relevance to the international arena.

However, the scope is broader. The methods and techniques of economic inquiry into competition carried out here are generalizable, offering the means to extrapolate them to pharmaceutical markets elsewhere. This also holds for any market where competition, innovation, monopoly, rivalry, and market power are relevant features.

Acknowledgments

This book was chiefly written during a research and lecturing tenure from 2000 to 2003 at the University of the Witwatersrand, Johannesburg, South Africa.

Most of all, I would like to thank my long-time counselor and intellectual mentor Professor W. Duncan Reekie for his suggestion of the topic, guidance, support, time, and stimulating discussions. His revisions of the early drafts of the script were invaluable.

Thank you also to my former colleagues and instructors at the University of the Witwatersrand, Mr. Henry Kenney and Dr. Daniel Leach, for their constructive input during the preparation of this work.

I am grateful to Mr. Jack Bailey, the former chief executive officer of Eli Lilly South Africa, and Mr. Jimmy Scheepers, the former vice president of IMS Health Southern Africa, for their assistance in providing the IMS Health data, without which the empirical work carried out here would not have been possible.

Thank you also to my former colleagues at the Pharmaceutical Manufacturers' Association (PMA)—former Chief Executive Officer Mrs. Mirryéna Deeb, for her ongoing encouragement, and Mrs. Maureen Kirkman, for sharing her knowledge on industrial research and development and mergers and acquisitions.

Last, but definitely not least, I thank my wife Hilary, whose many years of editorial experience have had to persevere over my own reluctance to submit to revision.

doi:10.1300/5505_c

Now, legal plunder can be committed in an infinite number of ways. Thus we have an infinite number of plans for organising it: tariffs, protection, benefits, subsidies, encouragements, progressive taxation, public schools, guaranteed jobs, guaranteed profits, minimum wages, a right to relief, a right to the tools of labour, free credit, and so on, and so on. All these plans as a whole—with their common aim of legal plunder—constitute socialism. . . . Legal plunder has two roots: One of them . . . is in human greed; the other is in false philanthropy. At this point I think that I should explain exactly what I mean by the word plunder. I do not, as is often done, use the word in any vague, uncertain, approximate or metaphorical sense. I use it in its scientific acceptance—as expressing the idea opposite to that of property (wages, land, money, or whatever). When a portion of wealth is transferred from the person who owns it—without his consent and without compensation, and whether by force or by fraud—to anyone who does not own it, then I say that property is violated; that an act of plunder is committed. I say that this act is exactly what the law is supposed to suppress, always and everywhere. When the law itself commits this act that it is supposed to suppress, I say that plunder is still committed, and I add that from the point of view of society and welfare, this aggression against rights is even worse. In this case of legal plunder, however, the person who receives the benefits is not responsible for the act of plundering. The responsibility for this legal plunder rests with the law, the legislator, and society itself.

Claude Frederic Bastiat
The Law, 1850

Chapter 1

Introduction

The work presented here examines and provides a framework for understanding the competitive process. The market structures that the competitive process generates are covered under the standard and well-known theories of perfect competition, oligopoly, and monopoly.

It should be noted that most of the time these market structures tend to be considered in isolation from one another. The result often is that markets or industries tend to be classified as perfectly competitive, oligopolistic, or monopolistic. This sort of classification, however, may be void of meaning if time is not taken into consideration, as will be shown.

The aim of this book is to illustrate that these market structures do not exist as mutually exclusive of one another or in isolation. Integrally, they form part of the competitive process, and which market structure prevails at any point in time depends on the stage of rivalry to which the market or industry has progressed.

In short, meaningful examination of the competitive process involves recasting existing theories of perfect competition, oligopoly, and monopoly into a single, comprehensive framework that highlights the dynamic nature of markets and how they change over time.

Because the literature does not define competition or the competitive process, the definition provided in this book is an attempt in that direction. The competitive process may be defined as the mechanism that over time moves markets through different market structures, retaining the efficient firms in an industry, while at the same time driving down market prices. The process is triggered by the profit motive, or the incentive for firms to make above-average profits or rates of return.[1]

doi:10.1300/5505_01

Two mechanisms underpin the working of the competitive process—the transfer mechanism and the innovation mechanism (Downie, 1958, pp. 63-96). The transfer mechanism involves the shift of market share from the firm whose total average cost is above the industry average to the firm whose total average cost is below the industry average.[2] Compared to the former, the latter will have higher profits and will therefore invest more in future production on things such as new equipment and research and development (R&D), with the aim of developing more efficient methods (thereby driving down cost) and lucrative new products.

The innovation mechanism involves the discovery of a new product or technology that enables the firm that uncovered it to amass greater market share compared to other firms in the industry. High total average cost relative to the industry average is one incentive for a firm to search for techniques that will reduce its costs and which can put firms on par or allow one firm to dominate others. Technological progress consists of creating cost differences, or "dispersion," and it is the tendency of cost differences to be eliminated over time that generates progress (Downie 1958, p. 95).

Thus, economic efficiency or superiority by some firms over others refers to the ability of some firms to exercise considerable total (average) cost advantages relative to others in the short and long run, the areas relating to capacity (or production), and the servicing of customers (old or new). Note that the average cost structure of a firm (whether in the short or in the long run) determines whether a firm is able to produce or service its customers altogether. However, the marginal cost structure of a firm (whether in the short or in the long run) determines how much a firm can produce or up to what point a firm is able to serve its customers.

The competitive process is usually considered in terms of either perfect or imperfect competition. This ignores the fact that the process entails both during the course of evolution of a market or an industry. Simply put, the time factor in the competitive process means that markets go through different stages or cycles of competition, one of which, in the long run, is perfect competition.

Perfect competition depicts markets that are characterized by the following conditions:

1. product homogeneity, meaning that the product supplied by different firms is the same;
2. perfect information, meaning that firms and consumers alike know the prices set by all firms;
3. equal access, meaning that all firms have access to the same production technologies;
4. price taking, meaning that firms and consumers take the price as given; and
5. free entry and exit, meaning that any firm may enter or exit the market as it wishes.

Markets which fulfill these conditions experience normal, i.e., average, rates of return where firms have profit rates or rates of return consistent with the average for the industry and matching market shares. Markets that do not fulfill these conditions are said to be imperfect in terms of competition. Markets falling in this category involve cases of monopoly (i.e., a single firm) or oligopoly (i.e., few firms). Some economists and antitrust authorities regard markets determined as "imperfect" as also being anticompetitive, because they make above-average or supernormal profits. As will be shown, this view may be unwarranted, theoretically unsustainable, and practically flawed.

In the long run firms can achieve market power in only two ways:[3]

1. government protection from competition, e.g., legalized monopolies, licensed entries, import duties, quotas, and so on
2. a long-lasting advantage enjoyed by the incumbent firm(s) over potential entrants, e.g., sole ownership of some necessary input or factor of production, access to superior techniques of production, established products, economies of scale[4] that render new entry uneconomic, and so on.

Thus, absent (1), market power is not permanent and firms must vie to achieve and retain it. Accordingly, only two alternative ways exist by which above-average rates of return (synonymous with market power) may be attained. These relate to

1. the occurrence of unexpected events—either generated by chance or (usually) stemming from the unexpected actions of other

firms—which magnify expected profits or convert them into losses; and

2. differences between firms in the ability to create or notice profitable opportunities that are, in principle, available to anyone. For example, the opportunity to develop a drug that considerably minimized the need for surgery in ulcer patients was open to any firm in the pharmaceutical industry, yet only GlaxoSmithKline with Zantac did so first.

Thus, assuming government protection is absent, the association of above-average rates of return and market power (in the short run) would chiefly reflect a market environment in which some firms, economically speaking, are manifestly stronger relative to others. This is consistent with what one may expect the competitive process to produce, for without some such process it is impossible to regard firm rivalry (or the vying for market share) as a means of selecting the fit from the unfit. As a consequence of this selection, market prices should decline over time, leading to the remaining firms having normal (or average) profit rates in the long run. In short, this is a reflection of the competitive process doing its work; in line with the tendency of above-average profits to dissipate over time is the tendency of market prices to decline over time.

For now it is important to remember that, due to the time factor, the competitive process guarantees that diverse market structures, i.e., markets, go through different stages, the final one being perfect competition, in which firms earn normal profits or rates of return. The corollary of this is that the competitive process ensures that there is "competition beyond perfect competition." The purpose of the work presented in the following chapters is to demonstrate this.

The book is structured as follows. Chapters 1 and 2 provide an introduction to the main thesis and an overview of competition and monopoly power.

Chapter 3 addresses the theory and meaning of perfect competition. It examines whether the theory is correctly understood in the context of new product development, showing that one must distinguish between the short run and the long run in judging the competitiveness of markets and proposing that the theory must be understood in the context of its roots.

Chapters 4 and 5 deal, respectively, with departures from perfect competition and rivalry under the competitive process.

As an extension of the discussion on perfect competition, Chapter 6 examines barriers to entry, economies of scale, product differentiation, and absolute cost advantages. These are usually regarded as instruments that foreclose rivalry among firms with the ability to disrupt markets from being perfectly competitive. The aim of this chapter is to show that this interpretation may be incorrect and that the orthodox understanding of what we classify as barriers to entry may also need to change.

Chapters 7 and 8, respectively, examine barriers to competition and competition with reference to market power, drawing attention to what the South African antitrust authority practically deems, as epitomized by its Report 73, to constitute market power. It is noted that this is consistent with what U.S. antitrust law considers to be market power and that South African competition law is identical to that of the European Union, which, with the recently enacted Articles 81 and 82 by the 1997 Treaty of Amsterdam, has been brought closer in line with American antitrust law.

Chapter 8 also looks at key aspects of market power, among them horizontal mergers and acquisitions, which the South African Competition Act deems to be outright or per se undesirable and anticompetitive. In addition, it examines price discrimination in the light of innovation and new product development. It is commonly assumed that price discrimination results in a reduction in the level of output, compared with the perfectly competitive output level. However, the actual effect of price discrimination may be either to leave output unchanged from the perfectly competitive point or to increase output and the servicing of otherwise underserviced or nonserviced markets compared to where price discrimination cannot take place. As was mentioned previously, new product development involves common costs, and price discrimination may be considered as an appropriate mechanism to recover these costs. Chapter 8 examines why this is so and why a competition policy that prohibits price discrimination per se and calls for uniform pricing may harm rather than improve consumer welfare.

Chapter 9 examines the underlying economic rationale for competition policy as exemplified by the structure-conduct-performance paradigm, which relies on the theory of perfect competition. In essence, the paradigm stipulates a positive relationship between market size and profitability (under market conditions in which incumbent firms have little or no exposure to entry, share identical cost structures, and face the same demand). Again, it is proposed that mere size does not constitute monopoly or market power. As will be shown, it is more plausible to interpret size as the consequence rather than the cause of profits. The credibility of the direction of causation the paradigm posits, namely structure leads to conduct, which in turn leads to performance, is also examined.

Chapter 10 discusses well-known and new measures of market concentration. These measures reflect how market shares are disbursed among firms at a point in time. The concentration ratio is a commonly used concentration measure and is the sum of the market shares of the largest firms in an industry based on sales, output, or assets. Concentration can be defined as the degree of disproportionate allocation of market share between firms. Horizontal mergers and acquisitions—which are commonly thought to increase market size—are discussed as an extension to the structure-conduct-performance paradigm.

Chapters 11, 12, and 13 put the theoretical expositions of the earlier chapters to the test by applying them to the South African pharmaceutical industry. If the industry complies with the theoretical expositions, then it should behave in accordance with the competitive process, and if so it may be regarded as contestable or competitive at the product and firm level.

Chapter 11 describes the South African pharmaceutical industry, while Chapter 12 comprises a macroindustry study of the industry's market (or monopoly) power. The aim here is to ascertain if such power exists, and if it does, whether it works to the detriment of all consumers of medicines or not. In short, the chapter examines whether on the aggregate the industry is close, and how close it is, to the perfectly competitive point.

Chapter 13 addresses the impact of mergers and acquisitions in the private and public markets, discussing the findings from an empirical perspective as to the effect these transactions have had on the level of concentration in the pharmaceutical industry.

Since the pharmaceutical industry is an aggregation of therapeutic markets within which firms compete in Chapter 14, a microindustry study is also conducted, assessing the level of competitiveness across therapeutic markets in both the private and public sectors. If the macroindustry study finds the industry approaches perfect competition, one would expect the microindustry study to reflect the same picture. Here it is imperative to understand that the microindustry study is undertaken to offset the possibility that the macroindustry study would mask the degree of competitiveness prevailing in the individual markets. This study examines the disbursement of the market shares of firms and their products, as well as their respective changes in ranking over time.

Chapter 15 draws a conclusion to both the theoretical expositions and the empirical findings presented, summarizing the preceding chapters and interrogating the initial hypothesis.

Chapter 2

Competition and Monopoly Power

All markets, in any industry, commence their existence with the introduction by a firm of a product, good, or service to meet previously unfulfilled demand. The introduction of new products involves expenditures (by the firms who make them) that produce common benefits for each market where the products are sold. For example, the costs that a pharmaceutical manufacturer faces to develop a new drug are one and the same, irrespective of whether the drug is sold in one country or another. Costs that cannot be allocated to any single or particular market are referred to as common costs. Common costs are fixed costs, and the amount of such costs depends on the technical complexities and risks involved in introducing a new product to the market. The more complex the new product is to develop and the higher the risk of failure (as in the instances involving product variety rather than homogeneous products) the greater the magnitude of the common costs (and vice versa). Creating product variety with long-lasting distinctiveness brings about large common costs. In such instances, if such expenditures are not incurred by the firm, the product may never be introduced to the market.

If the product is introduced and the firm has incurred these expenditures, then it seeks to recoup the common costs. Here the aim is to ensure that each market makes a contribution, according to its willingness to pay, to covering the common costs so that the firm at least breaks even, given that it has to incur such costs each time it begins the next round of new product development. Economics suggests that this should be done by means of price discrimination.

It has long been recognized (Robinson, 1934, p. 206) that price discrimination results in greater total output and surplus than uniform pricing and that price discrimination can work in favor of poorer (in income terms) markets, which may otherwise not be serviced under a

doi:10.1300/5505_02

regimen of uniform pricing. Recently Schmalensee (1981) and Varian (1985) have supported Robinson's work. Whereas the South African Competition Board was in congruence with this view of price discrimination, as exemplified in its Report 4 (1981), it did not support it in its Report 34 (1993). The new Competition Act Number 89 prohibits price discrimination on the grounds that it is outright anti-competitive behavior. Strong theoretical and practical grounds question whether such a view is warranted or desirable.

This work examines the competitive process in light of an industry that is, by its very nature, innovative, in which new product development is integral to firms in vying for market share. The pharmaceutical industry has been shown by Reekie (1978, 1981, 1995, 1996), Scott and Reekie (1985), Lu and Comanor (1998), and Cocks (1975) to comply with this definition.

In the industry there is rivalry for market share among highly innovative (patented) products which enable the firms that produce them to earn above-average rates of profit relative to the producers of homogenous products. In addition, these products provide the knowledge for the manufacture of homogenous or "me-too" products (also called generics), so that as time goes by the above-average rates of return decline until firms make no more than the normal rate of profit. In addition there is also rivalry for market share among the imitative products where the minimum efficient scale of a firm whether in the short or in the long run is decisive[1] In short, the pharmaceutical industry may be considered to provide a natural setting for the study of the competitive process in general.

This study specifically focuses on the South African pharmaceutical industry, aiming to establish whether the industry can indeed be regarded as competitive at a time when the South African Competition Board and government are skeptical of this. The South African Competition Board believes that the industry possesses significant monopoly power and that this impedes price competition between firms (Competition Commission, 2001, pp. 10-11).

The South African government has also come to regard the industry as anticompetitive by alleging that its products are priced in excess of what they ought to be and that its firms make supernormal profits (The Public Protector, 1997, pp. 10-17). So adamant is government in this regard that it has provided in legislation (Act 90 of 1997) for parallel importation (or its variant, reference pricing), generic substitution, and uniform (or single-exit) pricing in order to curtail the prices of medicines in South Africa.

The Competition Commission (2001, p. 11) has provisionally supported Act 90's provisions and has expressed the view that they "should increase competition, by reducing prices and promoting the affordability of health care for all South Africans."

Each of the previously mentioned provisions will be discussed at greater length; however, it is important to remember that the ostensible aim of introducing such measures was to curtail the supposedly high prices of products in the South African pharmaceutical market. Studying the competitive process with reference to the pharmaceutical industry will reveal whether pharmaceutical prices can and should be curtailed.

Given the objective of this chapter to analyze the workings of the competitive process within an innovative industry, the issue of pricing will be examined in the context of new product development.

Close to the competitive process is the creation of market power or monopoly. From our previous exposition of the components making up the competitive process, this can be regarded as depicting imperfect competition. Here it is imperative to remember that this does not mean that such markets are anticompetitive. As discussed previously, only two ways exist to build market power or monopoly in the long run. Of these, only one is consistent with rivalry, where some firms become, economically speaking, manifestly stronger relative to others, resulting in a discrepancy in ranking (or market positions) and differences in market share.

Some economists and antitrust authorities assume that an alternative way to acquire monopoly or market power is to engage in horizontal mergers and acquisitions, which presumably increase the market share of the combined entity. Such mergers and acquisitions are among rivals in the same line of business, so the joint entity should have a greater proportion of a market relative to other firms that have not merged. The joint entity could even end up being a monopoly if the only two firms in an industry merge. Accordingly, horizontal mergers and acquisitions may be undesirable, or anticompetitive, as they may foster an environment that enables firms to charge prices that allow them to make supernormal or above-average profits. Since horizontal mergers and acquisitions are linked to the creation of market power and thereby to the competitive process they are also examined.

However, it must be emphasized that mere size does not constitute monopoly or market power. Larger firms tend to earn higher profits compared with smaller firms, but it is more plausible to interpret size as the consequence rather than the cause of profits.

In examining horizontal mergers and acquisitions the focus is often on whether they should be regarded as anticompetitive, with empirical evidence presented (with reference to the South African pharmaceutical industry) to show whether horizontal mergers and acquisitions do lead to the creation of monopoly or market power. This also examines whether outcomes of mergers and acquisition in the industry are consistent with the view that market power is necessarily anticompetitive—a position adopted by the South African Competition Board in its Report 73 (1999) regarding the proposed acquisition of PharmaCare by Adcock Ingram. Report 73 stated that market power and anticompetitiveness are synonymous, although it was written under the old Competition Act Number 96, which did not deem market power as necessarily anticompetitive unless otherwise demonstrated. However, the report was heavily influenced by the publication—at the time in the form of a bill—of the new Competition Act Number 89, which incorporates the 1950 amendment to Section 7 of the Clayton Act of U.S. antitrust legislation, which readily permits the interpretation of market power as being necessarily anticompetitive.

Williamson (1968) has illustrated that horizontal mergers and acquisitions are likely to be consistent with achieving an improvement in productive efficiency, which may not occur at all if the merger does not take place.[2] In other words, a merger (or acquisition) is likely to enable the firms involved to experience a downward shift in their combined long-run average cost (curve) that would not occur without the merger (or acquisition). Thus, an empirical analysis of mergers and acquisitions in the pharmaceutical industry can determine whether they create market power by way of productive efficiency or market size, i.e., by the summation of market shares between the firms forming the union. If mergers and acquisitions take place in the industry in order to achieve gains in productive efficiency, then this answers the question, under what circumstances does productive efficiency, achieved by a union between firms, result in an increase in the proportion of the market covered by the joint firm? The pharmaceutical industry in South Africa provides an ideal environment in which to pose and seek an answer to such a question, because it operates in two distinct markets, i.e., the private and public (or state) sectors. Note that the former is highly innovative, and firms in this market obtain earnings primarily from new and innovative products, while the latter market is not innovative, with firms obtaining earnings primarily from imitating off-patent products (also called generics) which are sold at lower prices (De Villiers and Scott, 1986). Thus, where rivalry between firms is purely on the basis of price, as where homogeneous or imitative products are involved, then gaining productive efficiency through a merger or acquisition could enable the joint firm to achieve an increase in market share, relative to other firms. However, where rivalry among firms is focused on creating product variety through innovation, new product development, and product differentiation (which calls for advertising and marketing), achieving productive efficiency by a merger or acquisition may not be enough to allow the joint firm to gain a market share advantage.

A rise in market share stemming from the joint firm's improvement in productive efficiency may not materialize if other firms are able to learn—and match—with little or no delay what the improvement in productive efficiency entails. The joint firm may find it difficult to preserve the singularity of its superior production technique due to informal communications between personnel and movement of personnel from firm to firm, resulting in the knowledge of such a technique being diffused fairly rapidly.

In addition, the announcement of a proposed merger or acquisition may disseminate information that enables rivals to imitate the technological innovation motivating the acquisition. Alternatively, the introduction of public-disclosure requirements in competition law can result in extensive dissemination of technological information associated with the merger, thereby enabling other firms to gain and put into practice the knowledge from such information.

Chapter 3

Perfect Competition

The model of perfect competition is based on five central assumptions:

1. Product homogeneity, meaning that the product supplied by different firms is the same;
2. Perfect information, meaning that firms and consumers alike know the prices set by all firms;
3. Equal access, meaning that all firms have access to the same production technologies;
4. Price taking, meaning that firms and consumers take the price as given; and
5. Free entry and exit (i.e., no barriers to entry and exit), meaning that any firm may enter or exit the market as it wishes.

Markets that have characteristics consistent with these assumptions are said to be perfectly competitive. A perfectly competitive situation for a firm is depicted in Figure 3.1.

In a perfectly competitive market there are many firms. Firms sell identical or the same products, in the long run. Each firm's marginal revenue (MR) equals its average revenue (AR), which represents its demand (D). The firm will receive one and the same price (P) for each additional unit sold, such that its MR will equal P. Since the firm prices in order to maximize profits, i.e., where its MR equals its marginal cost (MC), only normal but not supernormal profits are earned, i.e., P just covers the total long-run average cost (AC), which at its minimum equals MC.

The equilibrium, E, under perfect competition is efficient in two senses. First, each firm sets the efficient output level, that is, the output level such that P equals MC. A lower output level would be less

doi:10.1300/5505_03

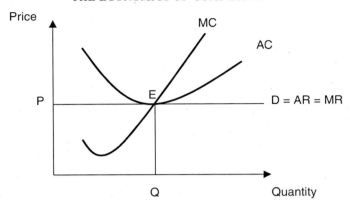

FIGURE 3.1. Perfect competition—long-run case.

efficient, as willingness to pay would be greater than cost; conversely, a higher output level would also be inefficient, for willingness to pay would be lower than cost. Second, the set (or number) of firms active in the long run is efficient; because of free entry, firms produce a long-run output such that price equals the minimum average cost. A higher or lower number of firms would imply a greater level of total cost for the same output level. Note that perfect competition leads to maximum efficiency given the existing or available technology. Thus, efficiency under perfect competition is static efficiency. In addition, what the model describes is the equilibrium that markets eventually reach freely, i.e., without government intervention. This is illustrated by Figure 3.2 (A) and (B), which is divided into two panels, illustrating how markets reach the perfectly competitive equilibrium over time.

We start by supposing that n identical firms sell homogeneous (or identical) products, and that no fixed costs can be recouped in the short run, which is a plausible assumption given that in the short run a firm can make little or no adjustment of its inputs to a change in supply or demand conditions. In the top panel the short-run market supply curve, S, is the horizontal sum of the supply curves of each firm, which is the MC curve above the minimum of the average variable cost (AVC) curve. The horizontal position of the market supply curve reflects that (1) no output is forthcoming if price is below the shutdown

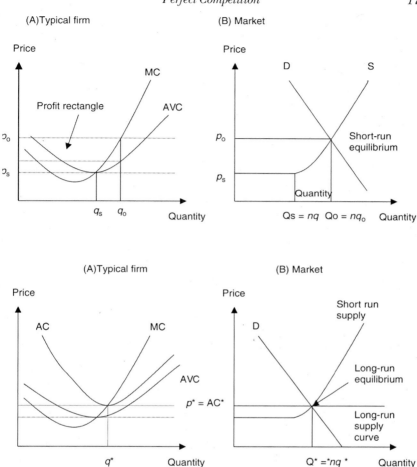

FIGURE 3.2. Transition to perfect competition. *Source:* Adapted from Carlton and Perloff, 2000, pp. 62-63.

point and (2) at price slightly above the shutdown point all firms produce.

The intersection of the demand curve with the short-run market supply curve determines the short-run equilibrium price p_0 and quantity q_0. The amount that firms want to supply at the equilibrium exactly equals the amount that consumers demand at that price. No unsatisfied buyers and no unsatisfied sellers exist. All buyers pay and all sellers receive the same price. In the short run equilibrium in Figure 3.2(A), top panel, a typical firm earns a profit, which provides an incentive for other firms to enter the market. However, such entry cannot occur in the short run, say, because firms cannot build new plants in the short run.

In the long run firms can adjust their levels of capital so that they can enter this market. Short-run profits or losses induce firms to enter or leave the market until price is driven to the minimum long-run average cost, AC^*, in the long run (Figure 3.2[A], bottom panel). In the top panel of Figure 3.2(A), firms are making a positive profit at the short-run equilibrium price p_0, which is determined by the intersection of the market-demand curve and the original short-run market-supply curve. In the long run these profits induce new firms to enter the market.

If the number of firms that can potentially produce at the same cost is very large, the long-run supply curve is horizontal at the minimum of the average cost curve AC^*, as the bottom panel of Figure 3.2(B) shows. The long-run equilibrium is determined by the intersection of the demand curve and the long-run market supply curve.

In the bottom panel of Figure 3.2(B) the market is in a new short-run and long-run equilibrium because the demand curve, D, intersects both the long-run supply curve and the new short-run supply curve corresponding to the equilibrium number of firms n^*. The equilibrium price is $p^*=AC^*$, and equilibrium output is $Q^* = n^* q^*$. In this long-run equilibrium firms make zero profit. Similarly, short-run losses induce firms to leave the market and reduce output until price rises again to yield normal (zero) profits. In long-run equilibrium firms receive economic profits of zero, which is just enough to induce them to remain in the market.

In summary, we could say that perfect competition is synonymous with price equaling marginal cost, i.e., P = MC. In South Africa as in the European Union and the United States, competition authorities often judge the competitiveness of markets on their compliance with the perfect-competition model, and especially its outcome of equality with MC. Any departures from perfect competition (whether they involve P > MC or P < MC) tend to be interpreted as implying a distortion in the efficient or appropriate number of firms an industry has or should have (refer to previous discussion on the efficiency of perfect competition). Consequently such departures are interpreted as a move of an industry toward monopoly, i.e., a single-firm situation, or the establishment of dominant firms. In short, departures from $P = MC$ tend be considered to give rise to monopoly or market power. Whether the authorities deem such power to be anticompetitive, i.e., to hurt consumers, involves a pure value judgment about equity (as to firm size), since there is no burden to show that such power does actually exist other than to establish that it is likely to be present. The following selected passages (ordered chronologically) from various legislations illustrate the point:

Every person who shall monopolize or attempt to monopolize, or combine or conspire with any other person or persons, to monopolize any part of the trade or commerce among the several States, or with foreign nations, shall be deemed guilty of a felony. (15 U.S.C. §2; §2 Sherman Act [1890], U.S. Antitrust Legislation)

No person engaged in commerce or in any activity affecting commerce shall acquire, directly or indirectly, the whole or any part of the stock or other share capital . . . of the assets of another person engaged also in commerce or in any activity affecting commerce, where in any line of commerce or in any activity affecting commerce in any section of the country, the effect of such acquisition may be substantially to lessen competition, or to tend to create a monopoly.[1] (§7 Clayton Act [1914], U.S. Antitrust Legislation)

The following shall be prohibited as incompatible with the common market: all agreements between undertakings . . . which have as their object or effect the prevention, restriction or distortion of competition within the common market, and in particular those which . . . control production, markets, technical development, or investment . . . and . . . afford such undertakings the possibility of eliminating competition.[2] (Article 81 [1997], EU Competition Law)

An agreement between . . . firms, or a decision by an association of firms, is prohibited if . . . it is between parties in a horizontal relationship and it has the effect of substantially preventing or lessening competition in a market.[3] (§4, South African Competition Act [1998])

However one reads these examples one thing is clear: competition authorities fear the social costs of monopolization of industries and by analogy the social costs of firm dominance, i.e., market power, and collusion, i.e., cartelization.[4] The obvious question here would be to ask why? The answer is illustrated with reference to monopoly power, but analogously the same principles hold for the cases involving dominant firms (and by extension mergers and acquisitions) and cartels. First, however, the meaning of the social costs of monopoly power is examined, and thereafter this discussion is examined in the context of a cartel. The link between monopoly power and mergers and acquisitions is examined at a later stage.

THE SOCIAL COSTS OF MONOPOLY POWER

Throughout the discussion on monopoly power in the present chapter the (naive) assumption is made that governments do nothing (whether by legislative or other means) to bring about monopoly power (in an industry). This chapter questions whether the conventionally accepted view of monopoly power is correct, and similarly if the accepted determinants of such power should not perhaps be considered as symptomatic of rivalry rather than encouraging its retardation. This requires touching on the concept of barriers to entry and arguing for its redefinition, which is to be done later.

In regard to the social costs of monopoly power, the following question is posed: "What would happen if a competitive industry, i.e., one where P = MC, producing homogeneous goods, were taken over by a single firm, which then operated as a multiplant monopolist?" Figure 3.3 shows how this question may be answered.

Under perfect competition LMC is both the industry's long-run MC curve and its supply curve. With constant returns to scale LMC is also the long-run average cost (LAC) curve of the industry. Given the demand curve, D, competitive equilibrium is at E. The competitive industry produces an output Q^c at price P^c.

When the industry is taken over by a monopolist, the monopolist recognizes that MR is less than price at each output. The monopolist produces an output Q^M at a price P^M, thus equating LMC and MR.

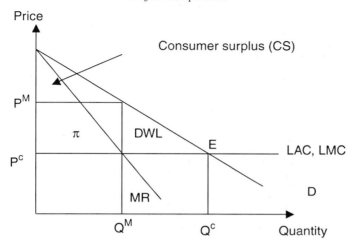

FIGURE 3.3. Social costs of monopoly power. *Source:* Adapted from Tullock, 1967, p. 225.

The area π shows the monopolist's profits from selling Q^M at a price in excess of marginal and average cost. The DWL triangle, as demonstrated by Harberger (1954, pp. 77-87), shows the dead-weight loss or social cost of monopoly power. Why? Because at Q^M the social marginal benefit of another unit of output is P^M, but the social marginal cost is only P^c (the perfectly competitive price level). Society would like to expand output up to the competitive point at which social marginal benefit and social marginal cost are equal. The DWL triangle measures the social profit or excess of benefits over costs from such an output expansion. Conversely, by reducing output from the perfectly competitive level of Q^c to Q^M the monopolist imposes a social cost equal to the area of the DWL triangle.

At the perfectly competitive point, E, productive efficiency is not an issue, as output is being produced in the least costly way. The concern is that if firms exercise monopolistic practices[5] or an industry is perceived to behave either as a theoretical monopoly (as described previously) or as if it were a monopolist, then it would charge at the monopoly level P^M where the corresponding output is Q^M.

By pricing in this manner the industry earns supernormal profit π, which represents a transfer of income from consumers to producers and induces allocative inefficiency (i.e., satisfying potential consumers would not cost extra at the margin, but they refrain from buying because P^M is above their willingness to pay). The DWL triangle measures this allocative inefficiency. The combination of allocative inefficiency and profit-making results in the reduction of consumer surplus.

This same result is also what is expected from a cartel, given it is an association of firms that agrees to coordinate its pricing and output activities. Simply put, a cartel takes into account the rise in profits to all its members from a reduction in each firm's output. Thus in the extreme case if a cartel includes all firms in a market it is in effect a monopoly, and the member firms share the monopoly profits. Anything close to this situation, such as the cartel involving many if not all firms in an industry, produces results reminiscent of those of monopoly power.

However, it is questionable whether the theoretical premise surrounding cartels holds upon close scrutiny.

THE PERSISTENCE OF CARTELS

Stigler (1961b, pp. 228-231; 1964, pp. 45-48) has noted that collusive conduct with the intent of achieving higher profits will not succeed for three reasons:

1. The supernormal profits a collusive agreement can produce will act as an incentive to entry and increase the number of entrants (assuming no barriers to entry). This would lead to lower prices (toward marginal cost) and the elimination of monopoly profits;
2. Firms participating in such cartel-based agreements can realize substantial increases in their earnings if they make a small (hard to detect) price reduction in relation to the other cartel members; and
3. Some cartel members may be operating at marginal cost levels that allow them to have a larger mark-up relative to other members. Such members have a greater ability to fluctuate their price, raising the likelihood that they may price below the cartel price for the same reason as noted in (2).

What follows from (1), (2), and (3) is that absent regulatory support a cartel or collusive arrangement would collapse, since there would always be members who would want to extract as much as possible from the gains of the price floor the cartel sets. As Stigler (1964, p. 46) observed, "the literature of collusive agreements, ranging from the pools of the 1880s to the electrical conspiracies of recent times, is replete with instances of the collapse of conspiracies because of 'secret' price cutting." Figure 3.4, adapted from Reekie and Crook (1995, p. 310), illustrates a case in point.

In Figure 3.4(B), Dc represents the industry demand curve. S is the market supply curve, obtained by aggregating horizontally the MC curves of the firms in the industry. Without collusion the market price would be P_1 and the total quantity produced and sold would be Q_1, where price equals marginal cost. Any single seller would produce and sell Q_4 units, where $Q_4 = Q_1/n$, where n = the number of (equal sized) firms in the market.

If any single seller were to sell an additional unit, his or her marginal revenue would be insignificantly different from P_1. For the group as a whole, however, MR would be significantly below market price; geometrically this is obscured in Figure 3.4 since the quantity axis in Figure 3.4(B) is a stretched-out version of the same axis in Figure 3.4(A).

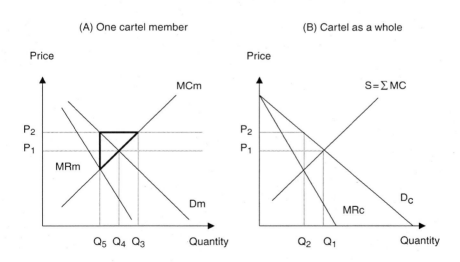

FIGURE 3.4. Do cartels last? *Source:* Adapted from Reekie and Crook, 1995, p. 310.

If the sellers collude as a single monopoly the profit maximizing price minus output combination is P_2Q_2, where MC = MRc. As long as all firms have identical MC curves, P_2 is also the optimum price for the individual cartel member. Since we are assuming that all sellers act in concert, when one reduces quantity there will be a perceptible effect on price. If a single seller acted alone, his or her demand curve would be almost horizontal at P_1, but since what any one does they all do, Dm, the residual demand curve is the relevant demand curve.

Had the two panels in the graph been drawn on the same (quantity) scale, the distance (Q_1-Q_2) would be n times as great as (Q_4-Q_5). Given concerted action, the profit-maximizing output for the single firm is Q_5 at the cartel price P_2, where MC = MRm. Each colluder is expected to supply only Q_5. This is a quota that the cartel must some-how enforce. However, each firm realizes that if it alone supplies more than Q_5 the effect on price will be negligible. P_2 is the price each firm must take.

If a firm acts alone P_2 is its MR curve. The quantity that then maximizes profit for the cheating firm is Q_3. The individual seller makes a profit gain shown by the bold triangle. Since this opportunity is open to all, the probability is very high that one or a few firms will seize it. Each firm will be tempted to gain a free ride on the anticompetitive behavior of the others. Unless a sufficiently powerful over-seeing body can enforce the output quotas and/or inhibit new entry, the cartel will inevitably crumble. Generally only government agencies have such powers of inspection and enforcement. As Von Mises (1949, p. 363) put it:

> the important place cartels occupy in our time is an outcome of the interventionist policies adopted by the governments of all countries. The great monopoly problem mankind has to face to-day is not an outgrowth of the operation of the market economy. It is a product of purposive action on the part of governments.

If marginal costs of cartel members vary, collapse is even more im-minent. Previously it was assumed that each firm's MC curve was in the same position, so that equal quotas resulted in equal marginal costs. Suppose, however, that marginal costs vary. Figure 3.5, adapted from Reekie and Crook (1995, p. 312), deals with this case.

Assume, as in Figure 3.5, that only two sellers exist and that the collusive agreement is that each will supply half the quantity

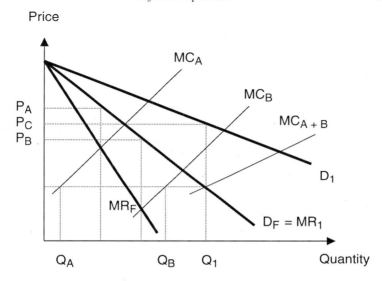

FIGURE 3.5. Cartel duration in the case of varying marginal costs. *Source:* Adapted from Reekie and Crook, 1995, p. 312.

demanded at each price. D_F is consequentially the residual demand curve for each firm and the MR curve for the group as a whole. MR_F is each firm's perceived MR curve for the group as a whole and MC_A and MC_B are the MC curves for firms A and B. The optimum prices for A and B are thus different, namely P_A and P_B.

They will disagree over which price should be set for the group. Moreover, the cartel's optimum price, P_C, is not the optimum for either of the two firms. Cartel profits are maximized, not when the quantity to be produced is necessarily divided equally, but rather where $MR_1 = MC_{A+B}$, giving optimum output Q_1 divided so that $MC_A = MC_B$ in order that each firm might have the same marginal cost. If MC_A does not equal MC_B at any output level, then output reallocation should take place between the two firms until the marginal equivalency condition again holds.

Without such reallocation the cartel would not be minimizing costs and so would not, even if operating at the profit-maximizing output level, be maximizing the difference between revenue and costs. Thus if an output of Q_1 and a price P_C could be agreed upon, the cartel would face formidable difficulties in allocating output in the profit-maximizing manner. Firm A would wish to produce more than Q_A and B less than Q_B. In such a situation only a body with strong enforcing powers could ensure that the cartel would not disintegrate. Once again, this seems to be more likely where a government exercises an industrial oversight.

It appears that the previous theoretical exposition as to the failure of cartels corroborates what is observed in practice. Suslow (2000; pp. 38-39), in examining seventy-one cartels, has demonstrated that the life of a cartel, on the average, is 2.8 years and that the most common cause of termination of the cartel arrangement is the inability of member firms to live by the cartel agreement. Causes of termination here include cheating, defection, and excess production. In short, because of rivalry, cartels seldom last.

Many regulators, however, tend to view matters differently as the extracts from the different legislation reveal. Monopoly power is considered harmful. If it exists, the aim of public (or competition) policies in such instances is to drive P^M to P^c (Figure 3.3), thereby adding to the existing consumer surplus (CS) area $\pi + DWL$. This, however, incorrectly assumes that government intervention has no costs. Accordingly, the gains the policies intend to deliver (i.e., the additions to the CS they would make) should be contrasted against the costs they would introduce. These costs can be thought of as the administrative/bureaucratic expenditure that would be sustained in adding to the existing CS area $\pi + DWL$.

If monopoly power is present in an industry one way to measure it and thereby gain an idea about how much the monopoly price P^M needs to fall for the perfectly competitive price P^c to be reached is to calculate the price-cost margin of the monopolist or monopolistlike organization.

THE PRICE-COST MARGIN

This margin is also known as the Lerner index of monopoly (or market) power and is given by:

$$L = [(p - MC)/p] = 1/\varepsilon, \qquad (3.1)$$

where ε = the elasticity of demand (determined from the demand curve)[6] and p = the price charged away from MC pricing.

L ranges between 0 and 1, with numbers close to 0 reflecting lack of monopoly power and numbers close to 1 indicating the presence of significant monopoly power. If no monopoly or market power exists demand is elastic, L = 0, and there is no DWL. However, with an inelastic demand implies that market power exists, L ranges are between 0 and 1, and the DWL is (numerically) a positive number.

Equation 3.1 also measures the presence of monopoly power in cases where there is more than one firm, assuming that each firm in an industry does posses some monopoly power, as implied by the price-cost margin it chooses and uses. Thus L = 0 would depict an industry with symmetrical firms and product homogeneity.

When we talk about symmetrical firms we refer to an industry containing firms that are identical with respect to costs, information about the market, and the objectives that they wish to pursue. In short, an industry of symmetrical firms is composed of roughly similar or identical firms, none of which has a strong operating advantage or leadership position. However, is the legislator's fear of monopoly power warranted, or put another way must or should firms be expected to price at MC, and if so under what circumstances?

To summarize, Chapter 3 began by defining a perfectly competitive market. In such a market all firms produce homogeneous goods, share the same technology and face no barriers to entry (or exit). In addition producers and consumers have full information, i.e., producers and consumers have all relevant information about the market, including the price and quality of the product. Perfect competition is characterized by the long-run result of P = MC. Deviations from this result in the form of P exceeding MC are viewed as representative of the presence of monopoly power. This power may either reveal itself through the presence of a single firm defining the industry or through any such arrangement with the same effect (e.g., cartels or horizontal integration).

Doubts were expressed as to whether the monopoly power concerns surrounding cartels are warranted. It was noted that the standard theoretical view of cartels is flawed. In the case of cartels, the profitable opportunities from not honoring the agreement in combination with the difficulty of getting firms to live by the agreement make it (almost) certain that any cartel is sure to crumble in the absence of government enforcement.

It was also noted that where the legislative intention may be to increase consumer welfare through the elimination of monopoly power, this makes the paradoxical assumptions that government intervention comes at no cost and consumers stand to receive less than what they may be getting. Towards the end of the chapter a fundamental question was raised regarding whether the consequence of monopoly power, i.e., P above MC, should be viewed as depicting a state inferior to the perfectly competitive nirvana. This question will be addressed in the following chapter.

Chapter 4

Departures from Perfect Competition

Should departures from perfect competition be viewed as anticompetitive? The perfectly competitive point, or point of static efficiency, $P = MC$, is attained for a given technology and homogeneous (matching) products. In short, perfect competition is silent on competition involving technical progress, e.g., new products, new production technologies, and so on. Thus, the perfectly competitive point, in fact, reflects the point of no competition, or, more specifically, the point where competition is exhausted or at its limit, given that firms compete for market share with the same technology and products (which in turn leaves firms to compete on one aspect only, namely price). This point was recognized and emphasized long ago by Hayek (1948; 1978) and Schumpeter (1949). Both reached it in different ways but concluded alike that given technical progress perfect competition either assumes the absence of all competitive activity in an industry or that perfect competition may not be an appropriate model of ideal efficiency. The passages below illustrate the point:

> economic theory . . . appears at the outset to bar its way to a true appreciation of the character of the process of competition, because it starts from the assumption of a "given" supply of scarce goods. But which goods are scarce goods, or which things are goods, and how scarce or valuable they are—these are precisely the things which competition has to discover. . . . The absurdity of the usual procedure of starting the analysis with a situation in which all the facts are supposed to be known . . . is a state of affairs which economic theory curiously calls "perfect competition." It leaves no room whatever for the activity called competition, which is presumed to have already done its task. (Hayek, 1978, pp. 181, 182)

doi:10.1300/5505_04

As soon as quality competition and sales effort are admitted into
the sacred precincts of theory, the price variable is ousted from
its dominant position. However it is still competition within a
rigid pattern of invariant conditions, methods of production and
forms of industrial organization in particular, that practically
monopolizes attention. But in . . . reality as distinguished from
its textbook picture, it is not that kind of competition which
counts but the competition from the new commodity, the new
technology, the new source of supply, the new type of organization (the largest-scale unit of control for instance)—competition
which commands a decisive cost or quality advantage and
which strikes not at the margin of the profits and the outputs of
the existing firms but at their foundations and their very lives.
This kind of competition is . . . much more effective than the
other . . . and so much more important that it becomes a matter of
comparative indifference whether competition in the ordinary
sense functions more or less promptly; the powerful lever that in
the long run expands output and brings down prices is in any
case made of other stuff. (Schumpeter, 1949, p. 84)

What follows from the Schumpeterian view on competition, which
Schumpeter succinctly coined "the perennial gale of creative destruction," is that profits can be earned by creativity and superior foresight
or simply by being first in the field. However, a profitable firm is always at the mercy of rivals attempting to develop new and better
products. In the absence of artificial restrictions, i.e., government
protection by law or some such thing,[1] the tendency is always for
profits to be competed away. With the Schumpeterian idea of competition in mind Littlechild (1981, pp. 357-358) has cast considerable
doubt over the conventional interpretation of monopoly power where
technical progress or new product development is involved.

INNOVATION AND COMPETITION

In the presence of technical progress or new product development
Figure 3.3 (see p. 21) represents and analyzes at a point in time the
behavior of a firm that discovers a new product (or production technique) before the rest of the market realizes its potential.[2] Assume the
firm charges a monopoly price P^M, since for the moment it is the sole

seller. It is true that the firm is restricting output compared to what it could produce, or compared to what would be produced if all its "rivals" shared its own insight. However, they do not share the firm's insight; this is not the relevant alternative. For the time being, the relevant alternative to the firm's action is no product at all. It would thus be inappropriate to characterize the firm's action as generating a social loss given by the welfare triangle DWL. On the contrary, the firm's action generates a social gain given by the firm's own profit π plus the consumer surplus (CS). This social gain is enjoyed from the time at which the firm discovers and exploits the new product (or production technique) until the time at which the market would otherwise have done so.

However, it is likely that through its discovery the first firm will stimulate the market to an earlier awareness of the situation, i.e., rivals will step in and compete P down to MC. This early awareness brings two different but simultaneous gains to consumers. The first, the obvious one, would involve the conversion of profit to CS given the entry of rivals to compete monopoly profits away, which would translate into a transfer of income from producers to consumers. The second one, is also a social gain, namely the earlier enjoyment of CS on output $Q^M Q^C$, which is equal in value to the area of the welfare triangle DWL. Shortly put, the DWL triangle measures the gain of consumers enjoying an innovation earlier from that firm able to achieve its innovation before potential rivals do so (if ever). This of course assumes that consumers would prefer to be exposed to innovations earlier rather than later. This is not different from reality, where innovation is highly likely to bring product variety and by extension increase the choice of alternatives (as opposed to a situation of homogeneity). Given, as we know from consumer theory, that consumers prefer more (versatility) to less there is a priori no reason to expect them to prefer innovations later rather than sooner if there is a chance to access them earlier.

Thus, in the case of industries that are innovative by nature, in which the focus of new product development is on producing products that represent drastic departures from accepted ways of performing a service, we may expect the existence of a DWL triangle. For example, in the case of the pharmaceutical industry Reekie (1995, pp. 50-51) has noted that the presence of such a triangle would illustrate that the pricing behavior of the industry suggests a competitive process with a welfare loss in the static sense, but where the monopoly rents implied are actually the sources of funds for the R&D which develops new products in the future.

In summary, from the assumptions of perfect competition it follows that an innovation would not satisfy the $P = MC$ condition. The perfectly competitive ideal, $P = MC$, reflects the point of output produced if all producers shared the same information. However, in the case of an innovation everyone does not share the insight of specialized knowledge and rivals do not have the alternatives to offer. In fact, the alternative is no product at all. Thus it is inappropriate to consider that innovations, whether in their technological, organizational, or product sense, that enable some firms to gain market advantage over others generate a social loss because they separate from "perfection." Here the action of the better-informed agent (i.e., the company able to put the innovation at use first) generates a social gain translated into the early enjoyment of consumer surplus (in addition to firm profit) from the output of the new offer. The disclosure of what is previously unknown enables the consumption of the discoveries. The point is that the providers of the innovative offer have drawn the attention of users to the possibility of obtaining Q^M at P^M.

The relevant alternative is not Q^c at P^c. Perfect competitors in equilibrium would never have noticed the possibility of change nor the opportunity for profit. The relevant alternative is for the good not to have been supplied at all. Thus, the very fact of production and sale implies a social gain equal to the firms' profits plus consumers' surplus. In general monopoly prices are paid to enjoy things that would not have been enjoyed at all under competitive prices. It is along these lines that the patent system can be justified as the best tool available in bringing about and disseminating inventions and for which reason proposals against it miss its influence on facilitating rivalry in the marketplace. The system does so by nurturing innovative competition and by predisposing the competitive process toward imitative competition. For instance, in the pharmaceutical industry the presence of the system highlights the difference between innovators (i.e., the leaders) and imitators (i.e., the followers). In the product market this distinction is reflected in the difference between product breakthroughs (i.e., the products with therapeutic advances) and generics (i.e., the products with identical therapeutic effect).

It is important to note that some argue that the patent system harms consumers by granting firms monopoly power, which enables them to charge monopoly rather than competitive prices. This, however, would be to ignore that such monopoly prices—which are temporary and reflect a superior offering—are offset by the fact that the patent system ultimately makes the knowledge of the invention a free good (through public availability) and exposes the conditions and ways of entry into a market. In short, contrary to popular opinion, patent protection does not make entry impossible or even unlikely, and functional knowledge on innovations (whether involving new products or production processes) is not a secret for long—it tends to disseminate fairly rapidly across an industry. This is what seems to happen in reality, as illustrated by Mansfield and colleagues (1981) and Mansfield (1985). These works have cast considerable doubt on the permanence of monopoly power acquired by firms through patents and innovations. Such power is always temporary and usually short-lived. The following discussion, drawing on the studies, helps illustrate this.

EROSION OF MONOPOLY POWER
UNDER INNOVATION

Mansfield and colleagues (1981, pp. 907-917) obtained data from randomly chosen major firms in four U.S. industries (chemicals, pharmaceuticals, electronics, and machinery) concerning the cost and time of legally imitating forty-eight randomly chosen product innovations (that were already introduced). The sample of products comprised both successful and unsuccessful new products, with about half of the innovations turning out to be successful in the sense that they were relatively profitable to the innovator. Of these, on the average, 71 percent were patented (81 percent for pharmaceuticals, 63 percent for chemicals, and 69 percent for electronics and machinery). The aim of the study was to determine the imitation costs and time it would take for the innovative products to be replicated in the form of variants (alternative versions) or me-too (prototype) products. Imitation costs were defined as all costs of developing and introducing the imitative product, including applied research, product specification, pilot plant or prototype construction, investment in plant and equipment, and manufacturing and marketing start-up. In addition, if the innovation was patented, the cost of inventing around it was also included. Imitation time was defined as the length of time elapsing from the beginning of the imitator's applied research (if any) on the imitative product to the date of its commercial introduction. Table 4.1 and Table 4.2 represent the findings of the study.

Mansfield and colleagues (1981, pp. 909-910) found that, on average, the ratio of the imitation cost to the innovation cost was about 0.65, and the ratio of the imitation time to the innovation time was about 0.70. The tables demonstrate considerable variation in these averages. In about half of the cases, the ratio of imitation cost to innovation cost is either less than 0.40 or more than 0.90. In about half of the cases, the ratio of imitation time to innovation time is either less than 0.40 or more than 1.00. Products with a relatively high (or low) ratio of imitation cost to innovation cost tend to have a relatively high (or low) ratio of imitation time to innovation time.

It may be surprising that imitation cost is no smaller than innovation cost in about one-seventh of the cases. In these cases the

TABLE 4.1. Imitation cost (divided by innovation cost) of forty-eight new products, by industry and cost of innovation.

Imitation cost (divided by innovation cost)	New products (weighted by innovation cost)(%)		
	Chemicals	Pharmaceuticals	Electronics and machinery
Less than 0.20	3	3	17
0.20 and under 0.40	0	11	0
0.40 and under 0.60	0	1	53
0.60 and under 0.80	44	54	0
0.80 and under 1.00	15	21	9
1.0 and over	38	9	22
Total	100	100	100

Source: Adapted from Mansfield et al., 1981, p. 908. *Notes:* The table refers to those innovations involving high development costs. Mansfield et al. distinguished between innovations costing more than $1 million (i.e., high development costs) and innovations costing less than $1 million (i.e., low development costs). New products are weighted by innovation cost. The weighted number of new products is expressed as a percentage of the column total (from the raw data table not supplied here). Due to rounding, percentages may not add up to 100.

TABLE 4.2. Imitation time (divided by innovation time) of forty-eight new products, by industry and cost of innovation.

Imitation time (divided by innovation time)	New products (weighted by innovation cost) (%)		
	Chemicals	Pharmaceuticals	Electronics and machinery
Less than 0.30	3	10	35
0.30 and under 0.50	2	28	17
0.50 and under 0.70	35	24	19
0.70 and under 0.90	22	0	0
0.90 and under 1.10	18	16	22
1.10 and over	19	23	9
Total	100	100	100

Source: Adapted from Mansfield et al., 1981, p. 909. *Notes:* The table refers to those innovations involving high development costs. Mansfield et al. distinguished between innovations costing more than $1 million (i.e., high development costs) and innovations costing less than $1 million (i.e., low development costs). New products are weighted by innovation cost. The weighted number of new products is expressed as a percentage of the column total (from the raw data table not supplied here). Due to rounding, percentages may not add up to 100.

Mansfield study found that this was not due to any superiority of the imitative product over the innovation, but instead due to the innovator having a technological edge over its rival(s) in the relevant field. Often this edge is due to superior know-how—that is, better and more extensive technical information based on highly specialized experience with the development and production of related products and processes. Such know-how is not divulged in patents and is relatively inaccessible (at least for a period of time) to potential imitators.

However, the results show that innovators routinely introduce new products despite the fact that other firms can imitate these products at about two-thirds and often less of the cost and time expended by the innovator. In some cases this is because, although other firms could imitate these products in this way, other barriers to entry exist (e.g., lack of a well-known brand name) that discourage potential imitators. However, to a greater extent, as Mansfield and colleagues (1981, p. 910) pointed out, "it seems to be due to a feeling on the part of the innovators that, even if imitators do begin to appear in a relatively few years, the innovation still will be profitable."

In short, the corollary from the findings is that patented innovations, which, given that they do encourage imitation, may be presumed to introduce above-average profits in an industry, do not appear to make entry impossible or even unlikely. On the contrary, they do seem to promote contestability between firms in an industry to meet consumer demand. This in turn may be expected to result in any above-average profits being competed away in time. That is, with imitation, over time, the market moves toward perfect competition.

Using a different methodology and a much larger number of industries (thirteen), Mansfield (1985, pp. 217-232) provided additional support for the previous findings by demonstrating that information pertaining to how innovations function and how they are made tends to diffuse fairly rapidly among firms in an industry, as illustrated by Table 4.3. In this study 100 firms were randomly selected from a list of firms in thirteen major U.S. manufacturing industries spending over 1 percent of sales on research and development. Mansfield (1985, pp. 219-223) investigated how soon after the development of a new product or production process the information is known to close rivals and/or other firms in the industry. As Table 4.3 shows, with the exception of processes in a few industries such as chemicals and pharmaceuticals, there seems to be little difference among industries in the rate of diffusion of such information. On average, the detailed nature and operation of new products leaks out to close rivals and/or other firms in the industry in about six to twelve months in virtually all industries, while information relating to the detailed nature and operation of new processes leaks out to close rivals and/or other firms in the industry in six to eighteen months in virtually all industries other than pharmaceuticals and chemicals.

This information spreads through many channels. Considerable movement of personnel from one firm to another occurs in some industires, and informal communication networks exist among engineers and scientists working at various firms, as well as professional meetings at which information is exchanged. In other industries input suppliers and customers are important channels (since they pass on a great deal of relevant information), patent applications are scrutinized, and reverse engineering is also undertaken. In addition to these reasons, Mansfield (1985, p. 221) also pointed out that for some

TABLE 4.3. Percent distribution of firms by average number of months after development before the nature and operation of a new product or process are reported to be known to the firm's rivals.

Industry	Products (Average number of months)				Processes (Average number of months)			
	≤ 6	6-12	12-18	≥ 18	≤ 6	6-12	12-18	≥ 18
Chemicals	18	36	9	36	0	0	10	90
Pharma-ceuticals	57	14	29	0	0	33	0	67
Petroleum	22	33	22	22	10	50	10	30
Primary metals	40	20	0	40	40	40	0	20
Electrical equipment	38	50	12	0	14	14	57	14
Machinery	31	31	31	8	10	20	30	40
Transporta-tion equip-ment	25	50	0	25	0	67	0	33
Instru-ments	50	38	12	0	33	33	33	0
Stone, clay, glass	40	60	0	0	0	22	20	60
Other	31	15	15	38	27	0	36	36
Average	35	35	13	17	13	28	20	39

Source: Adapted from Mansfield, 1985, p. 220. *Notes:* Due to rounding off the percentages may not add up to 100 (horizontally). "Other" represents a summation of the results for the industries of fabricated metal products, food, rubber, and paper.

industries "the diffusion process is accelerated by the fact that firms do not go to great lengths to keep such information secret, partly because they believe that it would be futile in any event."

Information regarding processes leaks out more slowly (in practically all industries). This is probably because a new process can be developed with less communication and interaction with other firms than can new products. Confirmation of these studies is provided in Levin and colleagues (1987, pp. 809-812).

The corollary of these studies is that innovative activity is very likely not only to facilitate rivalry but also to initiate it. The studies also suggest that in the presence of innovative activity industries tend to behave in accordance with Littlechild's view of monopoly power (discussed earlier). Here we can use Equation 3.1 (see p. 26) to detect whether an industry is characterized, at a point in time, by asymmetrical firms[3] and product heterogeneity. This would require that L be greater than 0 (but less than 1).

Given that innovative activity is very likely to initiate rivalry between firms in an industry, how does an industry reach the perfectly competitive point in time? This question is answered in the following chapter.

To summarize, this chapter revisits the theory of perfect competition and demonstrates that perfect competition is an end result. It depicts the exhaustion of competition in a market that has is no innovative activity and firms "compete" with homogeneous products, i.e., product variety is absent. Once again it is shown that a common concern to many antitrust authorities is their fear of monopoly power and by extension cartelization, but that such fears may not be warranted. Monopoly power is very likely to be the result of some firms being more efficient than others in the Schumpeter-Littlechild sense. Accordingly, the accepted barriers to entry may not represent impediments to reaching perfect competition. On the contrary, they can be viewed as symptomatic of rivalry and necessary if in the long run perfect competition is to be attained.

The competitive process in an industry commences with innovation. Innovative activity generates versatility (in products, processes, and forms of organization) relative to a situation of homogeneity, which in turn brings opportunities for above-average profits. These in turn attract imitative activity and entry until the above-average profits are competed away (or bidden down to normal levels). Some (probably many) regulators are likely to typically consider the DWL from monopoly power as a social loss. It is actually a gain (absent government protection/control) reflecting what consumers pay (voluntarily) to enable innovative competition between firms in an industry, without which consumers would not enjoy the surplus from receiving a new offer earlier rather than later. Nor would they be likely to enjoy the increase in surplus from consuming earlier rather than later (if ever) more of this new offer (without which subsequent imitations would not exist).

Three main points arise from this chapter. The first follows:

> Monopoly is a market situation in which intra-industry competition has been defined away by identifying the firm as the industry. Perfect competition, on the other hand, is a market situation which, although itself the result of the free entry of a large number of formerly competing firms, has evolved or progressed to the point (of equilibrium) where no further competition within the industry is possible, or . . . to the point where the effects of competition have reached their limit. (McNulty, 1968, p. 642)

Simply put, monopoly is a market situation in which competition within the industry has completed its task by identifying through rivalry the strongest firm, in the economic-efficiency sense, as the industry. Perfect competition, however, is a market situation which although itself the result of the free entry of formerly competing firms, has progressed to the point where no further competition within the industry is possible or to the point where the effects of competition have reached their limit.

The second point dealing with patents and closely linked to understanding competition and monopoly is as Mill ([1871] 1965, p. 928) summed it:

> The condemnation of monopolies ought not to extend to patents, by which the originator of an improved process is allowed to enjoy, for a limited period, the exclusive privilege of using his own improvement. This is not making the commodity dear for his benefit, but merely postponing a part of the increased cheapness which the public owe to the inventor, in order to compensate and reward him for the service. That he ought to be both compensated and rewarded for it, will not be denied, and also that if all were at once allowed to avail themselves of his ingenuity, without having shared the labors or the expenses which he had to incur in bringing his idea into a practical shape, either such expenses and labors would be undergone by nobody except very opulent and very public-spirited persons, or the state must put a value on the service rendered by an inventor, and make him a pecuniary grant. This has been done in some instances,

and may be done without inconvenience in cases of very conspicuous public benefit; but in general an exclusive privilege, of temporary duration, is preferable; because it leaves nothing to any one's discretion; because the reward conferred by it depends upon the invention's being found useful, and the greater the usefulness the greater the reward; and because it is paid by the very persons to whom the service is rendered, the consumers of the commodity. So decisive, indeed, are these considerations, that if the system of patents were abandoned for that of rewards by the state, the best shape which these could assume would be that of a small temporary tax, imposed for the inventor's benefit, on all persons making use of the invention. To this, however, or to any other system which would vest in the state the power of deciding whether an inventor should derive any pecuniary advantage from the public benefit which he confers, the objections are evidently stronger and more fundamental than the strongest which can possibly be urged against patents. It is generally admitted that the present Patent Laws need much improvement; but in this case, as well as in the closely analogous one of Copyright, it would be a gross immorality in the law to set everybody free to use a person's work without his consent, and without giving him an equivalent. I have seen with real alarm several recent attempts, in quarters carrying some authority, to impugn the principle of patents altogether; attempts which, if practically successful, would enthrone free stealing under the prostituted name of free trade, and make the men of brains, still more than at present, the needy retainers and dependants of the men of moneybags.

The third point, acting as a synthesis to the previous two points, relates to accepting a more holistic but perhaps not as orthodox view of what competition actually entails. As Clemens (1951, p. 9) has pointed out:

> Profit margins in the varying markets will differ due to localized monopolies, lags in competition and other factors. To assume conditions of competitive equilibrium where all profit margins are equal would be completely unrealistic. Normal profits, necessary to a firm's long-run existence, are obtained only in so far as average revenues under multiple-product production are

equal to average costs. This condition can only be attained by the continuous process of invasion and cross-invasion of markets, by the shuffling and reshuffling of prices and markets, which are so characteristic of economic activity.

Although one may be able to find examples that come close, it is doubtful whether any industry can aptly be described as perfectly competitive—and certainly not for any length of time.

Chapter 5

Rivalry and the Competitive Process

The perfectly competitive pricing norm is what one may observe in the case of homogeneous products. However, in the case where distinctiveness is present Dean (1951, p. 419) has submitted that

> The strategic decision in pricing a . . . product is the choice between: (1) a policy of high initial prices that skim the cream of demand; and (2) a policy of low prices from the outset serving as an active agent for market penetration.

Products with lasting distinctiveness, i.e., no acceptable or readily available substitutes, would be priced according to the price-skimming principle, whereby the product is sold at a high price in the early stages of its life cycle and at lower prices later on.[1] Put in economic terminology, a firm would opt for price skimming when demand for its product is likely to be inelastic in the early stages of the product's life cycle. This would be the case for a product that initially represents a "drastic departure from accepted ways of performing a service" (Dean, 1951, p. 419). Although with price skimming a firm may be imposing a market price above MC in the short (and possibly medium) term, this comes only by way of no other firm being able to supply the product the firm offers. Put differently, the high price and the firm's dominant market position (the consequence of its unique product offering) are temporary, given that product perishability increases over time.

The reverse pricing policy to that of price skimming is that of price penetration, which would be observed in the case of products of perishable distinctiveness, i.e., acceptable substitutes for a firm's products exist or are soon due to exist. Price penetration is likely to take place when the product is characterized by a "high price-elasticity of

doi:10.1300/5505_05

demand in the short run, i.e., responsiveness of sale to reductions in price should be great" (Dean, 1951, p. 422).

Given that a market commences with the introduction of a product or offer not previously available, one would observe that in industries characterized by innovative activity a new product of lasting distinctiveness would be priced by the firm in accordance with price skimming. With the passage of time, as the lasting distinctiveness switches to perishable distinctiveness, or with a product that is perishable from the outset, the firm would opt for pricing in accordance with price penetration. Such a move would enable the firm

1. to raise market share for its product in anticipation of alternatives that are soon to follow;
2. to preserve its market share lead by making use of the goodwill, i.e., continued customer patronage, the product has generated prior to the appearance of alternatives;
3. to gain market share for its product in the presence of (acceptable) substitutes; and
4. to maintain its presence in the market even if at lower market share by meeting or pricing close to the price of a rival.

In practice one may expect that in industries where innovation is present firms would use price skimming and price penetration interchangeably. To gain full understanding of how this may occur, the Clemens-Cocks model of pricing in the presence of new products is considered.

THE CLEMENS-COCKS MODEL

This model was first proposed in a static formulation by Clemens (1951, pp. 4-5). Cocks (1975, pp. 230-232) extended Clemens's model by providing a comparative static framework to highlight the dynamic characteristics of new product development. The Clemens-Cocks model rests on the following assumptions:

1. The development of new products is the primary objective of firms. As Dean (1951, pp. 419-423) has illustrated, the preferred market positions such new products can provide in terms of the price they can command is the main incentive for this objective.

2. Firms will expand output to the point where the least profitable unit is produced at marginal cost equal to price. Clemens noted that the firm would increase output if it has idle capacity, namely as Clemens (1951, p. 4) put it, "possessing excess capacity in the form of equipment, personnel, and organisation, it can increase production without an undue increase in marginal cost." However, Cocks (1975, p. 230) considered that firms would expand output by focusing on meeting unfulfilled demand for new products, which would vary in their uniqueness. Here Cocks distinguished between major, minor, or insignificant advances over existing products.

3. A high cross-elasticity of supply exists between the markets firms serve or supply, even though products are not homogeneous. This permits the output of heterogeneous products to be measured in terms of common units of the factors of production they require. This allows the demand curves (as per the output being produced) of the heterogeneous products to be considered in commensurate units (in input units required).

4. A low cross-elasticity of demand exists between products, i.e., the demand curves faced by a firm are not related. This assumption follows from (1). Since new product development creates product variety, i.e., differences in products, it follows then that the demands for different products are not related.

5. The market positions of a firm's various products range from ones with market power (as in the case of significant product advances) to pure or perfect competition (as in the case of insignificant product advances). This assumption highlights that new products have market power dependent on their uniqueness or long-lasting distinctiveness. As products mature commercially and substitutes become available, markets move to perfect competition.

Figure 5.1 represents the static Clemens model. It shows five separate demand curves, i.e., five markets, although the markets might well be innumerable.

It is assumed that the markets are entered according to their profitability. Profits are maximized when production is distributed between the five markets in such a manner as to make the MR equal in all markets and equal to MC. The EMR line in the figure refers to equal

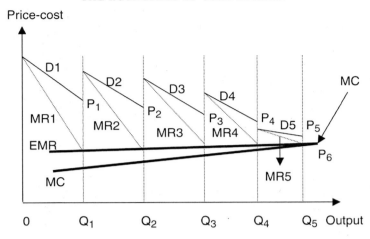

FIGURE 5.1. Pricing under innovative activity—Static view. *Source:* Adapted from Clemens, 1951, p. 5.

MR obtained by adding horizontally the MR curves of all the markets and set at a level determined by the intersection of the firm's MC curve and the MR curve for the last market that can be served profitably. This market is the one with the most elastic demand and the price established for it would be barely (if at all) in excess of MR and MC. This brings about equivalence of MC, MR, and demand in the marginal market. For a firm D1 could be the demand curve for the most recently launched and novel of five products. The demand for it would be relatively inelastic. The other demand curves could represent the demand for products at early or late stages of their maturity. Alternatively, the relatively more elastic demand curves could represent identical, or me-too, products that the firm produces to fill out excess capacity. Thus a firm may devise new products to gain a profitable market position and then fill out the rest of its productive capacity, or increase its capacity, in the manner shown. As long as a profitable market exists, a firm is encouraged to enter it. Because of the low MC (that idle capacity affords), an incumbent may enter markets that increase its profits but which would provide insufficient returns to a new firm with no existing plant or organization. Thus products are made available that would not be placed on the market if no firm had excess capacity or if there were no economies of scale or of learning.

Cocks took Clemens's model a step further. Specifically, Cocks (1975) noted that if the Clemens model is used on a comparative static basis it would highlight the dynamic characteristics of product innovation and its effects on price competition. Cocks (1975, p. 230) observed that price competition through product innovation "would be reflected by a shift of the demand curves D1 through D5 downward and towards greater elasticity." This price competition would arise in two ways.

In the first, demand for each of the firm's products is made more elastic by the competitive products introduced by other firms. In the second, demands facing other firms are made more elastic by the products introduced by the firm depicted in Figure 5.1. Figure 5.2 depicts the firm shown in Figure 5.1 in a subsequent period when it has introduced a new product significantly better than existing products.

Demand curve D6 represents this new product. While the firm was developing this product, competitors could readily see the profit potential of the products associated with, say, D5. They therefore had an incentive to enter with products of their own, and such entry would cause the elasticity of D5 to become greater. The introduction of the new product, D6, also alerts competitors to the profit potential of that new product. At the same time the firm in Figure 5.2 is introducing its

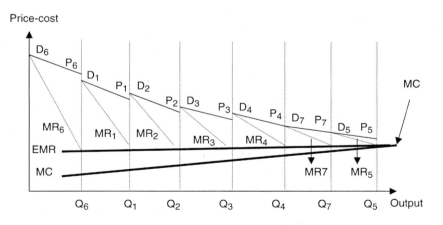

FIGURE 5.2. Pricing under innovative activity—Dynamic view. *Source:* Adapted from Cocks, 1975, p. 231.

significant new product, it could also be entering product areas of competitive firms (D7) with demand curves such as D5 in Figure 5.1, or any other area in which price is greater than MC. This increases the elasticity of the demand curves faced by these competitors. The equilibrium toward which this process would move would entail a price tending toward MC in every market where innovation took place.

Here it should be noted that the application and adaptation of the Clemens-Cocks model to an innovation-based industry does not predict that at some time we can expect a perfectly competitive equilibrium. The desire of (new) firms to develop significant new products and their successes in doing so prevents this. The model does show that given enough firms not being innovatively (or R&D) active a market environment is created that ensures results tending toward perfect competition. In addition, the model does show that as the number of product alternatives or substitutes grows firms tend to switch from using price skimming to using price penetration. Put another way, the model is consistent with the move of a market from innovative to imitative competition. As the market shifts from the former to the latter the difference between P and MC will shrink. Over time the persistence in the profit rate discrepancy (P > MC) will stimulate enough investment to make it possible to replicate the initiator's offering and collect as much as possible from the gains exposed by him. This explains the entry of imitative, i.e., me-too products and the disparity between innovative and imitative offerings. Imitative products are a by-product of their innovative equivalents. As such, if allowed to grow by their own account they would reflect the move of the market from innovative to imitative competition and contribute to the mitigation in the price difference between them and the innovative offers. This would persist until normal or zero profits are earned.

The Clemens-Cocks model illustrates the danger of compelling (in whatever way) markets to act in accordance with P = MC, as then no authority can pinpoint at what stage of the competitive process the rule is applied nor when it should be applied. This would result in a reduction of the number of iterative (competitive) stages being played out such that no consumer or user will ever know the potential alternatives missed. If firms are compelled to follow P = MC entry will be cut, resulting in less firms coming into the market, and no consumer or user will ever know the opportunities missed. In turn, the efficient and inefficient firms will not be discovered. Some expedient firms will lose the ability to remain in the market and would exit, as they would no longer be able to cover their total average costs of operation.

At this point it is worth asking whether the model works in practice. In the case of the pharmaceutical industry, including that in South Africa, empirical support for the Clemens-Cocks model has been provided by Reekie (1978, 1981, and 1996). Reekie's findings are especially valuable because they demonstrate, as a matter of principle, that in markets where competition is subject to innovation and limited or no government control on prices exists, firms tend in the long run to price in accordance with the perfectly competitive condition. Simply put, in such circumstances a firm's pricing behavior in the industry complies with what one would expect from simple price theory. Thus, many new products are priced at levels lower than leading substitutes. Those priced at high levels relative to competitors tend to be innovations providing important benefits that no product has provided before. Firms can charge higher price in those cases where consumers are willing to pay that price. Consumers will pay if the innovation is relatively more productive than alternative products. Minor variants, conversely, can only penetrate a market if their price is below that of existing rivals. Moreover, the evidence suggests that new product prices tend to fall over time, that prices of existing products tend to be cut in the face of innovations as firms attempt to gain a price advantage where a quality advantage has been lost, and that demand elasticity—being lower initially the more important the benefits represented by the innovation—increases as products mature (become subject to competition from later products). For ease of reference the product pricing process depicted by Reekie is referred to as "Reekie's product filter." This label is used to show how, for a given product innovation, over time, firm rivalry filters out any dissimilarity between the pioneering one and subsequent introductions. This results in gradually lesser departures from MC, leading in the long run to a market price consistent with this cost.

Building on Reekie's studies Lu and Comanor (1998) have provided strong evidence in support of Reekie's results. As a rule (in the case of the pharmaceutical industry) new products representing important advances in servicing or addressing consumer wants are priced significantly above their existing substitutes, while imitators are priced much lower. For new products offering modest gains to consumers in addressing their wants relative to existing products, the premium over existing substitutes is normally small. Over time, the price elasticity of demand increases as products mature (and so are subject to competition from later products).

In addition to providing strong empirical support for the Clemens-Cocks model, both Reekie (1978, 1996) and Lu and Comanor (1998) have provided support for Dean's (1951) price-skimming and price-penetration conjecture, namely that innovative products with lasting distinctiveness tend to be introduced by firms under a price-skimming strategy, whereas imitative or easy-to-copy products are launched by firms under a price-predation strategy.

In the public debate about whether patents result in high, i.e., monopoly-like, prices for pharmaceuticals, the evidence in support of the Clemens-Cocks model and Dean's conjecture illustrates that the proliferation of new patented drugs has not limited the extent of price competition. On the contrary, here prices fall because of competitive forces, which arise out of the quest for developing innovative products or because of the ability of some firms to make their offers available at a cost lower than their competitor(s). To gain full appreciation of this it is important to stress that what the Clemens-Cocks model describes is the competitive process itself. In an important way this represents an opportunity to link the Clemens-Cocks model to a bigger and comprehensive framework, first proposed by Downie (1958), as to what the competitive process entails. Downie's work links the Clemens-Cocks model to the Schumpeter-Littlechild view of competition into an integrated theory of what the competitive process encompasses even though Downie constructed his theory of the competitive process without knowledge of the Clemens-Cocks model or the Littlechild view of competition.

DOWNIE'S CONJECTURE
OF THE COMPETITIVE PROCESS

Downie's work forms the theoretical framework of this work. The graphs in Figure 5.1 and Figure 5.2 of the Clemens-Cocks model may also apply in explaining graphically the competitive process as hypothesized by Downie. So what did Downie conjecture about how the competitive process operates?

Downie (1958, pp. 31-96) focused on analyzing competition at the supply or firm level. He assumed that firms set prices via full-cost pricing, namely that the price is set by adding a normal profit margin to the weighted average of firms' total costs. The profit function for each firm then follows as the difference between the firm's total average cost and the market price multiplied by its output. Firms continue in existence only so long as profits are positive. This determines at any time the number of firms, n, that an industry will have. The second and more important part of Downie's conjecture concerns the way in which average costs will change over time. The change in average costs at a point in time in firm j is determined by the resources devoted to investment in physical capital, I_j, and to investment in research and development, $R\&D_j$, in the same period; I_j is determined directly as a given proportion of profits. However, investment in R&D is determined by two factors: (1) the availability of funds from profits and (2) the incentive to innovate arising from an awareness that the firm's costs differ from the industry average. The last assumes that a high-cost firm will make a special effort to reduce its costs by searching for lower-cost techniques. Putting these elements together we can discern two ways in which the current level of costs in firm j affects the rate of change in those costs over time. The first is the transfer mechanism, described by Downie (1958, pp. 63-80) to operate as follows: a firm with below-average (compared to the industry) costs will have higher profits and will therefore spend more on new equipment and on R&D, with a consequent decrease in its cost.

The second way is the innovation mechanism described by Downie (1958, pp. 81-96) as follows: high costs are an incentive to search for techniques, whether in production, product development, organization, or operations, that reduce total average cost. The typical situation, Downie suggests, will have the transfer mechanism outweighing the action of the innovative mechanism. In this case lower-cost firms will have average costs which decline faster than high-cost firms. If the industry starts out with a number of firms with different cost structures, it is clear that over time the least-cost firms will have a faster decline in costs than high-cost firms. As a result, the weighted average costs of the industry will decline and hence, via the (assumed) way prices are set, so too will the industry price. The decline in price will squeeze out the least-efficient firms, thus decreasing the number of firms in the industry and hence increase the market share of each surviving firm. So concentration would increase.[2] What would work against this is a strong innovation mechanism. The strength of this mechanism would depend on the rate or speed at which innovations in technique (i.e., how things get done), production, and organization (e.g., horizontal or other corporate arrangements) are disseminated or dispersed across an industry.

Downie (1958, pp. 93-94) describes the workings of the transfer and innovation mechanism as follows:

> The dispersion of efficiency at any particular moment of time results from the fact that innovations in technique (which may also be associated with innovations in production objectives) take place, that they are made by individual firms within the industry, and that knowledge of them is diffused only relatively slowly. The transfer mechanism . . . progressively reduces the average degree of cost dispersion, by exalting the low cost at the expense of the high. But the smaller the dispersion becomes the slower the rate at which it contracts further. This is all the more true because the rate of experimentation with new techniques will tend to intensify as the dispersion of costs is reduced. On the assumption of a self-financing industry . . . the cost of unsuccessful experimentation is something which has to be financed from the profits of the industry, so that the average rate of profit in the industry is higher. This acts . . . to slow down the rate at which the dispersion contracts. At some point the process of experimentation results in successful innovations. . . . The effect will be a disruption of the old cost-relatives and much of the redistribution of business between firms which the transfer mechanism has brought about it will now have to set to work to undo.

Thus, both the transfer and innovation mechanism of the competitive process work to impose differences in the rank and market share of individual firms and their products. Evidently, where these mechanisms are not at play the competitive process has done its work, i.e., reshuffling of the market positions of firms and their products is no longer possible and innovative activity has reached its limit, i.e., the process of discovery can uncover no more than it has already.

This theory of the competitive process makes an important contribution to our understanding of the Clemens-Cocks model and the

Schumpeterian-Littlechild view of competition. It illustrates that the process of relative growth of firms, of innovations by firms, and of changes in relative efficiency between firms is perpetual by nature. Thus, just as Cocks redrew (Figure 5.2) Clemens's curve (Figure 5.1) to show the effect of competition on prices and products in a subsequent period, this should be done in sequential periods as well, given that competition is a process where the constellation of demand and supply hardly, if ever, stays the same between any two points in time. Nonetheless, for illustrative purposes it should be recognized that both Figure 5.1 and Figure 5.2 may be used to show how the competitive process described by Downie works. However, it is important to realize that only if innovative activity plays itself out would one be able to graphically illustrate the point of P = MC. It should be noted here that Figure 3.3 (see p. 21) may also be used for graphical purposes to illustrate the workings of the competitive process formulated by Downie. Where the transfer mechanism considerably outweighs the innovation mechanism there would be a tendency for the price level in an industry to approach its MC level. However, for as long as the innovation mechanism functions one should expect an industry to conform as depicted by Figure 3.3. The strength with which this mechanism operates would determine how great the inequality P > MC should be.

A question arises in this regard as to which of the two mechanisms triggers the competitive process, or to put it another way, what the direction of causality is between the transfer and innovation mechanism. Downie (1958, p. 95) concludes that "progress consists in the creation of cost dispersion and it is the tendency of cost dispersion to be eliminated which generates progress." This corresponds to what has been outlined by this work thus far, namely that innovation fosters competition.

The stage has now been set to summarize the discussion on competition in the following axiom: competition is created by innovation. To some this fundamental principle may appear extreme. It nonetheless encapsulates the key element, i.e., progress, that explains why some markets cannot move beyond "perfect" competition and why others are constantly in a state of flux. Progress is embedded in the advances of technology, improvements in the use of the factors of production, the appearance of products and alternatives where none before existed, the creation of wealth, the change in consumer preferences for that which is novel and better, and the promotion of freedom of choice. In the absence of legislative barriers to entry where progress has ceased or entails insignificant changes, competition has reached its limit and the market at hand is in a state of perfect competition. Quite obviously, the reverse would apply where progress is at play. Here the market at hand would be subject to regular changes.

Here it is emphasized that there should be no legislatively imposed barriers to entry or trade (e.g., legalized monopolies, licenses, levies, and so on). As was noted earlier, in the absence of these barriers the only other way for such barriers to come in existence (and for market power to be present) is if an advantage is enjoyed by the incumbent firm(s) over potential entrants. Examples here include sole ownership of some necessary input or factor of production, access to superior techniques of production, beliefs by customers in the superiority of established products, economies of scale[3] which render new entry uneconomic, and so on. In general, the workings of the transfer and innovation mechanism would inevitably produce a situation where some firms foreclose or expose the limits of others, with the consequence that the former would have higher rankings and profits and greater market share relative to the latter. Should then barriers to entry so erected be considered as an impediment to markets arriving at perfect competition? This question is the topic of Chapter 6.

To summarize, Chapter 5 begins by stating that the perfectly competitive condition of $P = MC$ assumes away innovative behavior and applies to homogeneous goods. Departures from these conditions involve product distinctiveness, which may either be lasting or perishable. It was revealed that in the former instance firms are likely to employ a price-skimming strategy and in the latter instance a price-penetration strategy. To demonstrate how this may take place, the Clemens-Cocks model was presented. It was shown that as the number of product alternatives or substitutes increases, firms switch from price skimming to price penetration, or put another way, markets move from innovative to imitative competition. The Clemens-Cocks model was used to provide a formal framework of what the competitive process entails, demonstrating that the process works by means of a transfer and innovation mechanism. The innovation mechanism sets competition in motion by having firms search for new techniques, whether in production, product development, organization, or operations, which will reduce total average costs. Firms able to implement such techniques before any other would set the transfer mechanism in operation. This, as the name implies, involves the shift of market share and change in rank away from those firms that have become outmoded. The innovation and transfer mechanism portrays competition as a continuous process involving the invasion and cross-invasion of markets. It was noted that this, which is so characteristic of economic activity, may give rise to barriers to (new) entry. However, an important question here is whether such barriers should be treated as synonymous with retarding rivalry.

Chapter 6

Barriers to Competition

The conventionally accepted barriers to entry have been classified by Bain (1968, p. 255) in three groups:

1. *Product differentiation.* This covers long-established preferences of buyers for existing products, sometimes sustained by continuous advertising of brands and firm names, patent protection of products, product innovation through firm research and development programs, and control of particular distribution systems and retail outlets;
2. *Absolute cost advantages.* These arise from superior production techniques, either as a result of past experience; patented or secret processes; from control of particular inputs required for production, be it materials, labor, management skills, or equipment; and from access to cheaper funds because existing firms represent lower risks than new ones;
3. *Economies of scale.* These are also known as increasing returns to scale and refer to the case of falling total average cost (for a firm) as output increases. If economies of scale are important, then a new entrant faces the dilemma of going in at a small scale and suffering a cost disadvantage or taking a very large risk by entering on large scale. A large-scale entry will disturb the existing situation and may cause excess supply, lower prices, and retaliation. These effects will be exacerbated if (a) the existing minimum efficient scale of incumbent firms constitutes a large proportion of total industry demand and/or (b) the elasticity of demand is low, for then an addition to industry supply will depress prices more.

These are, as a matter-of-course, the legally accepted sources of barriers to entry by the competition authorities of many OECD[1]

doi:10.1300/5505_06

countries (OECD, 1996b, pp. 5-11; OECD, 1999, pp. 17-40). For instance, this is the case with the U.S. antitrust authorities (OECD, 1996b, pp. 41-47; OECD, 1999, pp. 199-212), their EU (OECD, 1996b, pp. 53-57; OECD, 1999, pp. 213-224) or South African counterparts (Competition Board, 1999, pp. 22, 39). By extension many OECD competition authorities hold the same sources to act as barriers to entry in the pharmaceutical industry (OECD, 2001, pp. 11-12, pp. 54-58). For instance, this applies in the case of the U.S. antitrust authorities (Balto and Mongoven, 1999, pp. 261-269; OECD, 2001, pp. 315-322), their EU (OECD, 2001, pp. 342-346) or South African equivalents (Competition Board, 1999, pp. 22, 39).

If one commences with the premise that these constitute barriers to entry it would be only a short stretch to argue that firms erecting them are in possession of monopoly power. Put another way, in the presence of such entry barriers incumbent firms are likely to harm competition by restricting market entry and thereby engaging in monopoly practices (e.g., monopoly pricing, tie-in sales, predatory pricing, and so on).

However, as Von Weizsäcker (1980, pp. 405-406) has pointed out, it is less than certain that the expenditures sustained to deter entry using the conventional barriers to entry are wasteful. They may well be socially productive in comparison with the equilibrium, which would prevail without them. Examples here may include making available an offer not previously provided or giving consumers alternatives that may provide them with gains they could not previously attain. Simply put, there is another way of viewing the conventional barriers to entry is as being symptomatic of rivalry.

To illustrate the case in point we draw reference to economies of scale.

ECONOMIES OF SCALE

Here the argument usually runs as follows. If low-cost production requires a large scale of output, then a new firm attempting to enter a market currently occupied by one or more incumbents faces the choice of producing a small amount at a substantial cost disadvantage or producing efficiently at large output, thereby swamping the market and driving the prevailing product price down. Either strategy might well be unprofitable, so economies of scale may discourage new firms from attempting entry. In that case incumbent firms will be protected from competition, which in turn may lead to (severe) monopoly distortions.

However, if economies of scale are accepted as a barrier to entry, then as Stigler (1968, p. 67) has remarked it is equally possible to say that inadequate demand is also a barrier to entry. Figure 6.1, adapted from Hay and Morris (1991, p. 87), is used to illustrate the argument. Consider an industry producing a homogeneous product with a long-run average cost curve, as shown by LAC in Figure 6.1 and industry demand curve DD. It is assumed that the industry operates in accordance with the "Sylos postulate," in that entrants may be considered to expect that firms already in the industry would maintain existing output levels if new entry occurs. This is justified on the basis that firms operating fairly near capacity with high fixed costs will find contraction of output very unprofitable and expansion on a significant scale impossible for a considerable period. In this case, only the industry demand curve to the right of the existing price/demand point will be available to the new entrant.

The entry-preventing price is the highest price consistent with no part of this residual section of the demand curve being profitable for the potential entrant. This can be found graphically by sliding the LAC curve and its axes horizontally to the right until no part of the

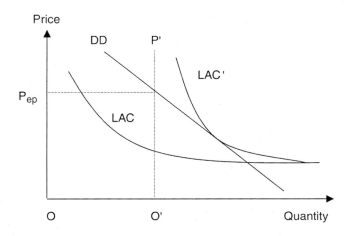

FIGURE 6.1. Economies of scale as a barrier to entry. *Source:* Adapted from Hay and Morris, 1991, p. 87.

LAC curve touches the industry demand curve (shown by LAC' and O'P'). The entry-prevention price is then given by the intersection of the new axis O'P' and the DD line. At this price the current output is OO'. Only output beyond O' is available for the new entrant. If it enters it will expand total industry output, depressing the price level. The industry will move down its demand curve, with the new firm meeting the increment of demand.

However, P_{ep} and O' have been chosen explicitly to ensure that no level of demand for the new entrant is sufficient to cover his or her costs, thus effectively impeding entry. A higher price, by reducing existing demand, would have made more of the demand curve available to the potential entrant (O'P' and LAC' would have been further to the left), and profitable entry could have been made at any level of output where DD was above LAC'. Thus, P_{ep} is the limit price. Any price above it would grant an entrant an adequate demand to enter the market and a price below it would, of course, still discourage all entry, but would sacrifice profits needlessly. However, a number of difficulties may be found with accepting that at P_{ep} entry is discouraged by virtue of inadequate demand.

First, if it prevails, P_{ep} would be a uniform price in a homogeneous product industry with significant differences in firms' costs. This either implies a collusive group of firms or a dominant firm, i.e., one which sets price and then meets all the demand not taken up by other firms in the industry at that price. In the former instance we know that prices set by collusive, i.e., cartel, arrangements seldom if ever last as chiseling by cartel members is too great to overcome or cartel-based price concealment always provides conditions rife enough to encourage entry. In the latter instance, where a dominant firm is present, this merely reflects that a more efficient, i.e., lower-cost, firm exists to meet the demand in question. Put simply, P_{ep} is consistent with a contestable market, i.e., one where entry is free but not without costs. In such a market, entry need not actually take place. The threat of it is sufficient discipline to ensure that the incumbent will never charge a price that implies profits in excess of the normal or perfectly competitive level. That is, the threat of entry would keep the market at the limit price, which in essence would act as an entry-deterring price only if it is below the entrants' average variable costs (whether in the short or long run). Obviously, such an arrangement does not work to the detriment of consumers.

It should be recognized here that P_{ep} is as much a limit price as $P = MC$ is, in the sense that at $P = MC$ any firm just breaks even and the motive for entry is completely eliminated. No firm with standard technology (i.e., that shared by other players in the industry) would be tempted to enter such an industry (where $P = MC$), any more than it would be tempted to enter one where scale economies and limited demand have resulted in only a single firm occupying the market with a price equal to the average cost required to supply the market at that price (Reekie, 1979, p. 88). Simply put, at $P = MC$ no (threat of) entry exists in the long run. By contrast, a price such as P_{ep} may have a preclusionary effect, but in a contestable market it would not be strong enough to foreclose entry altogether, especially if the entrant can demonstrate or credibly install the perception that he or she has a long-run average cost advantage compared to the incumbent.

Second, it may be asked why the price-setter should not maximize profits most of the time, reducing price to the limit level (P_{ep}) only when the threat of new entry occurs. If the threat of shifting to a limit price is insufficient, the time taken for entry to actually occur would usually be sufficient to make the threat a reality. However, the cost of expanding output to the limit level (given production or capacity constraints in the short run) might be very high, giving the new entrant considerable grounds for not expecting this reaction. This in turn would affect the pace of entry positively.

Third, it is questionable if incumbents would behave in accordance with the Sylos postulate. If the potential entrant does enter, it seems that the rational action for the existing firm(s) is to include the new firm in its price-leadership policy and to contract output somewhat. In this way a higher profit could be made in comparison with those profits (quite possibly negative) resulting from a policy of maintaining previous output levels so as to preempt the market. Knowing this, the potential entrant may not be deterred by the incumbent(s).

Fourth, whether the new entrant is able to claim a share in the market in which the incumbent operates depends on whether the entrant can capture any of the existing firm(s)' demand, on relative costs and on relative power, to survive a loss-making period. For instance, the cost of expanding output to the limit-price level with a plant geared to the smaller short-run profit-maximizing level might be very high, giving the new entrant considerable grounds for not expecting the incumbent's output-preempting tactic to prevail in the long run. In this case, although the entry may induce short-run losses, the entrant would be aware that the incumbent is unsustainably incurring such losses on a larger output than he or she is, effectively encouraging the entrant to wait out the loss-making period until a price level above P_{ep} prevails.

From this inspection of economies of scale it is doubtful whether they can be considered solely as a barrier to entry. What economies of scale do (along with demand) is determine the size of firms that will exist in an industry (Reekie, 1979, p. 88). If economies of scale are regarded as barriers to entry, then this is equivalent to saying that inadequate demand is a barrier to entry. However, as our discussion revealed, whether the new entrant is able to claim a share in the market in which the incumbent operates depends on whether the entrant can capture any of the existing firm(s)' demand, which depends on relative costs (between the entrant and the incumbent) and on relative power to survive a loss-making period (between the entrant and the incumbent). Only if the entrant can demonstrate or credibly install the perception that he or she has a long-run average cost advantage compared to the incumbent is his or her entry feasible. However, entry is not necessary if the market price is to be pushed toward the perfectly competitive level. Our discussion showed the incumbent can inhibit entry by pricing at a level sufficiently close to the perfectly competitive level, where entry is deterred all together.

We are now left with contemplating whether both product differentiation and absolute cost advantages are barriers to entry. Our discussion turns to the first of these sources: product differentiation.

PRODUCT DIFFERENTIATION

By definition product differentiation implies something unique about the product, i.e., that it has an attribute(s) others do not share. It is not enough for producers (sellers) to be aware of the differences in their products. This sentiment must also be shared by consumers (buyers), given that as a matter of principle the market eliminates from the entrepreneurial role those unable to anticipate better than others the future demand of consumers and that it is consumers who must accept the product as matchless (Von Mises, 1949, p. 288). The entrepreneur, according to Backhaus (1983, p. 108), is functionally defined as the originator of economic development and may be a person, a group, or an institution, such as a firm.

Going back to our discussion on product differentiation it should be noted that products are considered to be differentiated when physical differences or attributes (either real or perceived) cause buyers to prefer the product of one firm over that of a rival firm. In practice, product differentiation may occur in terms of physical appearance (e.g., packaging shape and color); features (e.g., safe and efficacious); durability (e.g., long-lasting); ancillary services (e.g., warranties, after-sales services, and information); image (e.g., prestige, healthy lifestyle); and geographic location (e.g., differences in attributes determined by location).

Product differentiation affects the degree of substitutability between products and in turn the constellation of demand and supply. How the constellation is affected depends on how distinct a firm's offer is, i.e., how much of an imperfect substitute the product is. If the product is new in the sense that it has no substitutes, then the firm is responsible for erecting both market demand (given by the firm's average revenue curve) and supply (given by the firm's MC curve above its shutdown point) where none existed before. Since the product has no substitutes, the demand curve would initially be downward-sloping and the supply curve would be upward-sloping. This would continue until such time that substitutes become readily available, thereby resulting in perfect elasticity for both the demand and supply curve in the long run. However, if a product's distinctiveness is insubstantial to begin with, then the firm would be working toward shifting or tilting the existing demand or supply curves (for the good). For instance, in improving an existing product a firm may have modified its existing production process to allow it to produce more of this product than it would have had it not modified its production process, which in turn would allow it to price this product below the one in use by consumers at present. In this way, the firm would shift both the market demand and supply curves to the right for the good in question. Alternatively, if the offer were no different from what is already offered, then the demand and supply curves would be tilted until perfectly elastic, i.e., horizontal. In the case of homogeneous products there is perfect substitutability and buyers see no real or perceived differences between the products offered by different firms. Here consumers are aware of the quality of the product, i.e., its ability in terms of the attributes it offers to satisfy or meet a customer's requirements, making price the single most important dimension along which firms producing homogeneous products compete. For such products any consumer search, i.e., seeking knowledge about the product, would involve buyers canvassing sellers as to the most favorable price they can obtain in the market (Stigler, 1961a, p. 213).

Things are different in the case of heterogeneous products. If a firm breaks away from offering what an existing product provides, uncertainty about the quality of its good arises, making it difficult for consumers to discern whether the product's quality is good or bad. From the firm's viewpoint, uncertainty concerning its product is clearly disadvantageous. In its presence consumers would be hesitant to commit to a purchase since, as Akerlof (1970, pp. 488-500) has demonstrated, if sellers know the quality of their product but buyers do not, then the price buyers face reflects the risk they take that they will end up with poor quality. In practice, in the case of novel products, firms attempt to mitigate this risk by resorting to advertising to draw consumer attention to the characteristics embodied in the product, such as product quality by means of a brand name, inducing consumers to try a new product via a free trial offer, tying the new product to an existing offer, and so on. Such practices are consistent with minimizing consumer search, which is a cost of purchase, given it is costly both in time and money and so inversely related to consumption. They are also a part of a firm's mundane activities to create goodwill, i.e., continued patronage by consumers without continued search (that is, no more than occasional verification), and reputation, which denotes the persistence of quality and commands a price (or exacts a penalty) because it economizes on search.[2] We may put our discussion on heterogeneous products in the context of goodwill and reputation with reference to the matrix classification in Table 6.1, dichotomizing each of the aspects considered into present (x) or absent (o).

Examination of all the possibilities enables us to eliminate 5 to 8 as a priori not applicable, i.e., in practice they would not hold. So, we are left with cases 1 to 4, which are a priori likely.

In the case of heterogeneous goods, whether the products compete on price alone would depend on what the consumer's search reveals about the substitutability between the novel and the existing product. In the case where the attributes of the products are such that consumers

TABLE 6.1. Heterogeneous products in the context of goodwill and reputation.

Possibilities	Product differentiation	Goodwill	Reputation	Profits (short/medium-run)
1	X	X	X	Supernormal (above average)
2	O	X	X	Normal (average), or Ricardian rent, or loss
3	X	O	O	Loss
4	O	O	O	Loss
5	X	X	O	N/A
6	X	O	X	N/A
7	O	X	O	N/A
8	O	O	X	N/A

classify them as near-neighbor or similar products, rivalry between firms would be based predominantly on price and vice versa. In the former case we should expect the transfer mechanism of the competitive process to be at play, whereas in the latter case we should expect the innovation mechanism to be at play. Here we saw how firms with distinct products earn temporarily supernormal profits and how over time their short-run profits dissipate. This is the situation that Row 1 in Table 6.1 depicts. However, we saw how firms with indistinguishable products were confined to normal profits, which is the situation Row 2 in Table 6.1 depicts. Our discussion on economies of scale and inadequate demand suggests that this confinement is not absolute. The imminent likelihood exists that in the case of entrants losses may actually take place. This would occur if the firms entering are incapable of covering their average variable costs in the short and long runs as the inadequate demand for their products or their inability to enter and sell at P_{ep} may be credited to the lack of distinctiveness of their offer(s).

However, it is likely that (some) incumbent firms may actually make a Ricardian, that is, economic rent (formally dealt with in the following section, but for the time being it may be simplistically regarded as a firm earning in excess of existing or potential rivals). This would be possible given that reputation denotes the persistence of quality and accordingly commands a price (or exacts a penalty) because it economizes on (consumer) search. Accordingly, some offers may have a greater fame amongst consumers than others, resulting in the firms producing them earning more than their existing or potential rivals.

The situation depicted in Row 4 is special because it highlights the fact that the aspects examined are not stationary. Row 4 has the characteristics of an opportunity waiting to be exploited, i.e., it reflects a new market potential. Here, in the immediate term, when uncertainty is rife, the introduction of a breakthrough product may place the market in a stage of infancy, which is what Row 3 depicts. In time the product breakthrough would acquire reputation and in turn goodwill, thereby transporting matters to Row 1. As the product's distinctiveness fades (recall supernormal profits are a condition of entry) and all that is left is reputation and goodwill, the market would shift to the state Row 2 depicts.

Our discussion on product differentiation and profit (and loss) makes due allowance for perfect competition in special circumstances only, namely where product differentiation is negligible or absent but goodwill and reputation are present. In addition, the matrix in Table 6.1 indicates that the presence of product differentiation alone does not amount to supernormal profits where the new offer is so different that it has no substitute. Here the firm making the offer would have to build reputation and by extension goodwill, i.e., essentially erect demand.

This would entail the firm alleviating the risk of consumers perceiving that they will end up buying a poor-quality item. As noted previously, in practice this would take the form of informative advertising, free trial offers, tie-in-sales, and so on. The possibility for supernormal profits exists in special circumstances only, namely where product differentiation is of high degree and goodwill and reputation is large enough to suppress the negative effects from uncertainty about the product's quality. As product differentiation comes to fall in degree over time, i.e., the once-breakthrough product becomes common in status, all that is left is reputation and/or goodwill. Under this environment normal profits should be expected, although as noted earlier it is likely that entrants exposed to it may incur losses, whereas incumbents may earn economic rents.

We have now come to the point of concluding the discussion on product differentiation. The conclusion drawn is simple, namely that there is no reason to presume outright that product differentiation is a barrier to entry. In fact, strong theoretical reasons exist for treating it as part and parcel of the competitive process, participating both in its transfer and/or innovation mechanism—either by involving the introduction of substitutes (in the former case) or novel products (in the latter case). In that way, product differentiation is consistent with market entry, i.e., it may facilitate entry into and penetration of markets by firms with products that buyers may prefer over existing ones. On the one hand, a potential entrant will scan the entire market looking for the most profitable niche between neighboring products in which to introduce a new product. Consumers are indifferent between neighboring products. If a new firm enters, it will depress the price of similar (or near-neighbor) products. Demand substitutability will result in lower prices and profits for other, somewhat less similar products (i.e., the transfer mechanism is at play). On the other hand, a firm may introduce a product so distinct that this creates a new market altogether where none existed before (i.e., the innovation mechanism is activated). Here the incumbent, initially the first entrant, exposes the conditions of entry and the gains that can emanate from actual entry. This in turn activates the transfer mechanism, which over time would involve firms competing away supernormal profits to the point of the marginal firm.

We are now left with contemplating whether absolute cost advantages are a barrier to entry.

ABSOLUTE COST ADVANTAGES

Absolute cost advantages may arise from reputation (as noted previously), superior production techniques (either as a result of past experience, patented or secret processes, or from control of particular inputs required for production, be it materials, labor, management skills, or equipment), and from access to cheaper funds because existing firms represent lower risks than new ones. Each of these can be viewed as representative of Ricardian, that is, economic rents. But should Ricardian rents be viewed as a barrier to entry?

The conventional definition of economic rent is that it is the excess a firm makes over the competitive rate of return (i.e., normal profit) attributable to owning a factor of production or resource whose supply is limited, at least in the short run (see, for example, Pindyck and Rubinfeld [1995, pp. 262-263]). This definition lends itself readily to equating economic rent with supernormal profit, which in turn standard economic theory affiliates with the absence of competition. However, is such association between economic rent and profit warranted? Let us consider the original text of Ricardo (1932, pp. 46-48) on this subject:

> The laws which regulate the progress of rent are widely different from those which regulate the progress of profits, and seldom operate in the same direction. In all improved countries, that which is annually paid to the landlord, partaking of both characters, rent and profit, is sometimes kept stationary by the effects of opposing causes; at other times advances or recedes, as one or the other of these causes preponderates. In the future pages of this work, then, whenever I speak of the rent of land, I wish to be understood as speaking of that compensation, which is paid to the owner of land for the use of its original and indestructible powers. . . . If all land had the same properties, if it were unlimited in quantity, and uniform in quality, no charge could be made for its use, unless where it possessed peculiar advantages of situation. It is only, then, because land is not unlimited in quantity and uniform in quality . . . land of an inferior quality, or less advantageously situated is called into cultivation, that rent is ever paid for the use of it.
>
> When in the progress of society, land of the second degree of fertility is taken into cultivation, rent immediately commences on that of the first quality, and the amount of that rent will depend on the difference in the quality of these two proportions. When land of the third quality is taken into cultivation, rent immediately commences on the second, and it is regulated as before, by the difference in their productive powers. At the same time, the rent of the first quality will rise, for that must always be above the rent of the second, by the difference between the produce which they yield with a given quantity of capital and labour. . . .

Rent is always the difference between the produce obtained by the employment of two equal quantities of capital and labour. If with a capital, of £1,000, a tenant obtain 100 quarters of wheat from his land, and by the employment of a second capital of £1,000, he obtain a further returns of eighty-five, his landlord would have the power at the expiration of his lease, of obliging him to pay fifteen quarters, or an equivalent value for additional rent. . . . If he is satisfied with a diminution of fifteen quarters in the return for his second £1,000, it is because no employment more profitable can be found for it.

Ricardo's text was written in the early 1800s, which would explain why his focus regarding the notion of rent was with reference to land. However, if we are willing to extract the principle of what rent as a concept entails using contemporary language, then several things can be discerned from the text.[3] First, rent in its Ricardian sense does not equal profit. Ricardo (1932, p. 45) notes that "this is a distinction of great importance . . . for it is found that the laws which regulate the progress of rent are widely different from those which regulate the progress of profits, and seldom operate in the same direction." Second, Ricardian rent is an issue only of relative productivity between different inputs (e.g., capital and labour) or assets (e.g., reputation or the lack of it) a firm employs or has in its possession. Third, an inspection of Ricardian rents should be governed only by marginal productivity analysis (in so far as using the inputs or assets is concerned) and opportunity cost assessment (in so far as adding or acquiring the inputs or assets is concerned). The addition of factors of production used or assets acquired is, strictly speaking, determined from an assessment of opportunity costs (i.e., the value of any benefit foregone, or given up, from an alternative action). This assessment is based on foreseen differences in productivity between different inputs and is not confined to the same line of business. Fourth, Ricardian rent definitely does not feature revenue (earnings). From the text we can define it to be the difference in productivity between firms employing alternative (scarce) factors of production in the same amount for the production of the same good under the same technology (in method and technique). The latter part of this definition may not be clear outright, since Ricardo (1932, p. 57) acknowledges the effects of technology later in the text:

> But improvements in agriculture are of two kinds: those which increase the productive powers of the land, and those which enable us, by improving our machinery, to obtain its produce with less labour. They both lead to a fall in the price of raw produce; they both affect rent.

Fifth, Ricardian rent is time-invariant, i.e., it is not confined to the short, medium, or long run, meaning that it exists throughout time.

This is to be expected in terms of the appropriate definition of Ricardian rents (provided in the preceding point) and simply reflects that differences in productivity between firms exist at any point in time and are bound to exist throughout time.

Relative to the appropriate definition we have awarded to economic (Ricardian) rent, the contemporary definition seems to depart from the notion of rent as manifested in its Ricardian sense. Simply put, contrary to popular belief it appears economic rent, in strict Ricardian sense, has an inverse association with supernormal profits.

Economic rent, in its Ricardian sense, is compatible with the production efficiency condition that applies to contestable markets (for a summary discussion of these markets see Baumol [1982, pp. 3-6]). Here a new firm would enter the market, attracted by the prospect of producing efficiently, undercutting the existing inefficient firms, and making a profit. Alternatively incumbents may alter their productive efficiency relative to other incumbents, thereby undercutting inefficient firms and making a profit. In any event production occurs up to the point where the MC of output equals its marginal benefit as measured by P. This compatibility with the production efficiency condition of contestable markets implies that we can regard the presence of economic rent as the propellant of the transfer mechanism of the competitive process. As illustrated earlier, this mechanism also works to the point of $P = MC$. Here what would explain the movement in market share between firms engaged in producing homogeneous goods facing the same or similar cost conditions and the same or similar levels in technology (in method or technique) would depend on the differences in productive powers in the inputs firms employ.

Compared to its rivals, a firm employing inputs with superior productive powers (arising either from differences in the quality of the factors hired or from the way they are organized into a productive whole) would meet more of consumer demand in the market which it supplies. In practice this would translate into the firm having greater profit, higher market share, and better ranking than its rivals. However, many channels of information spillover make the retention of these only temporary. For instance, publications or technical meetings, conversations with employees of rival firms, hiring employees from rival firms, reverse engineering a product, commissioning inquiries to determine what a competitor has done, and so on. Each of these informs competitors as to the way their more successful rivals operate and works toward spelling out the productive operations of these rivals. This in turn brings about an environment where firms undercut one another and where those with greater productive powers temporarily earn a profit, until in the long run any supernormal profits are bid away.

Thus, the presence of economic rents pushes markets toward the perfectly competitive point in the long run. However, the innovation mechanism (e.g., changes in technology, moving from product homogeneity to product heterogeneity, and so on) leads to a disruption of the old cost-relatives so that much of the redistribution of business between firms which the transfer mechanism has brought about would now in all likelihood be undone. This gives the competitive process its transient nature, where once the innovation mechanism has completed its work it kickstarts the transfer mechanism until the process repeats itself. This goes on, and on, and is the reason why, as noted earlier, economic rents exist throughout time. In each instance, i.e., during each cycle of innovation, their presence propels the transfer mechanism to push markets toward the perfectly competitive point before the innovation mechanism brings forth a new cycle of innovation.

This concludes the discussion on absolute cost advantages. On the one hand, such advantages may emanate from interfirm differences in productive powers that could be due to the quality of the factors they hire, the assets in their possession, or the way they organize either of these into a productive whole. On the other hand, they could emanate from interfirm differences in accumulated experience (learning by doing). Each of these sources of absolute cost advantages constitutes an example of economic, in the Ricardian sense, rent.

It has been shown that the contemporary definition of economic rent is not really an adequate interpretation of what the actual definition ought to be. In line with Ricardo's original work, we should consider economic rent to represent the difference in productivity between firms employing alternative (scarce) factors of production in the same amount for the production of the same good under the same technology (in method and technique). This makes economic rent, i.e., its presence, the propellant of the transfer mechanism of the competitive process. Given that a sine qua non of the process is having firms vie to place their inputs or assets in their highest-yield use from existing opportunities, this in all likelihood assures the presence of economic rents, which through the transfer mechanism would lead to markets approaching the perfectly competitive point in the long run.

If absolute cost advantages are associated with some firms having greater productive powers than others, and if this bestows them a higher market share and greater profits, then it is not at all clear why such advantages should be a barrier to entry or undesirable from the point of view of welfare.

If considerable doubts exist about treating product differentiation, absolute cost advantages, and economies of scale as a barrier to entry, and if theoretically strong reasons exist for casting doubt over these being barriers to entry, then what defines a barrier to entry? This is what we address in the following section.

REDEFINING BARRIERS TO COMPETITION

One answer, although partial, to the question posited in the previous section has been provided by Baumol (1982, pp. 3-5) with reference to the conditions of entry into contestable markets. Baumol (1982, p. 3) points out that the condition of free entry should not be taken to imply that it is costless or easy to enter, but rather that the "entrant suffers no disadvantage in terms of production technique or perceived product quality relative to the incumbent." This, however, as is well-known, presupposes an absence of sunk costs (i.e., irrecoverable expenditures). Examples of these entail capital requirements, including investments in capacity, proliferation of products, marketing expenditures, and so on. Thus, if such costs exist in practice, then they may place entrants at a competitive disadvantage, and if so competition authorities may hold them to be a barrier to entry (see barrier to entry references cited at beginning of chapter). This takes us full circle to the realm of barriers to entry discussed previously, where considerable doubt was cast over considering economies of scale, product differentiation, and absolute cost advantages to fulfill the role of barriers to entry. The same could be said for sunk costs. Given sunk costs entail capital requirements, such requirements, as pointed out by Stigler (1968), are not a barrier to entry. According to Stigler (1968, p. 67) "a barrier to entry may be defined as a cost of producing . . . which must be borne by a firm which seeks to enter an industry but is not borne by firms already in the industry." Applying his definition to the issue of capital requirements, Stigler (1968, p. 70) notes that "since existing firms also have to meet these requirements, they are not a barrier."

Two things are evident from the discussion on barriers to entry thus far. First, a barrier to entry must be something that interferes with competition or, specifically, the competitive process (Fisher, 1987a, p. 33). It follows that not everything that makes entry appear difficult or uninviting is necessarily a barrier to entry. The mere necessity of building a plant when incumbents have already built theirs is not such a barrier. Neither is the necessity of advertising (to inform consumers) or the application for registering a product to ascertain its safety and efficacy to the patient. A barrier to entry should permit an incumbent to earn supernormal profits continuously without inducing others to enter and bid those profits away. This, however, has been interpreted by some economists such as White (1987, p. 20) to mean that barriers to entry are costs that entrants have to bear irrespective of whether incumbents have borne them too. According to this view, significant economies of scale and investments in specialized resources that have limited alternative use are barriers. Similarly, relatively heavy advertising and other promotional costs are also not barriers to entry.

The type of barrier to entry envisaged is reminiscent of Bastiat's economic fable *A Petition*. Here the manufacturers of everything connected with lighting put their case for protection by the legislature as follows:

> We are suffering from the ruinous competition of a foreign rival who apparently works under conditions so far superior to our own for the production of light that he is flooding the domestic market with it at an incredibly low price; for the moment he appears, our sales cease, all the consumers turn to him, and a branch of . . . industry whose ramifications are innumerable is all at once reduced to complete stagnation. This rival . . . is none

other than the sun. . . . We ask you to be so good as to pass a law requiring the closing of all windows, dormers, skylights, inside and outside shutters, curtains, casements, bull's-eyes, dead-lights, and blinds—in short, all openings, holes, chinks, and fissures through which the light of the sun is wont to enter houses, to the detriment of the fair industries with which, we are proud to say, we have endowed the country, a country that can not, without betraying ingratitude, abandon us today to so unequal a combat. (Bastiat, [1845] 1996, p. 56)

Simply put, a barrier to entry must deny society the experience of a beneficial trading outcome. This is what Tullock's rent seeking portrays (Tullock, 1967, p. 228; Tullock, 1993, p. 22). Here the rent is not the one in its Ricardian sense, but a one that would be increased by regulatory capture, and accordingly one for which no socially valuable by-product exists. Such rent encourages rent-seeking costs or socially wasteful expenditures made by the rent seeker to achieve a gain to which he is the primary recipient. Tullock (1993, p. 22) notes that

Investing resources in order to obtain a rent is not necessarily rent seeking. For example if I were to invest resources in research and invent a cure for cancer, which I then were to patent, I should certainly become wealthy on the rents that would be generated. This however is not really what we mean by rent seeking. The result of my resource investment is not only that I am better off, but so is almost everyone else . . . If, on the other hand, I were to invest resources in obtaining a law prohibiting the import of a newly-devised cure for cancer because I am myself a manufacturer of an older and less effective one, then I might gain, but almost everyone else would lose. This is the kind of thing that we mean by rent seeking.

For politicians, as noted by Stigler (1988, p. 219), the rents are "success in election and the perquisites of office," whereas for lobbyists with commercial interest the rents include, among others, the results of import tariffs, subsidies, price fixing, restricting the modes of organizing, and at the extreme restricting rivalry itself. Graphically, the "gain" from the rent-seeking activity is represented by the π rectangle in Figure 3.3 (see p. 21). Thus, in studying the welfare losses from a monopoly essentially two kinds of losses exist: the well-known

Harberger or DWL triangle and the Tullock rectangle. It should be noted that usually the rectangle, which indicates the amount of rent-seeking taking place in order to obtain a monopoly position, is by far the larger of the two, and that it reflects a loss, i.e., it is "wasted," to the extent of not improving social welfare. In industries of a highly innovative nature (e.g., pharmaceuticals), rent seeking is successfully carried out mainly through R&D expenditure. Such industries represent those cases where expenditure in order to achieve a monopoly position is directly productive in the sense that it contributes to social welfare. In this connection it should be noted that the less elastic the demand curve, the less important will be the triangle relative to the rectangle.

Second, increases in market share and higher profit move in synchrony in any system where performance and reward go hand in hand (Demsetz, 1995, pp. 160-161). Superior ability in lowering cost or in improving products, irrespective of how it is achieved, will inevitably draw sales from the unsuccessful toward the successful and efficient firms (Demsetz, 1995, pp. 145-146, 160). Thus, the reason why some firms have a higher proportion of the market than others need not result from collusive behavior. If anyone doubts this "one should look for special privileges excluding actual and potential competitors granted via the political process" (Kenney, 1984, p. 50).

Our discussion on barriers to competition thus far leads us to the conclusion that this is a barrier imposed by regulatory intervention only. This assertion should not be taken lightly; neither should it be assumed to be extreme. In fact, excellent theoretical grounds support the opposite, which can be traced to the theory of economic regulation expounded by Stigler (1988, pp. 210-213).

In principle, when a firm or an industry seeks regulation the first question that arises is why they solicit the coercive power of the state instead of its cash. When requiring state support it would appear that the most straightforward approach is to ask for direct subsidies. However, several possible reasons exist for not doing so. The first and more obvious is that cash subsidies to a particular type of firm will attract further competitors into the industry, also seeking these subsidies. Therefore, a group of firms or an industry seeking public support would try to combine this strategy with an attempt to create entry barriers in order to keep unwelcome new rivals out of the market. First, regulation which creates entry barriers for new firms would be in the interest of existing firms, whether coupled with additional direct public support or not. Such barriers may be created through licensing of an entire firm (which can also be used as a means of preferring domestic over foreign competitors), of particular divisions of the firm, or of its products before they can be marketed.

Second, industries may try to invoke regulations affecting substitutes and complements to their products. For example, provided that a trade-off exists between treatment by drugs and other types of medication, producers of drugs could benefit if regulations induce price increases of those medications, and vice versa. Alternatively, a firm can also seek subsidization of complementary products, since this increases the demand for its products as long as new firms can be prevented from entering the market. For example, assuming the state is the national transport operator, the airline company may actively support state subsidies to airports so that resources be diverted away from other (new) modes of transportation (e.g., fast trains).

Third, firms may enlist the support of a regulatory agency in order to organize a cartel and fix prices while at the same time barring new competitors from entering the market. This, as revealed by Reekie (1997, pp. 282-285), is exactly what retail pharmacists in South Africa, the United Kingdom, the United States, Denmark, Holland, and Germany appear to have been able to achieve. Reekie (1997, p. 284) notes,

> The retail pharmacy cartel has recently proven it continues to possess political clout in the US market place. The USA, however, is not unique. The cartel's influence is pervasive in other parts of the globe as well. Retailers have influenced regulation and legislation in may other countries. Their success includes slowing down by legal process advances in distribution. Developments which are hampered range from conventional cost reducing devices such as attainment of scale economies, to more recent innovations designed explicitly to contain the costs of medicines.

It should be noted here that if a particular case of regulation is being analyzed it cannot be taken as given that the industry being regulated has actually sought that regulation. The political process admits outsiders (Stigler, 1988, p. 214). When resorting to the political level, a firm seeking regulation will no longer be on its own, as it would be if it had confined its activity to the marketplace. Political pressure groups which would not be able to command any leverage in the marketplace (boycotts being the remedy of last resort for such groups) may be able to influence the regulatory process, not necessarily to the benefit of the firm or industry under regulation. Thus, regulation may have come about as a consequence of the regulator's own desire to regulate (power and prestige may be deemed important objectives for civil servants), of competitors' political activity, of political activity on the part of interest groups only remotely connected with the industry, or of political activity on the part of the industry at some time in the past. This means that over time other interests may have gained control of the regulatory agency, the consequence being that regulation may work against the interest of the industry being regulated.

The major dissatisfaction with the theory of economic regulation is probably that expressed by Posner (1974, pp. 349-350), namely,

> The theory, pushed to its logical extreme, becomes rather incredible, because it excludes the possibility that a society concerned with the ability of interest groups to manipulate the political process in their favour might establish institutions that enable genuine public interest considerations to influence the formation of policy. . . . More generally the many features of law and public policy designed to maintain a market system are more plausibly explained by reference to a broad social interest in efficiency than by reference to the design of narrow interest groups.

However, if one were to follow the Posner argument to its logical extreme we would end up ascribing all kinds of superior properties to the regulator, relative to the competitive process, when it comes to directing the economy.

REGULATION AND ECONOMIC WELFARE

Here it should be borne in mind that it is not at all possible to assume that any feature of regulation, or any regulation of a particular industry, is necessarily enhancing economic welfare. There are three reasons for this. First, a problem exists with the definition of the public interest and what this means for economic welfare. The public interest includes, as pointed out by Reekie (1996, p. 50), the interests of labor, consumers, producers, and traders, as well as the national interest, and the latter itself contains, among others, the striving for economic growth, acceptable pattern of income distribution, and the efficient utilization of resources. In short, the public interest embraces "groups whose interests do not necessarily coincide, and economic goals which may be mutually exclusive" (Reekie, 1996, p. 50). With such a plethora of economic goals and special groups what is efficient for some may be construed as inefficient by others, in which case efficient would be what falls in the administrator's favored camp or favored economic goals.

Second, the move toward regulatory intervention necessarily involves the omission of property rights. This is a point Coase (1960, p. 17) emphasized by stressing that

> The government is . . . able to influence the use of factors of production by administrative decision. But the ordinary firm is subject to checks in its operations because of . . . competition. . . . The government is able . . . to avoid the market altogether, which a firm can never do. Just as the government can conscript or seize property, so it can decree that factors of production should only be used in such-and-such a way. . . . But the governmental administrative machine is not itself costless. . . . that direct governmental regulation will not necessarily give better results than leaving the problem to be solved by the market. . . .

Third, as noted by Hayek (1945, p. 527):

> The problem is precisely how to extend the span of our utilisation of resources beyond the span of the control of any one mind; and, therefore, how to dispense with the need of conscious control and how to provide inducements which will make individuals do the desirable things without anyone having to tell them what to do.

This is possible only by instituting a legal system of rights existing not for the purposes of government defining but formalizing such rights, given that life, liberty, and property are natural rights[4] and that their form can be modified by transactions on the market, as legal entitlements can be bought and sold just like any other product.

What follows from this is that government intervention comes at a cost and there is no reason to believe that its ramifications will be negligible. In spite of this, it is not uncommon to find administrative agencies, i.e., competition authorities, across countries being set in place to regulate the competitive process to ensure that the process does not produce a monopoly. What such agencies use to determine how competitive a market is will be the subject of investigation in Chapter 7.

It is not at all clear that the conventionally accepted barriers to competition, namely product differentiation, absolute cost advantages and economies of scale, are indeed barries to competition. Strong reasons, both in theory and practice, show that each of these is consistent with or symptomatic of rivalry. By definition, a barrier to entry or a barrier to competition ought to be that which is imposed by regulatory intervention only. Strong theoretical and practical reasons in the form of rent seeking and the economics of regulation exist to demonstrate that barriers so erected are both (1) undesirable from the point of view of economic welfare and (2) work against competition. Any presumption that regulatory intervention in the competitive process may be warranted (for whatever reason) has been shown to be unfounded. It is consistent with the regulator abrogating (whether partially or wholly) property rights and imposing on society costs that more than likely would not be negligible given that the regulatory claim of being motivated by the public interest is an ill-defined objective, and that the consumer exercising on a given day that choice he or she prefers is most certainly removed.

Essentially, two different ways exist to analyze competition in a market. On the one hand if we are interested in establishing an equilibrium point in studying an industry we will wish to focus on the familiar state of equilibrium, such as the fulfillment of marginal conditions (e.g., marginal cost = price = marginal utility). In equilibrium competition no longer exits. At this point the transfer mechanism has ceased to operate. What makes a disequilibrium in the long run not possible is competition among entrepreneurs. By definition these are the originators of economic progress that set the innovation mechanism in motion, which in turn produces short-run disequilibrium.

Over time competitors come to offer marginal improvements over the initial offer and thus by exhausting the potential for such impairments tend to work toward reestablishing an equilibrium in the long run. This process can be impaired when exchanges are not possible (e.g., for legal reasons) or when resources are owned by a monopoly, and entrepreneurs are not successful in proposing arrangements which would induce these owners to relinquish their monopoly.

Although the feasibility of certain prohibited exchanges is limited by the ability of legal authorities to enforce the rules, and although this is a consequence of public intervention in the marketplace, monopolistic resource-ownership as a barrier to competition is often a focus of public concern. In this context Backhaus (1983, pp. 108-109) has made two points. First, while the costs of prohibiting certain exchanges will not necessarily be borne by the legal authority, the private resource-owner must bear the opportunity costs of not realizing his or her product onto the market. When, for example, a producer is the exclusive owner of a commodity, he or she will have no particular advantage over any other producer, since the cost of using this exclusively owned good in the productive process (or of withholding its use) is equal to the opportunity cost of its alternative, i.e., of releasing it into the market and selling it to other producers.

Second, while prohibition of certain exchanges may often lead to clandestine, illicit exchanges that completely escape public attention and control, the reluctance to release exclusively owned resources or, alternatively, charging monopolistic prices for these resources creates incentives to develop substitutes. Consequently, artificial and imposed barriers to competition themselves create incentives to overcome these barriers; such incentives will in due course contribute to an erosion of the positions of either the owner of an exclusive resource or the authority which tries to prohibit exchanges. An interesting example is the presence of the retail pharmacy cartel in South Africa. Reekie (1997, p. 283) has noted that innovation in distribution has arisen from dispensing doctors and mail-order outlets, both of which have significantly encroached on the cartel's former preeminence. In the early 1980s nearly all private-sector sales passed through conventional retail pharmacies, but by 1993 this proportion had fallen to 41 percent by value, with 43 percent being paid out to dispensing doctors and the balance being accounted for by private hospital usage and the newly emerging mail-order distributors (Melamet Report, 1994, p. 41).

Although existence of a monopoly creates incentives to develop substitutes for a monopolistically controlled resource, attainment of a monopoly position may serve as an incentive to develop a scarce product in order to enjoy the monopoly thus created. This scenario entails two distinct possibilities. The monopolistic rent may be sought through either genuine innovation, e.g., the development of a product not hitherto known or available, or rent-seeking, when agents try to secure government protection of their economic status. The former is part and parcel of entrepreneurial activity, the latter is what creates barriers to competition. This takes us full circle to our earlier assertion that in the long run there are essentially two sources of monopoly:

1. Government protection of firms from competition, e.g., legalized monopolies, licensed entries, import duties, quotas, and so on.
2. A permanent advantage enjoyed by the incumbent firm(s) over potential entrants, e.g., sole ownership of some necessary input, access to superior techniques of production, beliefs by customers in the superiority of established products, economies of scale which render new entry uneconomic, and so on.

The transfer and innovation mechanism essentially creates two distinct markets describing completely different (1) groups of firms and (2) competitive situations. One group works in an environment where the basic knowledge required for the production process is available and it is only gradually improved upon. Here the market engages predominantly in price competition and the transfer mechanism outweighs the innovation mechanism, resulting in imitative competition.

The other group of firms works in an opposite environment. Here the innovation mechanism outweighs the transfer mechanism, resulting in innovative competition, which Schumpeter ([1911] 1961, p. 66) has noted covers the following areas:

1. The introduction of a new good—that is one with which consumers are not yet familiar—or of a new quality of a good;
2. The introduction of a new method of production, that is, one not yet tested by experiment in the branch of manufacture concerned, which need by no means be founded upon a discovery scientifically new, and can also exist in a new way of handling a product commercially;

3. The opening of a new market, that is, a market into which the particular branch of manufacture has not previously entered, whether or not this market has existed before;
4. The conquest of a new source of supply of raw materials irrespective of whether this source exists or whether it has first to be created; and
5. The carrying out of the new organization of any industry, such as the creation of a monopoly position (for example through trustification) or the breaking up of a monopoly position.

We expect the transfer and innovative mechanisms of the competitive process to work interchangeably, and profits to change over time. This, however, vitiates our conventional understanding of normal profits and requires that we confine ourselves to the Von Misian view, (1949, p. 295) where

> Profit and loss are entirely determined by the success or failure of the entrepreneur to adjust production to the demand of the consumers. There is nothing "normal" in profits and there can never be an "equilibrium" with regard to them. Profit and loss are, on the contrary, always a phenomenon of a deviation from "normalcy," of changes unforeseen by the majority, and of a "disequilibrium". They have no place in an imaginary world of normalcy and equilibrium. In a changing economy there prevails always an inherent tendency for profits and losses to disappear. It is only the emergence of new changes which revives them again.

Chapter 7

Regulating the Competitive Process

It is not uncommon to find administrative agencies, i.e., competition authorities, being set in place across countries to regulate the competitive process in an effort to ensure that the process does not produce a monopoly.

The OECD Committee on Competition Law and Policy (1996b, p. 5), on inspecting competition policy in OECD countries, remarked that

> There is general consensus that the objective of competition policy is to protect and preserve competition as the most appropriate means of ensuring the efficient allocation of resources—and thus efficient market outcomes—in free market economies. While countries differ somewhat in defining efficient market outcomes there is general agreement that the concept is manifested by lower consumer prices, higher quality products and better product choice.

The EU competition authority (OECD, 1996b, p. 53), on inspection of the competition rules it uses, remarked that

> Any efficiency issues are considered in the overall assessment to determine whether dominance has been created or strengthened and not to justify or mitigate that dominance in order to clear a concentration which would otherwise be prohibited. . . . If dominance is already existent on a market, i.e. competition is already fragile, the aim is to preserve at least the little degree of remaining competition.

No evidence suggests that this view has changed in recent times (OECD, 1999, p. 215). This fear of dominance is not unique to the

doi:10.1300/5505_07

EU. The U.S. antitrust agency (OECD, 1999, p. 199), on inspection of the antitrust laws in the United States, noted that

> Section 1 of the Sherman Act prohibits agreements that restrain trade, and thus can be used to attack active collusion, whether tacit or express. Section 2 of the Sherman Act prevents, among other things, conspiracies to monopolise. Section 7 of the Clayton Act forbids mergers and acquisitions that, among other things, substantially increase the risk of anti-competitive coordination.

The South African Competition Act of 1998 draws upon the U.S. Sherman, Robinson-Patman, and Clayton Acts and is identical to articles 81 (formerly 85) and 82 (formerly 86) of the EU Common Rules on Competition. The objective of the law is the same as that described by the OECD Committee on Competition Law and Policy with reference to the OECD countries. In particular, §2 (Act 89, 1998, p. 10) states that "the purpose of this act is to promote competition and maintain competition in the Republic [in order] to promote the efficiency, adaptability and development of the economy" (§2[a], p. 10) and "to provide consumers with competitive prices and product choices" (§2[b], p. 10).

Here, as in the previous cases, firm size and competition are considered to be the opposite sides of a coin. Specifically, §4 ¶1 of Act 89 (1998, p. 12) states that: "An agreement between . . . firms, or a decision by an association of firms, is prohibited if . . . it is between parties in a horizontal relationship and it has the effect of substantially preventing or lessening competition in a market." Report 73 (Competition Board, 1999), which examined the proposed acquisition of one pharmaceutical company by another, namely that by Adcock Ingram of PharmaCare, reinforces this view. In particular, in the Report (Competition Board, 1999, p. 28) the competition authority pronounced that "market power and competition can be regarded as the inverse of each other."

The South African competition agency may be deemed to consider large firm size as undesirable in terms of competition, i.e., something that might stifle the competitive process. In this regard, as we have seen, South Africa is not unique. However, from a consideration of such it is only a small step to come to argue that a dominance threshold exists at which competition is eliminated. In turn, this is likely to result in some competition authorities defining what the appropriate market size for a firm should be. For instance, with reference to the application of the EU competition law the EU competition agency (OECD, 1996b, p. 54) commented that "dominance is the absolute limit . . . which is a strong possibility from a market share of about 40%-45%." The South African Competition Act (Act 89, 1998, p. 14), per §7, takes the following stand:

> A firm is dominant in a market if:
> (a) It has at least 45% of that market;
> (b) It has at least 35%, but less than 45%, of that market, unless it can show that it does not have market power; or
> (c) It has less than 35% of that market, but has market power.

Each of the chosen market shares is arbitrary and, if anything, is reflective of a competitive rather than an anticompetitive market. None of the chosen market shares takes account of the nature or the structure of competition in a market or of the way markets are organized. For instance, a market may comprise a dominant firm and fringe firms, whereby the lack of impediment to entry (given there are fringe firms) and the lack of real cost advantages by the dominant firm over the fringe ones results in a perfectly competitive market price. Collectively the fringe firms may have a very large portion of the market— greater than that of the dominant firm. For example, a dominant firm in a market may have a 45 percent share, but the same market may well have 100 firms, making up the other 55 percent. Act 89 of 1998 is asking one to suppose, assuming one is willing to agree, that this is an unhealthy situation. The percentages listed in (a), (b), and (c) may be considered to depict a dominant-fringe–firm setting, for which it is known that a dominant firm (i.e., the one with the large market share) meets market demand alone or in combination with the fringe firms (i.e., the ones with the small market shares), depending on how great its cost advantage over the fringe firms is (Carlton and Perloff, 2000, pp. 113-118). Absent government support, a firm may gain dominance in only two other ways. The first way is by means of the dominant firm having lower costs than fringe firms. The three sources of lower costs are:

1. A firm may be more efficient than its rivals. For example, it may have better management or better technology that allows it to produce at lower costs;
2. An early entrant to a market may have lower costs from having learned by experience how to produce more efficiently; or
3. An early entrant may have had time to grow large optimally so as to benefit from economies of scale. By spreading fixed costs over more units of output, it may have lower average costs of production than a new entrant could instantaneously achieve.

If the dominant firm is dominant because of any or all of these possibilities, it would meet market demand alone. In such a case the dominant firm introduces a market price that is below the average costs of production of the fringe firms. If this results in the dominant firm being alone and likely to engage in monopoly pricing the threat of entry or actual entry from fringe firms would discourage it from doing so. However, if the cost advantages of the dominant firm in relation to the fringe ones is weak, and restriction on entry does not exist, then the dominant firm would meet market demand together with the fringe firms at the perfectly competitive price level.

The second way a firm may gain dominance is when it has a superior product in a market where each firm produces a differentiated product. This superiority may be due to a reputation achieved through advertising or through goodwill generated by its longer presence in the market.

Given that market dominance is a property associated with the competitive process, it is difficult to picture why competition law should deem it as the inverse of rivalry. The only possible explanation here is that some competition authorities perhaps hold the view that one way a dominant-fringe–firm market structure is created is by a group of firms collectively acting as a dominant firm. As we know, a group of firms that explicitly acts collectively to promote its best interests is a cartel. If all firms in a market coordinate their activities, then the cartel is effectively a monopoly; if only some of them do so, then the group acts as a dominate firm facing a competitive fringe of noncooperating firms. Thus, we have two direct implications from this regulatory view. The first is that cartels are presumed to persist. We already know that this does not stand up to scrutiny, both in practice and in theory. The second is that monopoly is necessarily not something competition should produce. On the basis of our discussion of the competitive process, the validity of this viewpoint is questionable and warrants further theoretical inspection. Its theoretical foundation is grounded in the structure-conduct-performance model advanced by Bain (1951), which is the subject of our discussion in Chapter 8.

Chapter 8

The Structure-Conduct-Performance Model

This examines the structure-conduct-performance (SCP) model, first outlining what the model encompasses and then tracing its theoretical antecedents, namely those of the Cournot and Von Stackelberg oligopoly models. The model is grounded in the belief that concentration emanates from collusion or collective monopoly, with the result that any transactions such as mergers and acquisitions that smack of "largeness" are likely to be classed by the model as anticompetitive, i.e., departing from the outcome of perfect competition. It is shown that the theoretical antecedents of the SCP model require, perhaps, greater latitude of understanding than is afforded to them at present, which in turn makes them unsuitable for upholding the model.

In conventional economic terms we can argue that the number of firms is irrelevant to the study of price behavior, since as the contemporary Bertrand model shows, two firms are enough in order to achieve perfectly competitive pricing. However, in the contemporary Bertrand model we have something quite different from the original model, which may warrant that we revise altogether our notion of this model.

Concentration in a given market is more likely to be the result of rivalry between firms, since the reward to performance, namely greater market share, for any firm is reflected in its market conduct. By extension, this notion is carried through in the inspection of mergers and acquisitions carried out in this chapter, given their closeness, from a public policy or public opinion perspective, with the perception that they may harbor collusion or monopoly intentions.

The SCP paradigm's ideal of competition is the perfect competition model. According to Bain (1951, p. 294), the model hypothesizes "that the average profit rate of firms in oligopolistic industries of a

doi:10.1300/5505_08

high concentration will tend to be significantly larger than that of firms in less concentrated oligopolies or industries of atomistic structure." This main hypothesis has two variations. Bain (1951, p. 295) formulated the first one as follows: "If we hold demand and cost conditions and entry conditions constant, monopoly or effectively collusive oligopoly tends to yield higher profit aggregates and prices in long-run equilibrium than competition or imperfectly-or non-collusive oligopoly." Bain (1951, p. 296) formulated the second variation as follows:

> There will be a systematic difference in average excess profit rates on sales between highly concentrated oligopolies and other industries. This difference should be found, strictly, even if there are on the average identical entry conditions in the two groups.

In a nutshell, the model hypothesizes that (1) the exercise of monopoly power should increase as concentration (i.e., the degree of disproportionate allocation of market share) increases and (2) the greater the barriers to entry, the greater the exercise of market power. In short, barriers to entry facilitate market power, which increases with concentration. Thus, when market concentration is growing some firms are perceived to be building monopoly power (i.e., the market deviates from the perfect competition structure), which results in positive profits (i.e., these firms charge above MC and behave as monopolists). As we already know, a move of a market in this direction in conventional, perfectly competitive terms produces allocative inefficiency measured by the DWL triangle. This is the concern of many antitrust authorities.

The SCP model is useful in explaining why some competition statutes and the agencies enforcing them may view dominance as undesirable and, by extension, why (horizontal) mergers and acquisitions may be construed by such agencies as a likely means to achieving market dominance or establishing a monopoly. At this point it should be noted that heavy emphasis in our discussion will be placed on (horizontal) mergers and acquisitions, given that they remain the area that is still to be addressed in this work; monopoly power and cartels have already been formally considered.

It may be argued, given Bain's postulation of the SCP paradigm, that theoretically the economic models of oligopoly, specifically those of Cournot and Stackelberg, provide support for this paradigm. However, it will be shown that this is questionable. Let us begin with the Cournot model of oligopoly.

THE COURNOT MODEL

According to contemporary economic theory (see, for example, Carlton and Perloff, 2000, p. 157) this model rests on the assumptions that in a given market:

1. Firms are exposed to no entry, i.e., no entry by other firms in the industry is possible.
2. Firms produce homogeneous (identical) goods.
3. Firms' actions are simultaneous (not sequential).
4. Firms know market demand, i.e., they have knowledge of the market-demand curve.
5. Firms have no fixed costs and each has the same (constant) marginal cost of production. Thus, firms also share the same average cost.

Under the assumption of a linear industry demand curve and a horizontal marginal cost curve Binmore (1992, p. 292) has derived the following formulae for output, consumer surplus, and profit under Cournot oligopoly:

$$Q^{CO} = (n/n + 1) \times Q^{PC} \qquad (8.1)$$

$$CS^{CO} = [n^2/(n + 1)^2] \times CS^{PC} \qquad (8.2)$$

$$\pi^{CO} = [2n/(n + 1)^2] \times CS^{PC} \qquad (8.3)$$

In these expressions Q^{CO} = Cournot oligopoly output, Q^{PC} = perfectly competitive output, CS^{CO} = Cournot oligopoly consumer surplus, CS^{PC} = perfectly competitive consumer surplus, π^{CO} = Cournot oligopoly total industry profit, and n = number of firms.[1] Equations 8.1, 8.2, and 8.3 were used to generate the results tabulated in Table 8.1, Table 8.2, and Table 8.3.

TABLE 8.1. Cournot output relative to perfectly competitive output.

Number of firms	Percent of perfectly competitive output
1	50
2	67
3	75
4	80
5	83
6	86
7	88
8	89
100	99
∞	100

Note: A similar table also appears in Reekie, 1979, p. 70. Results derived from Equation 8.1.

TABLE 8.2. Cournot consumer surplus relative to perfectly competitive surplus.

Number of firms	Percent of perfectly competitive surplus
1	25
2	44
3	56
4	64
5	69
6	73
7	77
8	79
100	98
∞	100

Note: Results derived from Equation 8.2.

TABLE 8.3. Cournot profit relative to perfectly competitive surplus.

Number of firms	Percent of perfectly competitive surplus
1	50
2	44
3	38
4	32
5	28
6	25
7	22
8	20
100	2
∞	0

Note: Results derived from Equation 8.3.

If we superimpose the results presented in the tables over Figure 3.3 (see p. 21) it can be seen that if markets are of the Cournot variety, then the number of firms in a market affects economic welfare. Specifically, a one-firm industry produces 50 percent of the perfectly competitive output (this also being how much the firm's profit absorbs of consumer surplus compared to perfect competition), with the resulting surplus left to consumers being only 25 percent of what it would be under perfect competition. The results illustrate that departures of price from marginal cost will be greatest when the number of firms is fewest. Conversely, an industry with a very large number of firms produces at the perfectly competitive level, although it appears that an industry with seven or eight firms produces results very close to this level.

The conventional Cournot model and its numerical results bode well with Bain's (1951, p. 296) supposition that, according to the SCP model, in highly concentrated oligopolistic industries, more express or tacit collusion will be found on average. In oligopolistic industries of lower concentration—as in industries of relatively unconcentrated structure—there will be, on average, less effective or more imperfect collusion, as well as more profit-destructive rivalry, whether open or secret, and thus a significantly closer approach to competitive pricing.

From this it can be readily inferred that any regulatory uneasiness regarding horizontal mergers and acquisitions can be explained in terms of them decreasing the overall number of firms in a given industry, which, as presented in Table 8.1, Table 8.2, and Table 8.3, is associated with moving firms apart from perfect competition and is likely to increase the odds of collusion (given that the Cournot model is said not to allow for entry).

However, does the conventional Cournot model stand up to scrutiny? From a historical perspective De Bornier (1992, pp. 623-645) provides evidence to suggest it does not. Let us reconsider the assumptions of the Cournot model. The first assumption is no new entry. Interpreted literally, this assumption states that actually competition does not exist in a Cournot-type market. Facing no pressure from the outside it is difficult to envisage why any incumbent should be interested in normal profits. From here it is only a small step to come to assume that with few firms, or analogously that a reduction in the number of firms by (horizontal) mergers and acquisitions, increases the likelihood of collusion or raises the odds of a cartel being formed. This may seem ever more imminent in the presence of homogeneous goods (the second assumption of the Cournot model), since a cartel agreement is easier to monitor (or enforce) where members sell identical rather differentiated products at the same point in the distribution chain. Thus, we have a self-fulfilling prophecy of collusion leading to concentration leading to supernormal profits "proved" by the Cournot model. This, however, is erroneous. Let us consider the original text (Cournot, 1927, pp. 79-83)[2] on this subject matter:

> Let us now imagine two proprietors and two springs of which the qualities are identical, and which, on account of their similar positions, supply the same market in competition. In this case the price is necessarily the same for each proprietor. If p is this price, $D = F(p)$ the total sales, D1 the sales from the spring (1) and D2 the sales from the spring (2), then $D1 + D2 = D$. If, to begin with, we neglect the cost of production, the respective incomes of the proprietors will be pD1 and pD2; and each of them independently will seek to make this income as large as possible. We say each independently, and this restriction is very essential, as will soon appear; for if they should come to an

agreement so as to obtain for each the greatest possible income, the results would be entirely different, and would not differ, so far as consumers are concerned, from those obtained in treating a monopoly.

Instead of adopting $D = F(p)$ as before in this case it will be convenient to adopt the inverse notation $p = f(D)$; and then the profits of proprietors (1) and (2) will be respectively expressed by $D1 \times f(D1 + D2)$ and $D2 \times f(D1 + D2)$, i.e., by functions into each of which enter two variables, $D1$ and $D2$. Proprietor (1) can have no direct influence on the determination of $D2$: all that he can do, when $D2$ has been determined by proprietor (2), is to choose for $D1$ the value which is best for him. This he will be able to accomplish by properly adjusting his price, except as proprietor (2), who, seeing himself forced to accept this price and this value of $D1$, may adopt a new value for $D2$, more favorable to his interests than the preceding one. Analytically this is equivalent to saying that $D1$ will be determined in terms of $D2$ by the condition $d[D1f(D1 + D2)]/dD1 = 0$, and that $D2$ will be determined in terms of $D1$ by the analogous condition $d[D2f(D1 + D2)]/dD2 = 0$, whence it follows that the final values of $D1$ and $D2$, and consequently of D and p, will be determined by the system of equations: (1) $f(D1 + D2) + D1f'(D1 + D2) = 0$, (2) $f(D1 + D2) + D2 f'(D1 + D2) = 0$. . . .

From equations (1) and (2) we derive first $D1 = D2$ (which ought to be the case, as the springs are supposed to be similar and similarly situated), and then by addition: $2 f(D) + Df'(D) = 0$, an equation which can be transformed into: (3) $D + 2 pdD/dp = 0$, whereas, if the two springs had belonged to the same property, or if the two proprietors had come to an understanding, the value of p would have been determined by the equation: (4) $D + pdD/dp = 0$, and would have rendered the total income Dp a maximum, and consequently would have assigned to each of the producers a greater income than what they can obtain with the value of p derived from equation (3).

Why is it then that, for want of an understanding, the producers do not stop, as in the case of a monopoly or of an association, at the value of p derived from equation (4), which would really give them the greatest income? The reason is that, producer (1) having fixed his production at what it should be according to equation (4) and the condition D1 = D2, the other will be able to fix his own production at a higher or lower rate with a temporary benefit. To be sure, he will soon be punished for his mistake, because he will force the first producer to adopt a new scale of production which will react unfavorably on producer (2) himself. But these successive reactions, far from bringing both producers nearer to the original conditions [of monopoly], will separate them further and further from it. In other words, this condition is not one of stable equilibrium; and, although the most favorable for both producers, it can only be maintained by means of a formal engagement; for in the moral sphere men cannot be supposed to be free from error and lack of forethought any more than in the physical world bodies can be considered perfectly rigid, or supports perfectly solid, etc. . . .

If there were 3,4, . . . ,n producers in competition, all their conditions being the same, equation (3) would be successively replaced by the following:

$$D + 3 \, pdD/dp = 0, \, D + 4 \, pdD/dp = 0, \ldots D + npdD/dp = 0;$$

And the value of p which results would diminish indefinitely with the indefinite increase of the number n. In all the preceding, the supposition has been that natural limitation of their productive powers has not prevented producers from choosing each the most advantageous rate of production.

Several points arise. First, each firm will initially use price as the means to control quantity demanded, quantity control being thereafter used as a tool of maximizing profit and of reaching market equilibrium, given that, in time, for a completely homogeneous product, there can be no difference in the selling prices of rivals. This is in contrast to the modern-day interpretation of Cournot's model, which tends to give the impression that firms make decisions only with respect to the volumes they produce and does suggest that a revision of this view may be in order.

Second, textbook orthodoxy (see, for example, Carlton and Perloff, 2000, p. 157) has it that the Cournot model describes rivalry among firms in a single period, i.e., it is appropriate for markets that last for only brief periods of time, so that rival firms compete once, but never again. The original Cournot model stipulates that symmetrical firms producing homogeneous (in quality) goods supply the same market in competition without there being a time restriction as to how long this may continue. This does suggest that a revision of the textbook orthodoxy may be in order.

Third, there is nothing strange about the algebra used. Cournot's work was first published in 1838, which may account for the choice of notation employed relative to the usual modern-day notation. Nonetheless, it is clear from his presentation that on the basis of the assumption of neglecting the cost of production the case of duopoly (or in general oligopoly) reduces to formulating expressions for revenue and thereafter using them to find the state of market equilibrium in both price and quantity by solving for the first and second derivative, namely, marginal revenue and maximization.

Fourth, of the five Cournot model assumptions listed, only the bottom four can be seen as historically correct. This has the implication that the contemporary assumption of "no entry" in the original Cournot sense is not valid. No reference in the original text states that entry may not occur. On the contrary, as contended by Cournot ([1838] 1927, p. 79), we may assert that firms "supply the same market in competition." This provision leaves no doubt that firms are exposed to rivalry all the time, which certainly does not allow for presumptions that there can be no competition from entrants.

Fifth, in the Cournot sense in a Cournot-type market collusion or cartel-type arrangements or anything that may lead to monopolizing a market has little chance of prevailing. Cournot ([1838] 1927, p. 83) dismisses the possibility of any of these prevailing, noting that in a two-firm industry the producer who pursues them "will soon be punished for his mistake."

Sixth, if firms make profit in a Cournot-type market, this can be credited as asserted by Cournot ([1838] 1927, p. 84), to the "the supposition . . . that natural limitation of their productive powers has not prevented producers from choosing each the most advantageous rate of production." Thus, in the Cournot sense a downward pressure on price (and hence on short-run profit) occurs only as the number of firms increases, and this is only because each firm has a limit on its productive capacity. This does suggest that Cournot may have downplayed the importance technology can play in overcoming a firm's shortcomings in production capacity. We can possibly attribute this to Cournot writing at a time when machinery or technology had not yet come to play an important role in the production of goods and services the way it does now.

All told, the Cournot model is not appropriate to use to confirm the SCP conjecture that concentration acquired by collusion, cartelization, or horizontal mergers and acquisitions done for the purpose of monopolizing would produce supernormal profits. In the strict Cournot sense, the possibility of any collusive-type arrangements being likely to occur is rejected on grounds that they would not come into existence for long. If such arrangements did come about, then bounded rationality (i.e., the limited human capacity to anticipate or solve complex problems) would make it difficult to enforce them, and out of their own accord they would create chiseling opportunities, increasing the odds of crumbling. In the strict Cournot sense, the gradual move toward perfect competition with respect to output, consumer surplus, and profit as the number of firms increases can solely be regarded as the result of rivalry (no restrictions on entry) and each firm in the industry having limited productive powers to begin with.

This has an important implication for our understanding of horizontal mergers and acquisitions, since it suggests that if we relax the Cournot supposition of limited productive capacity, then, contrary to popular belief, the Cournot model predicts that they would be exerting a downward pressure on price toward the point where the marginal cost of output equals its price.[3] This assumes that mergers and acquisitions are undertaken by firms for (productive) efficiency reasons. On the one hand the principal-agent framework, and on the other hand the Williamson trade-off conjecture appear to provide exemplary theoretical grounds for believing this to be the case. Let us first consider the principal-agent framework.

The Principal-Agent Framework

In this framework a firm's management (the agents) may pursue the maximization of its own self-interest, which may not coincide with maximizing the value of the firm and, thereby, the interests of shareholders (the principals). Examples here may include lavish consumption of office perquisites such as salaries, bonuses, pensions, and expense accounts; overpayment to suppliers; and so on. The principal-agent framework explains these agency costs. In particular it explains how they can be reduced, although some reductions themselves involve costs. They consist of the costs of writing and negotiating contracts with management and monitoring and enforcing managerial behavior by them. In practice this is (for instance) achieved by producing audited financial statements and devising and implementing compensation plans to reward managers for actions that increase shareholder wealth.

The agency costs tend to grow when the conflicts of interest in the principal-agent nexus are difficult to resolve or cannot be resolved to satisfaction. When these costs are large the threat of a takeover can reduce them. Normally the internal control mechanisms, through the board of directors, should encourage reluctant managers to restructure, but when this fails takeovers may be the only option left. The problem in the principal-agent dyad in essence becomes one of monitoring, with the monitor doing nothing if it is likely that he or she would perform worse than the firm's operating managers and intervening only when it is likely that he or she would perform better than the operating management. However, when the internal processes for change are slow or unable to bring about the required change or restructuring in managers efficiently, the capital markets, through the market for corporate control, are doing so. Manne (1965, p. 112) has emphasized this, stressing that

> A fundamental premise underlying the market for corporate control is the existence of a high positive correlation between corporate managerial efficiency and the market price of shares of that company. As an existing company is poorly managed . . . the market price of the shares declines relative to the shares of other companies in the same industry or relative to the market as a whole.

Mergers and acquisitions in this instance will occur in order to transfer the inefficiently utilized assets into the hands of those who can manage them more effectively. The potential capital gain in the share price will be the attraction that initiates this event since, as pointed out by Manne (1965, p. 113):

> Share price, or that part reflecting managerial efficiency, also measures the potential capital gain inherent in the corporate stock. The lower the stock price, relative to what it could be with more efficient management, the more attractive the take-over

becomes to those who believe that they can manage the company more efficiently.

Other management teams that recognize an opportunity to reorganize or redeploy an organization's assets and thereby create value can bid for the control rights of the organization in the acquisition market.

To be successful, such bids must be at a premium over current market value but short of the full posttakeover value of the shares. This would give the selling shareholders an opportunity to realize part of the gains from reorganization and redeployment of the assets. We talk about "part of the gains," since if the acquirer pays what the share is worth to him if the acquisition is successful, then the acquisition would not take place. In short, merger or acquisition targets have characteristics indicative of the need for external control, i.e., in the case where managers fail to shrink operations rapidly enough or to make the required adjustments (Schleifer and Vishny, 1988, p. 11).

In practice, the "evidence is consistent with the notion that these corporate transactions reflect economically beneficial reshuffling of productive assets" (Jarrell et al., 1988, p. 58). Here, in the short run, the acquirer buys an asset whose price reflects the weaknesses of internal and external control mechanisms and the resulting nonvalue maximizing behavior of managers. Taken to an extreme, such behavior could result in the firm becoming bankrupt, in which case mergers and acquisitions should be viewed as more desirable than the increased number of bankruptcies that would ensue if this avenue of taking control were totally closed.

Jensen (1988, p. 24) notes that cases exist where in an industry saddled with overcapacity exit is cheaper to accomplish through merger than by disorderly, expensive bankruptcy. However, as Reekie (2000, pp. 39-42) indicates, regulators are likely to ignore this, since if a large firm is doing the acquiring the reason will often appear to be one of merely increasing market power. It is difficult to offer a readily available explanation for this other than to state that it seems to corroborate the SCP model or the conventional Cournot model being used by some regulators as the analytical yardsticks of market competitiveness. However, suppose that in a given industry a horizontal merger is proposed that yields economies of scale, for instance, by displacing ineffective management or stimulating technological progress, while at the same time it might also have some market power effects by reducing rivalry between the merging firms but possibly enhancing their market position with respect to their rivals. Such a merger could supposedly introduce a DWL but this needs to be contrasted against the productive efficiency it creates. This takes us to the Williamson trade-off conjecture.

The Williamson Trade-Off Conjecture

Williamson (1968, pp. 21-23) examined the effects on resource allocation of a merger that yields economies but extends market power in a partial equilibrium context. He used a graph such as Figure 8.1 under the assumption that the postmerger market price for a product is higher than the premerger one.

The horizontal line labeled AC_1 represents the level of average costs of the two (or more) firms before combination, while AC_2 shows the level of average costs after the merger. The price before the merger is given by P^1 and is equal to AC_1. The price after the merger is given by P^2 and is assumed to exceed P^1.

The firms to a merger are likely to view the premerger average cost level AC_1 as high which provides them with an incentive to merge to attain the lower average cost level AC_2 in the long run.[4] Following the merger the joint firm may face little or no competition, which would

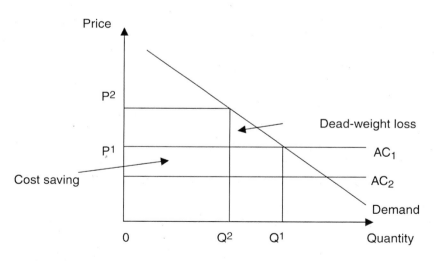

FIGURE 8.1. Williamson trade-off conjecture. *Source:* Adapted from Williamson, 1968, p. 21.

allow it to charge P^2, which would be above the competitive price P^1. This would generate a DWL, shown by the DWL triangle. However, DWL is not the only thing to come out of the merger. An improvement in productive efficiency is reflected by the cost-savings rectangle. As a result, the net welfare effect (or the net allocative effect) of the merger is shown by the difference in the areas of the cost-saving rectangle and the DWL triangle. The former may be deemed to be greater than the latter. Thus, if there is any allocative inefficiency from mergers and acquisitions it is highly likely that this would be made up for with the improvement in productive efficiency generated by the merger.

The assumption that price is set at P^2 following the merger or acquisition is restrictive. This price stimulates entry by any firm that can produce at AC_1 and that in time may even come to produce at AC_2, given that by virtue of their amalgamation the joining firms would be exposing to outsiders the possibility of attaining this cost level. In time firms would come to make available their offers at this new lower level. This if anything stands to enlarge rather than lessen consumer welfare, as revealed by the larger consumer surplus triangle to be had under the AC_2 than P^1 level.

The Williamson efficiency conjecture appears to be recognized under the South African competition statute as a means to rebut otherwise per se prohibited mergers and acquisitions. Under the statute §4¶1(a) states that:

> An agreement between, or concerted practice by, firms, or a decision by an association of firms, is prohibited if it is between parties in a horizontal relationship and it has the effect of substantially preventing or lessening competition in a market, unless a party to the agreement, concerted practice, or decision can prove that any technological, efficiency, or other pro-competitive, gain resulting from it outweighs that effect.

The recognition afforded to the conjecture is important since as Williamson (1968, p. 20) has remarked, "there is no way in which the trade-off issue can be avoided. To disallow tradeoffs altogether merely reflects a particularly severe a priori judgment as to net benefits."

In practice this is what seems to be occurring with the South African competition enforcement agency, which in Report 73 (Competition Board, 1999, pp. 69-70) came to the conclusion that:

For purported efficiency arguments to prevail over a substantial lessening of competition in a given case, it is necessary for a competition authority to be convinced that such efficiency gains outweigh the detrimental anti-competitive effects of the transaction. . . . Parties to a merger often do not fully appreciate that efficiency gains must be judged on their overall welfare-enhancing attributes. A focus on purely enterprise-centric pecuniary or managerial economies does not suffice as a determinative or adequate efficiency gains argument.

It is difficult to come to terms with such a view, since it looks as though it is contrary to what the Williamson conjecture signifies. White (1987, p. 18) renders an explanation of how this may be. He argues that efficiencies are easy to promise yet may be difficult to deliver. All merger proposals will promise theoretical savings in overhead expense, inventory costs, and so on. However, diseconomies of scale caused by managerial limitations may also be present and can overtake the promised synergies. Nevertheless, diseconomies of scale owing to managerial incompetence can be as much a reason for a merger or acquisition as economies of scale that each aims to deliver. In spite of this, it appears that the goal of the competition authority is to stop a merger or acquisition that fits White's description. In such a judicial process it is hardly possible to differentiate between what is and what is not efficient. This can be observed only when firms are put to the market-share test, which reveals winners and ploughs away losers.

The alternative is to trust that a bureaucratic apparatus can achieve exactly the same. However, in such a case an administrator promises as much efficiency by banning the merger or acquisition judged to be inefficient as do the firms that propose to merge. The public policy choice here is between confidence in the operation of market forces and the need or desirability of government intervention to diffuse apparent "market power." Our discussion on barriers to entry suggests that the former choice is likely to be better for economic welfare. A powerful argument in this regard is made by Reekie (2000, pp. 41-42). Reekie explains that, other things equal, if two firms refuse to merge or demerge in order to gain lower costs, then their joint output is produced at a higher cost than it need have been. This is a social loss, but is borne entirely by the owners of the firms in their lower incomes. Alternatively, if, for instance, a merger takes place in order to save costs but managerial judgment is proved faulty and costs rise, then the loss again is borne entirely by the owners of the firms who made the mistake in the first instance.

The decision of whether to merge or not resides with those most intimately involved with the situation, i.e., those who have considerably more knowledge compared to a regulator of a firm's and industry's cost structure, including its demand conditions and prospects. Falling in this category are the members of industry who have the most to lose from a poor merger or demerger decision and therefore who have the greatest incentive to make correct choices. It should not thus be expected that the outcome in response to mergers and acquisitions is the stifling of competition.

For firms, success and survival depends on how they pass the market-share test. Enlarging the product spectrum, producing at lower cost, and giving the goods and services that consumers (users) demand are all things that can be pointed to and examined. Either a benefit accrues from them or not, neither of which can be determined *ex ante,* which is what the administrator does. In contrast to the firms, the profit motive is not well entrenched in the administrator. His or her decision about whether or not a merger or acquisition will take place has little to do with the tangibles described. It tends to be based on "whether the merger can or cannot be justified on substantial public interest grounds" (Act 89 of 1998, §16¶1(b), p. 24). However, as we have already established, the public interest embraces the interests of labor, consumers, producers, and traders, as well as the national interest, which itself contains, amongst others, the strive for economic growth, an acceptable pattern of income distribution, and the efficient utilization of resources. With such a plethora of economic goals and special groups what is efficient for some may be construed as inefficient by others, in which case a proposed merger or acquisition would be deemed efficient as long as it falls in the administrator's favored camp or favored economic goals. For instance, in the proposed acquisition of PharmaCare by Adcock Ingram the public interest, among others, leaned toward existing and potential competitors. Here the competition agency (Competition Board, 1999, p. 37) came to the conclusion that

> On the face of it, the combined entity would be supplying a much wider range of products than its major competitors. . . . The combined product mix of the merged entity would allow

much more aggressive pricing with the view to either eliminating competitors from existing categories of dominance, or from gaining significant market share by pricing products in groups (tying the pricing of one product to the pricing of another).

At this point it would be useful to remember that the discussion concerns the inspection of the SCP premise regarding whether concentrated industries exhibit abnormally high profits (or rates of return), and whether in turn this is a result of collusive-acquired monopoly power. Put another way, the structuralists' view or SCP contention is that market concentration is based on an intuitive relationship between high concentration and collusion (with the ability to collude increasing with an increase in concentration). Our starting point in examining this premise was to demonstrate that the contemporary Cournot model usually used to support it is, in the strict Cournot sense, inappropriate for this purpose. It was shown that the original Cournot model discards the possibility that arrangements with the intent of monopolizing a market will be successful. In the strict Cournot sense the Cournot model actually prognosticates that firms with superior productive capacity (however acquired) compared to rivals in the same line of business would move a market toward pricing at MC in the long run. Our discussion on the market for corporate control and the Williamson trade-off conjecture demonstrated that mergers and acquisitions between firms in the same line of business usually involve, or are undertaken for the purpose of, improvement in (productive) efficiency. Combining this with the original Cournot model we should expect, at least theoretically, such transactions to be compatible with moving a market toward the perfectly competitive point rather than away from it. This is in stark contrast to what would be concluded with the contemporary Cournot model, and as shown is the price to pay for not strictly adhering to the original Cournot text.

However, an alternative way exists by which some regulators may believe harm can be bestowed on nonmerging rivals. It involves arguing that the aggregation of two or more firms can create a dominant firm, with the remaining firms being too small to counteract the joint firm's monopoly-like practices.[5] The theoretical underpinning of an argument such as this can be found in the conventional Von Stackelberg model of oligopoly. The following section deals with this model.

THE VON STACKELBERG MODEL

Here the market or industry has the leader firm, i.e., the dominant or large market-share firm, pick its output level first. Thereafter the other firms, i.e., the followers or small market-share firms, are free to choose their optimal quantities given their knowledge of the leader's output. Hay and Morris (1991, p. 61) have come to actually restate the orthodox view that: "The difficulty with this solution is that the theory is incomplete. It does not specify which firm will be the leader, and why the other firm should accept the passive role of follower." The absence of such specificity provides a fertile ground to claim that the Von Stackelberg model can support the SCP premise that market concentration is based on an intuitive relationship between high concentration and collusion (with the ability to collude increasing with an increase in concentration or a decrease in the number of firms in a market). However, should the Von Stackelberg model be used as part and parcel of such a premise? Let us examine the original text on this subject. Von Stackelberg ([1934] 1952) proposed his model by way of questioning the way firms behave in the Cournot model, emphasizing that if both duopolists are resolved to capture the market a struggle for market position will ensue in which each will compare the dependent and independent supply positions and attempt to obtain the one that is more favorable. The first duopolist will notice that the second always follows suit and adjusts to its total supply, in reaction to which it will then release on the market a product amount—in Cournot's case mineral water—that will maximize its profits after the resultant adjustment of its rival's supply. This is the independent supply of the first duopolist. As this occurs, the second duopolist could then offer its own independent supply, selling at a price that will in response make the first duopolist likewise succumb and adjust its own supply. The first duopolist will then occupy the dependent supply position. Under such rivalrous interchange, Von Stackelberg ([1934] 1952, p. 194) demonstrated that,

> As a rule, the position of independence will be more favorable for both. If this is the case, then each duopolist will put that amount of the commodity on the market that will correspond to his independent position and will seek to maintain it until the other decides to give up. A regular trial of strength emerges and no equilibrium position is reached. This can be called "Bowley's

Case" . . . In special cases, however, it may be more advantageous for each one to adopt the dependent position. In this case, each simultaneously tries to induce the other to offer his supply first, so that the latter . . . is . . . taken as a datum. . . . We can call this situation "Cournot's Case". But this result offers just as little chance of an equilibrium . . . as the first case.

Equilibrium is first attained if one duopolist offers his independent supply and the other his dependent supply. We can call this case "asymmetrical duopoly". But this equilibrium is unstable, for the passive seller can always take up the struggle again at any time. Only if one duopolist is, economically speaking, manifestly stronger than the other will he know that he can take up the most favorable market position and that the second will have to content himself with a less favorable one. It is possible, of course, that the duopolist may attempt to supplant one another in the market so that "cut-throat" competition breaks out. Only the formation of a collective monopoly or State regulation of the market can bring the battle to an end and restore equilibrium.

A number of important points arise from the Von Stackelberg text. First, which firm gets to be a leader and which a follower is not at all unclear and the theory is not incomplete in that regard.

In the strict Von Stackelberg sense ([1934] 1952, p.198):

The conditions of demand must be of a very special character and the costs of each producer must be widely different, if, in the same market, one duopolist is going to find it advantageous to take up his independent position at the same time as the other finds it most profitable to adopt his dependent position. The origin of asymmetrical duopoly is likely to . . . arise if one duopolist renounces the struggle with the other and is prepared to be content with the place which the former allots to him in the market. This result is to be expected if the two duopolists differ in strength economically, for in such a case the weaker competitor would be unable successfully to keep up the struggle against his more powerful adversary.

Second, textbook orthodoxy (see for example Pindyck and Rubinfeld, 1995, p. 427) has it that in the Von Stackelberg model firms act sequentially, i.e., at different points in time. However, in the original Von Stackelberg model, as stressed by Von Stackelberg ([1934] 1952, p. 198), equilibrium will occur only if one duopolist tries to reach an independent position at the same time the other tries to reach the dependent position.

Third, textbook orthodoxy (see, for example, Carlton and Perloff, 2000, p. 172) also has it that the Von Stackelberg model depicts firm rivalry in a single period, i.e., it is appropriate for markets that last for only brief periods of time, so that rival firms compete once, but never again. In the original Von Stackelberg model (Von Stackelberg, 1952, p. 194) if competitors are "determined to capture the market, then they will compare the dependent and independent supply positions and seek to attain the more favourable one." without there being a time restriction as to how long this may take. This does suggest that a revision of the textbook orthodoxy may be in order with respect to the Von Stackelberg model being a single-period model.

Fourth, in the Von Stackelberg model, in the strict Von Stackelberg sense, the leader-follower allocation in the absence of barriers to entry (as defined in this work) is mainly a result of market forces in which the weaker competitor would be unable to maintain his struggle against the stronger rival. This suggests that the outcome of firm rivalry in the original Von Stackelberg model is to lead to a market situation in which pure (perfect) competition can be obtained in the long run. This point has been illustrated by Von Stackelberg ([1934] 1952, pp. 199-201). Such an end result may not be possible to obtain under the conventional Von Stackelberg model but is the price to pay for not strictly keeping to the original Von Stackelberg text.

Fifth, the Von Stackelberg model as Von Stackelberg intended suggests that if a merger or acquisition results in the joint firm becoming a leader, this would chiefly be a result of the joint firm being economically superior, for instance, by means of product differentiation, economies of scale, or absolute cost advantages relative to its rivals who would, in turn, have to settle with being followers. In conjunction with the fourth point this also suggests that we should expect, at least theoretically, such transactions to be compatible with moving a market toward the perfectly competitive point rather than away from it.

All things considered, the conclusion we should draw at this point is that the Von Stackelberg model, in the strict Von Stackelberg sense, is not appropriate to use to support any theories that firm dominance retards rivalry, as such dominance, according to Von Stackelberg, is not the likely result of collusion or cartelization.

Finally, for the sake of completeness it is recalled that Von Stackelberg refers to A.L. Bowley's *Mathematical Groundwork of Economics,* published in 1924.

To illustrate that the number of firms in an industry is irrelevant to the study of price behavior or that dominance need not stifle rivalry (i.e., its presence does not preclude a market from moving toward perfect competition), it is really necessary only to point to the contemporary Bertrand model of oligopoly, where "the unique equilibrium has the two firms charge the competitive price" (Tirole 1998, p. 210).

In the conventional Bertrand model the perfectly competitive outcome of standard theory is to be expected given that homogeneous goods are produced by firms sharing the same marginal and hence the same average cost, in which case no difference is possibile in the selling prices of the firms; a slight price cut on the part of one firm relative to another would result in the former meeting all or most of market demand. To correct for this and restore demand for its offer, the other firm will match this reduced market price. Given that the firms share the same MC and that the profit-maximizing decision requires that MR = MC, this gradual reduction in prices would play itself out until P = MC. All of this indeed provides an effective means to cast doubt on the notion that the number of firms is essential if any competitive activity in a market or industry is to occur. However, let us review the original text on this subject.

THE BERTRAND MODEL

In response to the Cournot model of oligopoly all Bertrand ([1883] 1992, p. 649) had to say was this:

> The results seem to be of minor importance; occasionally, I must admit, they appear unacceptable. Such is the study made in chapter VII of the rivalry between two proprietors, who without having to worry about any competition, manage two springs of identical quality. It would be in their mutual interest to associate or, at least, to set a common price so as to make the largest possible

revenue from all the buyers, but this solution is rejected. Cournot assumes that one of the proprietors will reduce his price to attract buyers to him, and that the other will in turn reduce his price even more to attract buyers back to him. One major objection to this is that there is no solution under this assumption, in that there is no limit to the downward movement. Indeed, whatever the common price adopted, if one of the owners, alone, reduces his price, he will, ignoring any minor exceptions, attract all the buyers, and thus double his revenue if his rival lets him do so. If Cournot's formulation conceals this obvious result, it is because he most inadvertently introduces as D and D' the two proprietors' respective outputs, and by considering them as independent variables, he assumes that should either proprietor change his output then the other proprietor's output could remain constant. It quite obviously could not.

Two important conclusions may be drawn from this passage. A comparison between the Cournot work on the one hand and Bertrand's critique on the other indicates that Bertrand did not follow the assumptions of the original Cournot model. This has prompted De Bornier (1992, p. 631) to conclude that: "In many respects, it is impossible to believe that Bertrand seriously read Cournot."

The issue of contention is that Bertrand's critique assumes, mistakenly, that in the original Cournot model the producers in a market do not have to worry about any competition, with the obvious result that the only possible market equilibrium then is where producers find it "in their mutual interest to associate or at least to set a common price so as to make the largest possible revenue from all the buyers (Bertrand, [1883] 1992, p. 649). Bertrand's critique centers on undoing this assumption (of no competition) and its end result (of collusion). The text designed to address this reads as follows:

> Whatever the common price adopted, if one of the owners, alone, reduces his price, he will, ignoring any minor exceptions, attract all the buyers, and thus double his revenue if his rival lets him do so. If Cournot's formulation conceals this obvious result, it is because he most inadvertently introduces as D and D' the two proprietors' respective outputs, and by considering them as independent variables, he assumes that should either proprietor

change his output then the other proprietor's output could remain constant. It quite obviously could not. (Bertrand, [1883] 1992, p. 649)

The transgression in the text from competition based on price to competition based on quantity seems explainable on the premise that there cannot be two prices for the same good, as dictated by Jevon's law of price indifference, i.e., in the same open market, at any one moment, there cannot be two prices for the same kind of article (Jevons, 1957, p. 91). Thus, a reduction in price by one firm from the common market price adopted by all firms results in the remaining firms changing their output to meet this new price level if they are to prevent the rival who first reduced his or her price from attracting all of consumer demand and increasing (doubling) his or her revenue.

If it is possible to conceive of a Bertrand model, given that Bertrand published only a review of Cournot's work, then from Cournot's and Bertrand's work it should be deduced that such a model actually follows the assumptions of the original Cournot model. The distinction here is that in the original Bertrand model (Bertrand, [1883] 1992, p. 649) "there is no solution . . . in that there is no limit to the downward movement" in competing away a collective (monopoly) price if it exists in a market.

Simply put, in the Bertrand model, in the strict Bertrand sense, firm rivalry does not yield the perfectly competitive point, which is not to say that the competitive process does not take place but that this process does not produce an equilibrium, i.e., it is characterized by disequilibrium. In Bertrand's text, the term "no solution" qualifies this point and no other. From a historical perspective De Bornier's (1992, p. 633) account on this matter is instructive:

Did Bertrand mean that, in duopoly, competition must lead to a situation where price is equal to marginal cost? Probably not, because he believed that competition would lead to no solution. Here I think that we must trust his wording to understand him, keeping in mind that he was an excellent mathematician for whom "no solution" certainly did not mean "a solution with zero profits," as he is interpreted now. He may have had the idea that in a price war, price will fall below marginal cost, or he may not have given any thought to the problem.

All told, if the original Bertrand model has an outcome substantially different to that of the conventional Bertrand model, this is mainly a result of not strictly abiding by the original Bertrand text.

Our discussion of the Bertrand conjecture indicates that in addition to the requirement to reexamine our understanding of the Bertrand model as we know it today, we may also need to revise the textbook orthodoxy that the model depicts firm rivalry in a single given period: "Bertrand's crucial condition that players are assumed to play only once" (Tirole, 1998, p. 212). The original Bertrand text contains no statement to that effect at all. If anything it does suggest that competition between firms is not limited by time, and irrespective of time the competitive process results in markets (for a given product) being continuously in disequilibrium.

Our description of the Bertrand model as prognosticating that competition produces no equilibrium fits our description of the competitive process and of the Von Misian view of profits. This process is guided by the innovation mechanism, which produces short-run disequilibrium, with the transfer mechanism working toward imposing an equilibrium in the long run, given the new conditions of rivalry the innovation mechanism has bestowed on firms at the outset. Since the transfer and innovative mechanisms work interchangeably, we expect the innovation mechanism to resume working again upon completion of the transfer mechanism. Here the original Bertrand model suggests that what constituted an equilibrium, derived from the operation of the transfer mechanism, turns into disequilibrium as soon as the innovation mechanism becomes operational. In this case the transfer mechanism is set in motion to find a temporary equilibrium to the rivalry produced by the new good, method of production, market, source of supply of raw materials, and/or form of organization that has arisen out of the innovation mechanism. In essence, mobility from one state to another occurs with the initial equilibrium point, which, although continuing to exist, is no longer attractive given that the innovation mechanism has brought about a new competition point. The implication is that "There is nothing 'normal' in profits and there can never be an 'equilibrium' with regard to them" (Von Mises, 1949, p. 295).

Altogether it seems that under the pressure of rivalry and in the absence of barriers to entry (as defined in Chapter 6) concentration of an industry's output in the hands of a few firms could come only from their superiority in producing and marketing products (relative to their rivals). An industry will become more concentrated under competitive conditions only if a differential advantage in expanding output develops in some firms. Such expansion will increase the degree of concentration simultaneously with an increase in the rate of return that these firms earn. The cost advantage that gives rise to increased concentration would be reflected in scale economies, downward shifts in positively sloped MC curves, better products that satisfy demand at a lower cost, innovations in new products or methods of production, and so on. None of these things yield monopoly power but merely reflect how one rival can outperform another, both in market share and rank. The conclusion we should draw from this is that the structuralists' proposition runs in reverse. Performance (low cost or product innovation) leads to conduct (fulfilling the conditions of rivalry), which in turn leads to structure (concentration of industry). Two convincing pieces of evidence corroborate this direction of causality, one by Brozen (1970, pp. 281-288) and the other by Demsetz (1973, pp. 1-9). In the section that follows we examine this shift from structuralism to competition, beginning with the Brozen study.

CONCENTRATION IN PRACTICE

Brozen (1970, pp. 285-286) contended that if collusion (cartelization) or mergers and acquisitions are geared to raise profits above average (normal) levels, then the above-average profits should persist over time. The above-average profits would represent a noncompetitive disequilibrium in the sense that if they persist, then no competitive forces are at play that would bid them away. By contrast, if the profits do not persist, an industry is in a state of transition where above-average rates of return would tend to decline and below-average rates of return would tend to rise. New entrants with above-average returns would be attracted by the prospect for higher profits. This would stimulate an increase in capacity and supply, leading to decreases in price and the move of the above-normal rates of return to average or normal levels. Conversely, capacity would contract and rates of return would rise if an industry, other things being equal, offers below-average returns. In this case, some firms would be driven to their MC level while others would leave. For the firms that stay, their high rates of return would attract entry so that eventually the industry's rates of return would move to average levels. Thus, if there are no barriers to entry the result of rivalry in the long run is to move concentrated and unconcentrated industries toward a point of convergence, i.e., on the average little or no difference exist in the rates of return the industries make. Using the industry groups Bain (1951) studied over the periods 1936 to 1940 and 1953 to 1957, Brozen (1970, p. 286) found that the above- and below-average return industries performed as stipulated: "The gap between the more and less than 70 per cent concentrated industries closed from a 4.4 percentage point gap in 1936-1940 to a 1.1 percentage point gap in 1953-1957, a statistically insignificant difference between the two groups."

However, if in the long run convergence does not take place (i.e., there is absence of rivalry) and high (above-average) profits are the result of collusion (cartelization) or mergers and acquisitions with the same effect, then we should expect all firms in a particular industry to share in such profits. This is the position adopted by Demsetz (1973), and it is the focus of our discussion in the following section.

Demsetz (1973, p. 5) contended that a successful collusion ought to benefit smaller firms much like larger firms, suggesting a positive correlation between the degree of industry concentration and the rate of return earned by small firms. However, once efficiency comes into play the picture alters. Here, other things considered, the positive correlation is between industry concentration and the difference in the rate of return earned by large and small firms, in turn affected by the real dissimilarity or superiority in their respective cost structures of supply.

The premise here is that if superiority is expressed in terms of firms having horizontal MC curves, then in the long run rivalry would lower industry price to the superior firms' cost, eliminating inferior firms from the industry. The expansion of the superior firms may be constrained by rising MC curves, in which case price will be unchanged or will not fall enough to eliminate all inferior firms. The superior firms will then earn higher rates of return (representing economic rents) than the inferior firms as a result of their superior efficiency. Small firms should earn rates of return equal to that of large firms if they are able to produce at the same cost as the large firms. Then for an industry overall profitability would not correlate with concentration, as small and large firms alike have identical rates of return. The positive correlation would only arise in an industry if its rate of return is dominated by the rates of return of the large, superior firms. Simply put, according to the competitive/efficiency view, if a particular firm size earns a higher rate of return than another size, given any collusive price, then differences in the cost of production must exist which favor the firm that earns the higher rate of return.

Alternatively, Demsetz (1973, p. 4) has noted that

> If there is no single price upon which the industry agrees, but, rather a range of prices, then one firm can earn a higher rate of return if it produces a superior product and sells it at a higher price without thereby incurring proportionately higher costs; here, also, the firm that earns the higher rate of return can be judged to be more efficient because it delivers more value per dollar of cost incurred.

Demsetz (1973, pp. 6-9) presented empirical evidence consistent with the competitive/efficiency viewpoint, contending that this increases doubts about the benefits of an active deconcentration or anti-merger policy.

The Demsetz position (efficiency hypothesis) has been confirmed of all places in South Africa too, an economy traditionally seen as depicted by dominant (monopoly-like) pyramid groups deemed to give rise to an "unhealthy over-concentration of economic power" (Mandela, 1990). This widespread belief has been dealt a severe blow by Leach (1992, 1997) who has shown that the South African manufacturing industry as a whole, which includes the pharmaceutical industry, complies with the Demsetz efficiency view.

In his first study Leach (1992, pp. 151-152) demonstrated that a positive correlation exists between concentration and the difference between the rate of return earned by large firms and that earned by small firms. This can only prevail if the large firms are efficient (i.e., able to operate at lower average cost levels). In his second study Leach (1997, pp. 18-21) strengthened his initial finding by demonstrating that small- and large-sized firms in concentrated industries earned no more than their equivalent counterparts in unconcentrated industries. These findings have prompted Leach (1997, p. 23) to reach a conclusion not dissimilar to that struck by Demsetz:

The point . . . is that the source of . . . substantial monopoly power is not the concentration of industry. Thus, a policy of deconcentration of industry . . . as a possible antitrust remedy would destroy large firm efficiency and produce no corresponding gain in the form of lower prices to consumers. Public policymakers should become more concerned with removal of the real source of monopoly power in South Africa: government protection, especially high tariffs that shield many industries from international competition.

The corollary of our discussion is that large firms can raise price only to the extent of their cost advantage over smaller firms. Otherwise, smaller firms would earn higher profit rates in concentrated industries than in unconcentrated industries. Since the costs of smaller firms already determine price, breaking up the large firms will destroy large-firm efficiency with no benefit to consumers in the form of lower price and greater output. In the context of mergers and acquisitions, strong evidence has been presented in this regard by Stillman (1983), Eckbo (1983), and Mitchell and Mulherin (1996).

Horizontal mergers and acquisitions are a vibrant area of business. Evidence by Church and Ware (2000, p. 716) illustrates that the pace of merger and acquisition activity has been accelerating throughout the 1990s in both the United States and Europe. In South Africa evidence by the Competition Commission illustrates that of all the mergers (of which the Commission received notification) that took place in the period 2001-2002, 66 percent were horizontal (Competition Commission, June 2002, p. 9). We now turn to examining individually the Stillman, Eckbo, and Mitchell and Mulherin studies.[6]

Concentration and Mergers and Acquisitions

Stillman's (1983, pp. 225-240) study is an extension of the Demsetz efficiency hypothesis being applied to horizontal mergers and acquisitions by means of testing for its inverse, i.e., the inefficiency or so-called collusion hypothesis. Stillman (1983) noted that under the conventional Von Stackelberg or dominant firm model (when the merger involves the dominant firm) and the Cournot model, horizontal mergers tend to result in higher prices in equilibrium for homogenous goods. If the industry produces heterogeneous goods this translates to higher quality-adjusted prices following a merger. A price-increasing horizontal merger also benefits other firms in the industry if the inefficiency hypothesis holds. In the tacit collusion models, the competing firms limit output and share in the profits that result across the industry, whereas they are protected by a price umbrella in the dominant firm model. The implication is that the value of rival firms should increase as the result of anticompetitive, horizontal mergers, making stock market data appropriate to study the inefficiency hypothesis. As Stillman (1983, p. 227) remarks:

> Maintaining a "rational expectations" or "efficient markets" assumption, today's stock prices represent the capital market investors' best estimate of the present discounted value of a share in firms' expected future net income. If the announcement of a horizontal merger changes investors' expectations about future product prices and hence firms' income, the announcement will coincide with an abnormal rise or fall in stock values. The inefficiency hypothesis predicts that events that raise the probability of a merger occurring should coincide with abnormally high returns on the stock of rivals to the merging firms, while probability-decreasing events (such as judicial decisions against the merger) should coincide with abnormally low returns on rivals' stock.[7]

Stillman (1983, p. 235) tested this set of predictions, examining their effect on the other firms (in a market) that the authorities alleged would have been adversely affected by the challenged mergers. Specifically, Stillman (1983, p. 235) studied the "abnormal returns on portfolios of the stock of rivals to firms engaged in challenged horizontal mergers for days on which the perceived probability of the mergers evidently changed." Stillman (1983, p. 240) found that in general the rivals exhibited no abnormal returns, suggesting that the government is likely to have precluded horizontal mergers that would not have had any anticompetitive effect on product prices.

Simply put, the evidence suggests that mergers and acquisitions do not appear to comply with the traditional view of monopoly power (or market dominance), i.e., they have no anticompetitive effect. The same has been found by Eckbo (1983).

In an investigation identical in its theoretical scope to that of Stillman's, Eckbo (1983, p. 268) used stock market data to study the daily abnormal returns of major horizontal competitors in relation to merger proposal and antitrust complaint announcements to determine whether merger gains originate from collusion. Eckbo proposed that rival firms can benefit from the announcement of a horizontal merger that will result in considerable reduction in the costs of enforcing tacit collusion within the industry. Accordingly, news that the government has subsequently challenged the merger would be expected to reverse monopoly rent expectations, resulting in negative abnormal performance for the rivals. Thus, so long as productive efficiency is the underlying reason for firms or enterprises coming together, the positive performance displayed by the rivals of the challenged mergers reflects discounted projected savings made possible by information indicated in the initial announcement. Eckbo (1983, p. 269) found:

> No significant evidence that proposed horizontal mergers are expected to reduce the value of the competitors of the merging firms. Thus, if mergers typically take place to realize efficiency gains, we can not conclude that the "synergy" effect is expected to produce a significant expansion of the merging firm's share of the market along with an increase in industry rate of output. If scale economies are involved, then these seem on average to be insufficient to make the rivals worse off.

In a nutshell, the evidence opposes the collusion hypothesis pattern of abnormal returns across the proposal and complaint announcements. The results show that the rivals of the horizontal challenged mergers on average earn significantly positive abnormal returns at the time of the merger proposal announcement, and that while the subsequent news of the antitrust complaint causes a reduction in the market value of the merging firms, the rivals on average show positive abnormal returns performance, i.e., their performance at the time of the antitrust complaint is independent of the corresponding performance around the merger proposal. Furthermore rivals of the horizontal challenged mergers are found to earn on average larger abnormal returns at the time of the merger proposal than the rivals of the horizontal unchallenged mergers, whether or not the two merger categories take place in the same industries. The same is found for the merging firms, namely that both bidder and target firms in challenged mergers perform better than firms in mergers that go unchallenged.

Eckbo concluded that antitrust policy or regulatory activity that presupposes mergers or takeovers for collusion alone serves as a regulatory tax distorting the allocation of corporate resources by making some efficient mergers unprofitable.

These findings on mergers and acquisitions may be hard to come to terms with if we find it difficult to dislodge as a theoretical proposition the link between concentration and collusion (tacit or explicit). However, the Mitchell and Mulherin (1996) study's theoretical premise and findings correspond to the previous two studies. Mitchell and Mulherin (1996, p. 194) set out to study how industry shocks that "include deregulation, changes in input costs, and innovations in financing technology . . . induce or enable alterations in industry structure." In their inquiry Mitchell and Mulherin (1996, pp. 220-221) came to contend that linking industry shocks with takeover activity implies that a positive revaluation of industry members should follow the announcement of a takeover of one firm within a particular industry. They set about testing this implication by taking the month of announcement for each of the firms subject to restructuring or takeover and computing the abnormal return for the value-weighted portfolio of firms within the industry. The results concur with Eckbo's (1983) findings. Mitchell and Mulherin (1996, pp. 220-221) concluded that:

> These spillover effects of merger announcements are often interpreted by antitrust regulators as evidence of anticipated market power. Our analysis points to a more benign explanation. Since we find that takeovers and restructuring are driven by industry shocks, the positive response to takeover announcements by industry members could represent the anticipation of ongoing restructuring throughout the industry. . . . Takeovers . . . and related restructuring activity are the message bearers of the more fundamental changes facing an industry. In such cases, more business failures may occur if takeovers are inhibited.

It probably would be of use to highlight here that since the Mitchell and Mulherin (1996) findings are consistent with Eckbo's (1983), they are also supportive of Stillman's (1983).

A number of things emerge from the works presented thus far in regard to horizontal mergers and acquisitions. First, the evidence shows that the announcement of a merger or takeover at one firm in an industry is accompanied by a positive revaluation of other industry members. This is not incidental. Given that the production technologies of close competitors are by definition closely related, the news of a proposed efficient merger can also signal opportunities for rivals to increase their productivity. For example, the proposal announcement may disseminate information that enables the rivals to imitate the technological innovation motivating the acquisition. If such innovation activity requires merger, then the stock prices of the rivals will be bid up in anticipation of the expected gains from the future merger activity. The proposal announcement by the merging firms or the firm doing the acquiring is not the only channel of information spillover. For instance, publications (media or press releases); meetings (industry gatherings, conferences, and technical workshops); hiring employees from the merged firms, public disclosure laws (e.g., patent laws and any disclosure provisions contained in competition statutes); conversations with employees of the merging firms; judicial decisions (legal precedents); and so on.

Each of these channels informs competitors about the way their merging rivals intend operating and works toward spelling out the productive operations of the joint firm. In turn this makes it unlikely that mergers and acquisitions would produce a significant expansion of the merging firm's share of the market compared to its rivals.

Second, if horizontal integration appears not to act to the detriment of rivals, then a market's overall concentration cannot be expected to increase. This and the first point should not be regarded as only an artifact of the work we have examined here. In summarizing the empirical evidence on (horizontal) mergers and acquisitions, Jensen (1988, p. 23) noted that in general it tells us that merger and acquisition activity has not increased industrial concentration and that takeover gains do not come from the creation of monopoly power.

Third, the bulk of the evidence fails to confirm the collusion hypothesis in mergers and acquisitions. The implication of this is that it is likely that more business failures would occur if regulations inhibited takeovers. This seems especially imminent in a statutory environment such as that in South Africa, where horizontal mergers and acquisitions are per se prohibited. This in all likelihood would have a detrimental effect on competition by distorting the allocation of corporate resources by making otherwise efficient mergers unprofitable (i.e., illegal).

This suggests that from a public policy perspective a statutory per se prohibition on mergers and acquisitions should be undone or that competition policy control over horizontal mergers and acquisitions should be unequivocally abandoned, since it appears market forces already do what this control is intended for, i.e., nurturing competition.

To summarize, the discussion began with an inspection of the SCP premise that concentrated industries exhibit abnormally high profits (or rates of return) and whether in turn this is a result of collusive-acquired monopoly power. This represents the "structuralists" view, where market concentration is based on an intuitive relationship between high concentration and collusion (with the ability to collude increasing with an increase in concentration). Our starting point in examining this premise was to demonstrate that the contemporary Cournot and Von Stackelberg models usually used to support it are, in the strict Cournot and Von Stackelberg sense, inappropriate for this purpose. It was shown that the original Cournot model discards the possibility of the success of arrangements undertaken with the intent of monopolizing a market. In the strict Cournot sense, the Cournot model actually prognosticates that firms with superior productive capacity (however acquired) compared to rivals in the same line of business would move a market toward $P = MC$ in the long run.

We also demonstrated that the Von Stackelberg model, in the strict Von Stackelberg sense, is not appropriate to use to support any theories that firm dominance retards rivalry, given that in the original model it is deemed to arise only if firms differ in economic strength. In the Von Stackelberg model rivalry leads to markets approaching the perfectly competitive point in the long run.

The one recourse, i.e., the conventional Bertrand model, we had available to illustrate that the number of firms in an industry is irrelevant to the study of price behavior or that dominance need not stifle rivalry was shown not to be employable for this purpose, since it is not what we know it to be at present. The Bertrand model, in the strict Bertrand sense, prognosticates that competition does not yield the perfectly competitive point in the sense that rivalry produces a situation of disequilibrium. This aspect of the original Bertrand model matches with our description of the competitive process and of the Von Misian view of profits, in the sense that what constitutes an equilibrium derived from the operation of the transfer mechanism turns into disequilibrium as soon as the innovation mechanism becomes operational.

It was shown that in general the source of substantial monopoly power is not to be found in the concentration of industry, but rather in government protection. Large firms can raise prices only to the extent of their cost advantage(s) over smaller firms. Otherwise, smaller firms would earn higher profit rates in concentrated industries than in unconcentrated industries. Since the costs of smaller firms already determine price, breaking up the large firms via an antitrust policy of deconcentration of industry will destroy large-firm efficiency with no benefit to consumers in the form of lower price and greater output. Our discussion on the market for corporate control and the Williamson trade-off conjecture demonstrated that mergers and acquisitions between firms in the same line of business usually involve, or are undertaken for the purpose of, improvement in (productive) efficiency. The productive-efficiency hypothesis covers a wide range of possible specific reasons for merger, including realization of technological complimentarities, replacement of inefficient management teams, and avoiding bankruptcy costs.

Mergers and acquisitions carry potential efficiency gains. On the one hand is the obvious possibility of complimentarities in production, research and development, and distribution. For example, a merger announcement may signal the existence of hitherto unappreciated economies of scale in any of these three areas that can be realized by rivals as well as by the merging firms. Investors might speculate that the rivals themselves are likely to merge and realize the same scale economies and, thus, investors could react to news of a socially efficient merger that would actually lower product prices by bidding up the stock price of rival firms. On the other hand, managers in the same industry may have a comparative advantage at identifying mismanaged firms that takeovers (through the market for corporate control) or the threat thereof can turn around.

The empirical evidence points to (horizontal) mergers and acquisitions not having increased industrial concentration. This is in line with mergers typically taking place to realize efficiency gains, which in turn leads, as discussed earlier, to positive revaluation of other industry members. This creates a situation where it may not be possible for a merger to produce a significant expansion of the merging firm's share of the market relative to its rivals. Here the evidence indicates that if scale economies are involved, then these seem on average to be insufficient to make the rivals worse off.

Since the evidence shows that market forces already do what competition policy control over horizontal mergers and acquisitions is intended to do, i.e., nurture competition, our discussion suggested that from a public policy perspective the abundance of such control is probably warranted. This proposal does go at the heart of a strong ideological bias against apparent concentration of economic power that underpins public policy in competition and on the basis of which it could be contended that the market for corporate control is little in evidence under a concentrated ownership. Recent evidence by Kaplan (1997, p. 91) representing a synthesis of Kaplan's (1994a,b) previous work impugns this contention and points out that the diffuse ownership (weak proprietor) system of corporate governance displays no signs of automatic superiority to its concentrated ownership (powerful proprietor) counterpart.

In particular, Kaplan (1997, p. 87) found that for both systems alike:

> Executive turnover . . . increases significantly with poor stock performance and earnings losses. Executive compensation . . . is also related to stock returns and earnings losses. . . . The fortunes of . . . top executives . . . are strongly affected by stock performance and current cash flows. Sales growth, a measure of market share, plays a similar role.

These results originated from the United States, Germany, and Japan, where the corporate landscape of the first is characterized by diffuse ownership and that of the latter two by concentrated ownership resembling in nature that observed in South Africa. These, in view of being market economies, led Kaplan (1997) to conclude that successful market economies will inevitably produce such similarities. As long as the market for corporate control exists within a competitive or market-based economy, it will impel governance systems to become relatively efficient, and different systems will therefore generate analogous results. Thus, as Kaplan (1997, p. 91) put it,

> Governance differences should be less important when firms can not survive if they don't maximise their value. That will be true when product markets are competitive, government subsidies are small, and few (economic) rents are available. In those circumstances, managers face two basic choices: maximise or

fail. Managers who do not maximise, and often their firms, will not survive.

Kaplan's findings are complimentary to Manne's (1965) work, which as we know argues that the takeover market functions to discipline managers who might otherwise have behaved in ways inimical to the owners of a firm. They are also complementary to this work, as they show that market concentration appears to matter most when firms operate under conditions of noncompetitive product and capital markets (i.e., when barriers to competition exist as elaborated on in Chapter 6), government protection (in the form of subsidies) is large, and the scope for rent-seeking is immense.

However, somehow it always seems that, when assessed through the prism of the regulator, monopoly brought about by the competitive prices tends to be good for monopolists but bad for consumers. We already know the South African competition regulator, not unique to itself, sees polarity between competition and market power. In line with this the South African competition agency sees market power as

> The ability to raise prices significantly above the competitive level, or to exclude competition, or a position of economic strength enjoyed by an economic undertaking which enables it to hinder the maintenance of effective competition by allowing it to behave to a significant extent independently of its competitors and customers, and ultimately of consumers. (Competition Board, 1999, p. 29)

Accordingly, firm dominance (for instance gained by a merger or acquisition) may bring with it practices such as monopoly pricing, price discrimination, and predatory pricing that must be quelled by legislation. This, for example, is the case under the South African Competition Act.

Chapter 9

Firm Dominance and Price Decisions

A closer inspection of the statutory prohibitions of monopoly pricing, price discrimination, and predatory pricing that apply with regard to dominant firms under the South African Competition act 89 of 1998 shows that the act stipulates that each of the aforementioned practices constitute per se prohibitions:

- §8(a) of the act (1998, p. 14) states, "It is prohibited for a dominant firm to charge an excessive price to the detriment of consumers."
- §8(d, iv) of the act (1998, p. 14) states, "It is prohibited for a dominant firm to . . . engage in . . . selling goods or services below their marginal or average variable cost."
- §9 of the act (1998, p. 14 and p. 16) states,
  - (1) An action by a dominant firm, as the seller of goods or services, is prohibited price discrimination, if—
    - (a) it is likely to have the effect of substantially preventing or lessening competition;
    - (b) it relates to the sale, in equivalent transactions, of goods or services of like grade and quality to different purchasers; and
    - (c) it involves discriminating between those purchasers in terms of—
      - (i) the price charged for the goods or services;
      - (ii) any discount, allowance, rebate or credit given or allowed in relation to the supply of goods or services;
      - (iii) the provision of services in respect of the goods or services; or
      - (iv) the payment for services provided in respect of the goods or services.

doi:10.1300/5505_09

(2) Despite subsection (1), conduct involving differential treatment of purchasers in terms of any matter listed in paragraph (c) of that section is not prohibited price discrimination if the dominant firm establishes that the differential treatment—

(a) makes only reasonable allowance for differences in cost or likely cost of manufacture, distribution, sale, promotion or delivery resulting from the differing places to which, methods by which, or quantities in which, goods or services are supplied to different purchasers;

(b) is constituted by doing acts in good faith to meet a price or benefit offered by a competitor; or

(c) is in response to changing conditions affecting the market for the goods or services concerned, including—

(i) any action in response to the actual or imminent deterioration of perishable goods;

(ii) any action in response to the obsolescence of goods;

(iii) a sale pursuant to a liquidation or sequestration procedure; or

(iv) a sale in good faith in discontinuance of business in the goods or services concerned.

A careful reading of Section 9 of the Competition Act reveals that it follows almost word for word the Robinson-Patman revision of Section 2 of the Clayton Act of the U.S. antitrust legislation on discrimination in price, services, or facilities, which reads as follows:

It shall be unlawful for any person engaged in commerce, in the course of such commerce, either directly or indirectly, to discriminate in price between different purchasers of commodities of like grade and quality, where either or any of the purchases involved in such discrimination are in commerce, where such commodities are sold for use, consumption, or resale . . . , and where the effect of such discrimination may be substantially to lessen competition or tend to create a monopoly in any line of commerce, or to injure, destroy, or prevent competition with any person who either grants or knowingly receives the benefit of such discrimination, or with customers of either of them: Provided that nothing herein contained shall prevent differentials which make only due allowance for differences in the cost of manufacture, sale, or delivery resulting from the differing methods or quantities in which such commodities are to such purchasers sold or delivered: Provided . . . further, that nothing herein contained shall prevent persons engaged in selling goods, wares, or merchandise in commerce from selecting their own customers in bona fide transactions and not in restraint of trade: And provided further, That nothing herein contained shall prevent price changes from time to time where in response to changing conditions affecting the market for or the marketability of the goods concerned, such as but not limited to actual or imminent deterioration of perishable goods, obsolescence of seasonal goods, distress sales under court process, or sales in good faith in discontinuance of business in the goods concerned. (15 U.S.C. §13)

This chapter will show that these prohibitions either contradict economic theory or theoretically do not stand up to scrutiny.

EXCESSIVE PRICING

This prohibition is the same as an outright ban on all (collective) monopoly pricing. It is strange why this should be, given that, as advocated in this work, the source of such pricing is usually not the competitive process. As Von Mises (1949, p. 677) put it,

Almost all . . . instances of monopoly prices are the outgrowth of government interference with business. They were not created by the interplay of the factors operating on a free market. They are not products of capitalism, but precisely of the endeavours to counteract the forces determining the height of the market prices.

We have said much on the topic of monopoly pricing and it is not necessary to repeat all of it. Nonetheless, it should be recalled that in the absence of barriers to competition as created by government protection (control) or rent-seeking, such pricing comes from the innovation mechanism of the competitive process, where rivalry takes place along Schumpeterian-Littlechild lines. A firm may feel that its offer is a rare innovation not previously offered and warrants the imposition of a premium. In essence, we have a situation of temporary price skimming tied to "monopoly power" that either reflects the supply of a new offer that no rival can yet mimic or the creation of a new market where none previously existed. In time, in the absence of barriers to entry, the working of the transfer mechanism erodes this price skimming and "monopoly power" to bring (in the long run) the familiar "pure" competition outcome of P = MC.

A price above those of rivals, tied to product attributes (or quality) may simply reflect the repositioning of a firm in a market. In such a case if a firm anticipates lower-price entry it may be segmenting the market ahead of the changes in demand by positioning itself toward the inelastic segment of the market, where consumers perceive little or no substitutes for its offer(s). Alternatively, if a firm anticipates that the future demand for its product would not be as high as it has been, it may set a high price in order to price ahead of the product's new demand, thereby smoothing out any fluctuations in the product's earnings stream. Here, although a monopoly price may prevail, this price is essential if the product is to be offered in the future.

In addition, another possibility to consider is if for a given offer buyers face a monopoly price, this may be sufficient to prompt them to look for product surrogates; in such an instance, although no actual entry may occur, this would very likely impel the price to crumble. This exhibits the workings of the transfer mechanism.

PRICING BELOW MARGINAL COST OR AVERAGE VARIABLE COST

This prohibition follows almost word for word that of its proponents, Areeda and Turner (1975, p. 733), who proposed that in the short run a price below normal marginal cost or average variable cost should be considered "predatory," and therefore the monopoly may not defend its pricing practice by saying that it was "promotional" or equal to the low price of a competitor. Thus

> Recognising that marginal cost data are typically unavailable, we conclude that:

(a) A price at or above reasonably anticipated average variable cost should be conclusively presumed lawful.
(b) A price below reasonably anticipated average variable cost should be conclusively presumed unlawful.

So the theory behind this prohibition is that the dominant firm may be able to charge a price below (short-run) MC. Since

> the incremental cost of making and selling the last unit cannot readily be inferred from conventional business accounts, which typically go no further than showing observed average variable cost . . . it may well be necessary to use the latter as an indicator of marginal cost. (Areeda and Turner, 1975, p. 716)

Accordingly, any price charged should be regarded as predatory if it falls below average variable cost. Since nonpredatory prices are well above average variable cost, no entrant or incumbent equally as efficient as the incumbent should be driven out by such prices. It follows that the predatory price must be below the shutdown point of rivals. The situation here corresponds to that considered in the treatment of scale economies, where in describing Figure 6.1 (see p. 59), we noted that any price above P_{ep} would grant an entrant an adequate demand to enter the market and a price below it would, conversely, discourage all entry but sacrifice profits needlessly. This is our predatory pricing problem, where "A necessary . . . condition of predation is the sacrifice of short-run profits" (Areeda and Turner, 1975, p. 703). However, we pointed out that P_{ep} is consistent with a contestable market in which the threat of entry would keep the market at this price, which in essence would act as an entry-deterring price only if it was below the entrants' average variable costs (whether in the short or long run). Obviously, such an arrangement does not work to the detriment of consumers.

The predatory view has three fundamental problems. First, the proposition that any price higher the average variable cost level will not threaten an equally efficient rival is based on the assumption that the rival could produce at the same scale as the incumbent. If significant economies of scale are involved, a price at the average variable cost level is unlikely to allow a smaller rival sufficient market share to produce profitably in the sense of covering its own variable costs. This, however, does not mean that the larger rival presiding in the market stifles competition, since no other viable competitor can do better.

Second, assuming that predation is successful, then every costly period of predatory pricing would have to be followed by a period of recoupment—high prices to recover the losses experienced in the predatory price war. This in itself illustrates why predation is an improbable strategy for the deterrence of entrants and for the elimination of existing rivals. If the predator raises prices after the predation period, an entrant will come, lured by the profits. For the predator the decision then is either to follow predation and incur short-run losses that could turn into long-run losses given the high chance of entry or allow entry outright. For the incumbent (the predator), this last option appears plausible to adopt, given that the "victim" of predation (the entrant) can in all likelihood foresee the gain to come after predation, i.e., monopoly prices, which will give it the incentive to stay in the market so as to be able to benefit from them in due course. Thus, entry takes place rendering predation ineffective.

Third, an automatic prohibition of predatory pricing could unnecessarily render price penetration practices by firms, i.e., the use of low prices as the principal instrument for penetrating mass markets early, illegal. If this were to happen it would actually hurt consumers, especially those with low incomes, since, as Dean (1951, p. 422) has pointed out, a penetration price permits "quick sales to the many buyers at the lower end of the income (or preference) scale who are unwilling to pay any substantial premium for novelty or reputation superiority."

In addition, we may consider another possibility. It concerns horizontal mergers and acquisitions and predatory pricing, where it has been shown that mergers typically take place to realize efficiency gains, and that these gains are not only confined to the merging parties but also extend to rival firms. Thus, on the average, mergers and acquisitions do not produce a significant expansion of the merging firms' share of the market relative to the nonmerging rivals. If the latter are not made worse off following the merger (or acquisition), then quite obviously, as noted by Eckbo (1983), the same evidence contradicts the argument that the merging firms will initiate a monopolistic or predatory price war after the merger. If this were not the case, i.e., horizontal mergers and acquisitions fulfilled the predatory pricing theory, then nonmerging rivals would have been subjected by such mergers (or acquisitions) to negative abnormal performance in terms of their rates of return, market share, or rank. However, it must be stressed that if such negative performance is observed and if it can be tied to predatory pricing, this must not be seen as evidence of an anticompetitive deed. It merely reflects how the merger or acquisition produces a joint firm able to produce below the nonmerging rivals' average variable costs, i.e., the merger has produced the most efficient firm in the market. This, in line with the treatment of barriers to entry offered in Chapter 6, is not what we have in mind when we talk of lack of competition. The sources of this must be looked for elsewhere, namely in government protection or control and rent-seeking.

PRICE DISCRIMINATION

As we have already established, this prohibition is a replica of the U.S. Robinson-Patman Act. The EU common rules on competition contain a provision under Article 82 (formerly Article 86) similar to that of the South African Competition Act and the U.S. Robinson-Patman Act that appears to render price discrimination per se illegal. In particular Article 82 states that

> Any abuse by one or more undertakings of a dominant position within the common market or in a substantial part of it shall be prohibited as incompatible with the common market insofar as it may affect trade between Member States. Such abuse may, in particular, consist in . . . applying dissimilar conditions to equivalent transactions with other trading parties, thereby placing them at a competitive disadvantage.[1]

The prohibition contained in §9(1) of the South African Competition Act automatically forbids price discrimination. The section, by its wording, in conjunction with §9(2) of the act, implies that the regulator views price discrimination as anticompetitive in that it is something that results in lower consumer surplus than does an instance of single, i.e., uniform, pricing at MC. Simply put, compared to this latter standard, price discrimination produces a situation of monopoly pricing that the regulator deems would result in compromising consumer consumption.

This reasoning can be traced to the traditional classification of the forms of price discrimination, in which Pigou ([1920] 1960, p. 279) distinguished between

> three degrees of discriminating power, which a monopolist may conceivably wield. A first degree would involve the charge of a different price against all the different units of commodity, in such wise that the price exacted for each was equal to the demand price for it, and no consumers' surplus was left to the buyers. A second degree would obtain if a monopolist were able to make n separate prices, in such wise that all units with a demand price greater than x were sold at a price x, all with a demand price less than x and greater than y at a price y, and so on. A third degree would obtain if the monopolist were able to distinguish among his customers n different groups, separated from one another more or less by some practicable mark, and could charge a separate monopoly price to the members of each group. . . . These three degrees of discriminating power, though all theoretically possible, are not, from a practical point of view, of equal importance. On the contrary, in real life the third degree only is found.

Thus, if (third-degree) price discrimination enables a firm to charge each customer group a monopoly price for its offer, then by elementary monopoly theory this must mean that the price and output level are not at the perfectly competitive point and buyers pay more and consume less than they ought. Or must it?

Before we proceed, it is imperative that we make a number of important comments. First, the focus in this section is on third-degree price discrimination only, which, if not the only one found in practice, is probably, as pointed out by Varian (1989, p. 617), the most common.[2] Examples of it abound, e.g., regular versus "special" airline fares, premium versus nonpremium brands of chocolate, discounts to students and senior citizens, and so on. In practice consumers are frequently divided according to time, that is, impatience (cinema versus video movies), geographical location (foreign versus domestic), income (luxury versus standard), ability to shift to other products (industrial versus home use), and quality (first versus second grade).

Second, if third-degree price discrimination involves the firm charging each customer group a monopoly price, then in the absence of barriers to entry as erected by rent-seeking or government control, such a price constitutes a motive for initial and subsequent entry. Accordingly, price discrimination ought to be seen as representative of demand creation and demand diversion, and this in turn means either of two things. The first of these is that, through demand creation, price discrimination amounts to expansion of total market supply due to firm entry into new or additional markets, which results in a firm meeting more of consumer demand for the good or service in question, i.e., it supplies more instead of less markets. The second is that, through demand diversion, price discrimination amounts to extending the product spectrum by increasing consumer choice between different alternatives for the good or service in question, which results in a firm servicing more rather than less consumers.

These two things taken together have two implications. The first is that the difference between markets where price discrimination is practiced and where it is not, i.e., the case of uniform pricing, affects the number of firms in an industry differently. If price discrimination is consistent with demand creation and demand diversion, then it must be that in all those markets where price discrimination is present compared to where it is not these markets probably have more firms in them. We say "probably" since it is not necessary that this be the case all the time. In fact, it need not be the case where markets are contestable or entry is free, as rent-seeking or government protection impediments to competition do not exist. Here the threat of entry would propel the incumbent(s) to engage in price discrimination for purposes of demand creation and demand diversion in order to enter a new market before someone else does or to establish a new product among those already existing—all of which is meant to create a preemptive first-mover advantage.

The second of the implications is that assuming no legislative impediments to price discrimination abound (as in it is not prohibited), then its practice is highly unlikely to operate against consumers' interest. This is in response to price discrimination being manifested in demand creation and demand diversion. We can thus view price discrimination as all about the unfolding of supply and opening up of access to the goods and services firms make, especially where significant fixed or common costs (to be defined later) are involved as in the relevant case where investment in innovation (and infrastructure) are high.

Previous mention was made of common costs. We may define these, to use Brown and Sibley (1986, p. 44), as costs which cannot be allocated in a clear, cost-related way to any single market. Simply put, these costs are unattributable to a particular market. Common costs are thought of as a fixed cost. A good example of a common cost can be found in the R&D cost of new pharmaceutical products. This cost is the same regardless of the number of countries or consumers who use the medicine. Hence, the cost cannot be causally attributed to particular patient groups or countries. In addition to R&D costs for new product development in those industries where it is common apart from pharmaceuticals (e.g., computer software, semiconductors, aerospace and defense industries, and so on), primary production and some administration also entail costs that are joint across many countries and products. For instance, taking into account R&D costs, capital expenditure (plant and equipment), and administrative and overhead costs, evidence from Danzon (1997b, p. 305) demonstrates that in the case of a new pharmaceutical product common costs account for around 46 percent of the product's total launch costs with R&D costs alone comprising 31 percent of these costs. Recent research by Tollman and colleagues (2001, p. 12) estimates that the average cost that a typical research-intensive firm incurs to develop a new drug is U.S. $880 million. DiMasi (1995, p. 377), however, has shown that the total capitalized—clinical plus preclinical—cost per approved new chemical entity grows at an average annual rate of 8.7 percent.

The point that is emphasized with these figures is that in the short run the firm with such costs faces the situation of its average fixed cost exceeding its MC, so expanding total market sales via price discrimination through demand creation or demand diversion allows it to spread its fixed costs over more markets or buyers. This in turn implies that in those instances where fixed or common costs are significant, by the invasion and cross-invasion of markets, third-degree price discrimination would approach the perfectly competitive price/output point in the long run. Clearly then, if prices in the short run are set to cover only MC, which is the norm in "pure" competition and may occur with strict regulation, firm revenues will not cover fixed or common costs, and if these can be tied to innovation, as seems very probable, then in the long run innovation will not be sustainable. Simply put, in the short run, a higher level of innovation can be sustained under price discrimination than under MC pricing, which reinforces the point we made earlier, that in "pure" competition innovation is absent.

If the invasion and cross-invasion of markets underpinning third-degree price discrimination seems indistinguishable from that in the Clemens-Cocks model this is because, as Stigler (1961b, p. 217) reminds us, the theory of price discrimination is a variant of the theory of the multiproduct firm where the Clemens-Cocks model is rooted. The closeness between the theories is not difficult to spot. In the theory of the multiple-product firm, the firm sells different products in different markets. In the theory of price discrimination, the firm sells a single product in different markets, which cannot really be the same for the different markets the firm supplies if it is to extract the monopoly price from each of them. This point would be pursued in the upcoming third and final commentary, which will outline the conditions under which price discrimination is possible. For now, for ease of reference, we wrap up the second commentary in the following four statements:

1. If price discrimination creates short-run profits, then absent barriers to entry (of the rent-seeking or government protection variety) this brings entry and downward pressure on prices toward the perfectly competitive point in the long run;
2. It follows that the raisons d'être for price discrimination are demand creation (opening up of new markets) and demand diversion (expanding consumer choice). These two are more likely to expand rather than contract total market supply, or as Robinson (1934, p. 206) put it, "price discrimination must be held to be superior to simple monopoly in all those cases in which it leads to an increase in output, and, . . . these cases are likely to be the more common."
3. Opening up new markets or increasing the product spectrum allows firms to spread out fixed or common costs such as R&D over more markets and buyers, which ends up helping consumers in those cases where these costs are initially high. Then, by the invasion and cross-invasion of markets, third-degree price discrimination expands total market supply, thereby approaching the perfectly competitive price/output point in the long run.
4. It follows that in the short run, spontaneous price discrimination (i.e., the firm's freedom to practice price discrimination is not

impinged upon statutorily or likewise) nurtures a higher level of innovation compared to those cases where, via regulation or anything similar, prices are set at MC. Here, as we know, no product variety is yielded.

Third-degree price discrimination, to quote Pigou (1960, p. 275), is feasible only

> when the demand price for any unit of a commodity is independent of the price of sale of every other unit. This implies that it is impossible for any one unit to take the place of any other unit, and this, in turn, implies two things. The first of these is that no unit of the commodity sold in one market can be transferred to another market. The second is that no unit of demand, proper to one market, can be transferred to another market.

For a firm to practice price discrimination there must be no arbitrage (i.e., no resale) between the markets the firm serves, otherwise it is to charge them a single (uniform) price. Where the condition of no arbitrage is associated with the transferability of the product this literally means that no physical transfer of the product can occur between the different markets the firm supplies. That is, in acquiring the product, consumers in the different markets ought not to be able to exploit the differences in price between themselves. The second condition of no arbitrage is no transferability of demand. This condition merely reinforces the first one in that it permits for its fulfillment. Here no physical transfer of the product occurs, but instead the consumer chooses between the different options the firm offers, with the result that each market has little or no chance of buying the product meant for the other market.

Thus, as noted earlier, we may deduce that under third-degree price discrimination the product for which this discrimination applies is not strictly homogeneous given that if the monopoly price for it is to be extracted from each market, then this requires the sealing off of these markets from each other. As proposed by Stigler (1961b, p. 215), the best compromise to account for this lack of complete homogeneity across the markets seems to be "to restrict the term, price discrimination, to the sales of technically similar products at prices which are not proportional to marginal costs." In plain language, this definition tells us that price discrimination accounts for any differences in the elasticity of demand between the markets to which the firm sells. This emanates from the firm's markup for its product (above the original competitive price) being inversely proportional to its elasticity of demand.

In order to answer the question posed earlier, we have now to compare the output and price of third-degree price discrimination with that of simple ("pure") competition.

The Nature of Price Discrimination

In accordance with the inverse elasticity principle, a firm's markup above the original competitive price for a product it sells is inversely proportional to that product's elasticity of demand. Reekie (1979, p. 45) has demonstrated that an extension of this principle in the case of third-degree price discrimination has the firm price in n markets in accordance with the following rule:

$$Z_i = 1/(1 + \varepsilon_i) \qquad (9.1)$$

where Z_i = markup above the original competitive price in the ith market, i.e., $Z_i = [(P_i - MC_i)/MC_i]$; and ε_i = product's elasticity of demand in the ith market.

If, for instance, we have two markets to which a firm sells, then, by division of Equation 9.1 for each of the markets, we have the firm price between them in accordance with the markup expression:

$$Z_1/Z_2 = (1 + \varepsilon_2)/(1 + \varepsilon_1) \qquad (9.2)$$

Equation 9.1 tell us is that the more inelastic the demand for the firm's product, the greater should be the percentage deviation from MC. Specifically, the higher a market's elasticity of demand, the lower the markup and the closer the price is to MC. By analogy, Equation 9.2 tells us that the firm sets its markup in such a manner that the market whose demand is relatively sensitive to price is charged a lower price. Alternatively stated under price discrimination, the market that has the higher elasticity of demand receives a discount. To visualize Equation 9.2, the determination of prices is displayed graphically in Figure 9.1.

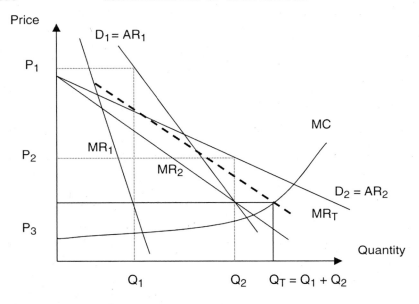

FIGURE 9.1. Price discrimination. *Source:* Adapted from Stigler, 1961b, p. 217.

As per Equation 9.2 it is assumed that the firm supplies to two independent markets, i.e., the demand in the one market does not depend on the price set in the other market. Otherwise stated, the cross-
price elasticity between the markets is zero. Annotate the one market
(segment) as the stronger market and the other as the weaker market
to reflect that the former is price inelastic (made up of price-insensitive
buyers) and the latter is price elastic (made up of price-sensitive buyers). It is customary now and then for these two types of markets to be
referred to as high demand in the case of the stronger market and low
demand in the case of the weaker market, simply to reflect that the
former's marginal willingness to pay exceeds the latter's.

Let the demand curves in the two separable markets be D1 and D2,
with corresponding marginal revenues MR1 and MR2. Then, if the
marginal revenues are added horizontally to get MR_T, we obtain the
curve of aggregate quantities that can be sold at given marginal revenues. Output will be set where total MR equals MC (itself assumed to
be the same in each market, otherwise the firm would reduce its costs
and increase its profit by reallocating to the market with the lower

MC). The output so determined will be sold in the two markets at prices P_1 and P_2, for at these prices marginal revenues are equal. The total quantity, Q_T, sells for an average price of P_3, which equals MC. Thus, notwithstanding the limitation that practical considerations impose upon the number of markets than can be formed and upon the firm's freedom to make up the several markets in a way that hinders arbitrage, it appears, on the whole, that price discrimination can yield an output as large as that of simple competition.

Figure 9.1 shows that under price discrimination an overall price and output unchanged from that of perfect competition is achieved in the long run. It may actually be more accurate to say that Figure 9.1 depicts this to be the case where initially high common or fixed costs are involved, as seems the more likely scenario, given such costs are present virtually in all productive and innovative activity. Over time these costs subside as they come to get absorbed by the opening up of markets and the expansion of the consumer pool, which price discrimination encourages, which in turn pushes total market output toward the perfectly competitive point in the long run. However, the disbursement of this output across the different markets varies.

In the market (segment) with inelastic demand Q_1 is supplied for the price of P_1, and in the market with elastic demand Q_2 is supplied for the price of P_2. This difference in pricing merely takes cognizance of the differing elasticities of demand between the markets given that a high-demand elasticity generally means ready availability of substi-. tutes whereas a low-demand elasticity tends to mean that people who want a certain product have few alternatives available to them and regard the product as a "necessity" (Reekie, 1979, p. 43). Accordingly in the former instance, as shown in Figure 9.1, price is lower. This way of pricing for differing elasticities of demand holds in general (recall Equation 9.2). Essentially, the market with the relatively inelastic demand—the stronger market—is charged more than the market with the relatively elastic demand. If this discrepancy in price sensitivity between buyers in the different markets can be tied to income, as seems most probable, then there is a prima facie welfare rationale for price discrimination. The reasoning behind this rationale is just as Robinson (1934, p. 204) described it, namely that "members of the more elastic markets (for whom price is reduced) may be poorer than members of the less elastic markets, and we may consider a gain to poorer buyers more important than a loss to richer buyers. In this case price discrimination must always be considered beneficial."

In its early existence the South African Competition Board shared this same equity view of price discrimination and viewed its consequences in much the same way as portrayed in Figure 9.1. On account of examining its welfare implications, in Report 4 (Competition Board, 1981, p. 9) the agency held that: "It seems safe . . . to assume that discrimination . . . with little or no prejudice to efficiency, produces a shift of income in favour of the poorer classes in a community." This discrepancy between what the agency views on the subject matter were at one point in time, and what the present Competition Act stipulates on this matter represents how far the legislator has departed from understanding this topic. Hopefully Report 4 can serve as a legal precedent to reverse this.

This equity justification for price discrimination extends to a pivotal case, that of addressing the difference between consumers having a choice and not having a choice, which tends to ultimately transpire into the difference between consumption and no consumption for a product. Restated alternatively, we are talking about product variety.

Product Variety and Price Discrimination

To understand price discrimination and how it affects product variety and consumer choice, consider a firm selling one good in each of two markets. From this illustration, generalizing to cases with more than two goods or more than two markets is straightforward.

Product variety by its definition invokes innovation. In the short run, innovation is typically accompanied by high common costs that are usually manifested in R&D costs, with low marginal costs of production following once the product is developed. Such a situation has the property that once a new (breakthrough) product is uncovered, producing additional units of it costs little, possibly next to nothing. In the short run, the firm that developed the product operates under conditions of the product's fixed costs, which encompass its common costs, exceeding its MC. In response to this, as Reekie (1979, p. 40) reminds us, the price the firm would set for the product in the short run would "exceed its marginal cost of production in order to contain its . . . overhead . . . and . . . common costs." This manner of pricing could, however, draw forth a political response against the price in which it is to result, given that by elementary price theory such price is not perfectly competitive, i.e., it is in excess of MC. This political response would usually be conveyed by legislatively banning outright price discrimination and requiring that either P = MC be instigated or that a single price across different markets, independent of their level of consumption, be administered.

The former case will necessarily have the firm suffering a loss in the short run in the presence of high common or fixed costs. Assuming the firm's losses cannot automatically be covered by taxes, given constraints on the use and imposition of tax subsidies, this in turn makes it more likely that a regulation by uniform price would prevail. This would in essence allow the firm to cover its common costs as part of the coverage of its fixed costs, and hence set P above MC, but with the reservation that the final price so determined cannot vary between the markets to which the product is sold. We graphically present in Figure 9.2 what this does for the well-being of consumers. The figure is similar to that employed by Schmalensee (1981, p. 246), but also emanates from an excellent discussion on this topic by Reekie (1979, pp. 40-45), and from subsequent discussions offered by Varian (1985, pp. 873-874), Holmes (1989, pp. 247-249), and Train (1994, pp. 123-125). For ease of exposition we shall maintain our assumption that MC is the same and that demands are independent. Under these assumptions we can analyze pricing in each market in isolation from the other markets. As before, we assume the firm supplies a

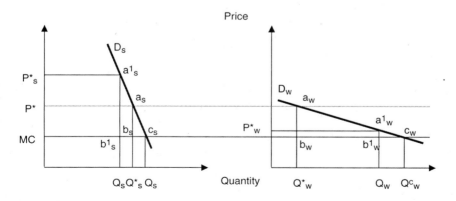

FIGURE 9.2. Short-run welfare consequences of price discrimination. *Source:* Adapted from Schmalensee, 1981, p. 246.

single (technically similar) product to two different markets, which, in accordance with the price sensitivities of the buyers they contain, are labeled the strong market (represented by demand curve D_s) and the weak market (represented by demand curve D_w).

Recall that in our exposition discrimination is impossible due to a statutory imposition (or something similar) requiring that all buyers be charged one price, which, due to the presence of high common (fixed) costs in the short run, is allowed to be P* to allow for the coverage of these costs and prevent the firm from operating at a loss. In such a case, the firm's pricing policy would quite obviously be positioned in a manner that focuses on drawing sales from the stronger rather than the weaker market. The implication of this is that those buyers who are more price sensitive will reduce their use of the product by more and hence experience a greater loss in welfare than would the less-price-sensitive buyers. Very price-sensitive consumers may drop out of the market either entirely or almost so. In our graphical illustration we see that under P* the market with inelastic demand experiences a relatively smaller decrease from the perfectly competitive level of consumption (P = MC) than the market with elastic demand. In the former instance the contraction of output is from Q^c_s to Q^*_s, whereas in the latter instance the contraction of output is from Q^c_w to Q^*_w, leaving the market with elastic demand on the brink of not consuming at all.

It can be easily inferred from this that a legislative policy of uniform pricing harms consumers by reducing their overall consumer surplus by the magnitude of the area $a_s b_s c_s + a_w b_w c_w$, representing the sum of the DWL triangles for the strong and weak market at the uniform price, P*. Allowing for price discrimination can reverse all that. When discrimination is allowed, the firm raises profits by imposing high markups in those markets where they will matter least, where quantity demanded is not too sensitive to price changes. That is, it would increase prices in markets where price elasticities of demand are relatively low and vice versa. This would actually alter markets as little as possible from the P = MC equilibrium, since in the strong market consumption would depart little from that point, whereas in the weak market it would move closer to it.

Thus, the net effect from the difference in the change in consumption between the strong and weak market would be positive, which in turn implies that the summed area of the DWL triangles under uniform pricing would be higher to that under price discrimination. Consequently, overall consumer surplus in the latter instance would exceed that in the former. This is what we observe happens in our portrayal of price discrimination in Figure 9.2.

When discrimination is allowed, price in the strong market increases from P^* to P^*_s, while in the weak market it drops to P^*_w. This in turn results in output in the price-elastic segment moving closer to the perfectly competitive point and in the price-inelastic segment departing little from it. In the former instance the move is from Q^*_w to Q_w, with this last output level being close to the perfectly competitive point Q^c_w. In the latter instance the move is from Q^*_s to Q_s, with this last output level not being far off from the perfectly competitive point Q^c_s. The net effect of these movements is that overall consumption (as measured by the difference between fragments $Q^*_wQ_w$ and $Q^*_sQ_s$) is increased. So, too, is overall consumer welfare, given that area $a^1_sb^1_sc_s + a^1_wb^1_wc_w$—representing the sum of the DWL triangles for the strong and weak markets under price discrimination—is smaller compared to area $a_sb_sc_s + a_wb_wc_w$ under uniform pricing, thereby resulting in more consumer surplus as a whole being exalted under price discrimination than uniform pricing.

The discrepancy in output between price discrimination (where it is higher) and uniform pricing (where it is lower) suggests that it is possible for uniform price regulation to decrease the number of firms supplying the product compared to where price discrimination is allowed. This seems more likely for the weak market, where the construction in output under uniform pricing far exceeds that of the strong market.

In addition, we can see that price discrimination results in higher profits for the firm than uniform pricing. This can be spotted by noting the difference in the profit rectangles between the uniform and price discrimination cases in Figure 9.2. The summed area $P^*_sa^1_sb^1_sMC + P^*_wa^1_wb^1_wMC$ of the strong and weak markets for the profit rectangle under price discrimination is greater than the corresponding area $P^*a_sb_sMC + P^*a_wb_wMC$ under uniform pricing. Hence, a higher level of innovation, i.e., more product variety, can be sustained in the short run if price discrimination is permitted, given it would yield higher profits for firms than uniform pricing.

Here we must bring to attention an important point relating to the recoupment of common and overhead costs. What we have presented in essence demonstrates two different ways of how this recoupment of costs can be achieved. One is having the regulator allow for spontaneous third-degree price discrimination, i.e., leaving the firm to do what it would do naturally, and the other is having the regulator assume the role of a dirigiste and bestow a single, nonvaried price across markets. Under the uniform price case, recovery of the common and overhead costs would be guaranteed by regulation, whereas under the price discrimination case coverage of these costs would be subject to the profits the firm makes. This in itself ought to raise alarm bells as to whether, from a public policy perspective, pursuit of the dirigiste route is desirable, given it is a peculiar feature of those cases involving rates of return guaranteed by regulation to invite lack of market discipline and organizational slack.

More important, however, given that we have already established that the case of price discrimination has the advantage of producing more product variety than that of uniform pricing, price discrimination should then be seen as essential for the functioning of the innovation mechanism of the competitive process. Hence, in addition to the equity rationale for price discrimination, an innovation (or product variety) rationale can also be added. We have demonstrated that price discrimination is very likely necessary if product variety is to exist at all. Since product variety is synonymous with choice, a consumer choice rationale also can be made for price discrimination. This is strengthened by the chief assumption, inter alia, of the theory of consumer behavior, that is, consumers always prefer more of any good to less. Therefore, more choice made possible by more product variety is always more desirable than less.

Jointly, the equity and consumer choice rationale give rise to another rationale for price discrimination: consumption. If a market comprised of low-income (poor) individuals is to enjoy product variety as does a market made up of high-income (rich) individuals, then price discrimination is a prerequisite if the former is to be supplied at all, and its members enabled to enlarge their consumption where little or none existed before. In our discussion, this was demonstrated with reference to the increases in consumption (and improvement in consumer surplus) the weak market undergoes relative to the strong market under price discrimination instead of uniform pricing.

Before we proceed any further, we should question whether, in response to price discrimination, a price of P^*_s for the strong market is a viable price. If the market is competitive, i.e., subject to the competitive process, then under the transfer mechanism a monopoly price such as P^*_s (which qualifies as such more than P^*_w) cannot prevail for long. Thus, it may be possible for a strong market (where no barriers to entry abound and firms have to recover their common and overhead costs) to face in the short run under price discrimination a price lower than that from uniform pricing but higher than that from price discrimination in a weak market. In Figure 9.1 this would involve drawing a horizontal line between P^* and P^*_w on the ordinate for the strong market schedule. Such a price would arise either as a result of rivals bidding away by demand diversion the monopoly price P^*_s or the firm that has imposed this price opting to set a price identical to of its rivals. Still, we must be mindful that, whatever the price competition, here it applies to an inelastic market. Since the quantity demanded is not too sensitive to price changes (reductions), the increase in consumption (output) from lower prices is unlikely to have the same bearing as it might have for the weak market.

Before proceeding any further, we should also consider the decline in price for the market with elastic demand—the market that is more price sensitive—in response to which consumption for this market gets to move very close to that attainable under perfect competition. For this market, under uniform price regulation, the resulting price, in our case P^*, effectively constitutes a monopoly price by decree. If uniform price regulation for this market is removed, this amounts to subjecting the market to the competitive process, where under the transfer mechanism a monopoly price such as P^* cannot prevail for long. A downward pressure would be imposed on such a price. This may arise either from rivals competing away such a price by expanding supply, or by the original firm opting to set a price identical to its rivals.

We should recognize at this point that, as a matter of principle, where pricing is not subject to regulation and a firm is allowed to price freely, it would then naturally engage in price discrimination since this would yield it higher profits than uniform pricing by dictate. This implicitly assumes that a firm can fulfill the condition of no arbitrage. Given that price discrimination comes with higher profits than does single, nonvaried pricing, it can be safely assumed that this encourages the firm to keep the markets it serves independent from one another.

The exposition on price discrimination offered here hopefully makes it easier to see how it is that a firm can engage in demand creation and demand diversion via price discrimination. Supplying a product to a price-elastic segment, which would have only made abysmal or no use of the product if price discrimination were not possible, can be seen as an example of the former instance. Driving down the monopoly price applicable to a price-elastic or -inelastic segment under a regimen of free pricing, where spontaneous price discrimination thrives by means of switching to competing alternatives, can be seen as an example of the latter instance. It should be noted here that the spectrum proliferation for a given product would most probably vary in range across the segments, since in accordance with the equity rationale of price discrimination referred to earlier, the market with elastic demand is very likely to be affiliated with low-income individuals in contrast to the market with inelastic demand. As incomes grow, people have more discretionary income. Thus, it is possible that the spectrum for a given product would be greater in the market with the more price-insensitive buyers (users). However, we need not be so cautious by asserting that this is a possibility. It is in fact a matter of principle, as proven by the Koutsoyiannis product variety rule (Koutsoyiannis, 1982, p. 86). This rule is an extension of the Buchanan-Dorfman-Steiner (price-advertising) theorem, and has been expanded by De Villiers and Scott (1986, pp.198-199) to show that, for a firm operating in n markets, its optimal (profit maximizing) product variety decision in each is given by:

$$V_i / R_i = \varepsilon_{V_i} / \varepsilon_i, \qquad (9.3)$$

where V_i = expenditure required to produce the product variety in the ith market (in practice this is none other than the expenditure on R&D; R_i = sales in the ith market; εV_i = elasticity of demand with respect to the change in V_i for the ith market; and ε_i = price elasticity of demand for the ith market.

Equation 9.3 represents nothing more than the mathematical formulation of the product variety rationale for price discrimination. To understand it, it must be examined jointly with the price discrimination rule depicted in Equation 9.1. For the case of a firm launching a new product into two independent markets, it tells us that the firm would recoup its expenditure on R&D from which this product emanated by levying a higher price in the stronger market. This would be so since the elasticity of R&D expenditure, namely the relative change in quantity demanded consequential on a change in R&D expenditure will be positive in the less-price-sensitive market, and this market will thus encourage innovative expenditure. Conversely, the elasticity of R&D expenditure will not be positive in the highly price-elastic market, and this market will therefore not be conducive to innovative expenditure. Simply put, most of the contribution to the firm's spending on R&D will come from the market with the relatively less-elastic demand. By extension, markets whose buyers are not so sensitive to price compared to those whose are would experience more R&D on the part of firms and correspondingly a greater product assortment. All this takes us back to our illustration of price discrimination in Figure 9.2, which signals that in the short run price departures from MC for the former market would exceed those of the latter market.

However, if we are prepared to accept the workings of the competitive process in lieu of government-set prices, then it has to be acknowledged that monopoly power is only temporary. Its presence in the absence of government support or legislative means of like effect need not result in high market (monopoly) prices at all.

Under the competitive process, profit maximization is not unconstrained but subject to a constraint imposed by actual entry or the threat of it, where incumbents would tend to be disciplined by potential entrants with access to the same technology and with no rent-seeking or government-imposed impediments to entry. What this means for the way firms price in contestable markets is just as Baumol and colleagues (1982, p. 222) described it: "Potential competition can . . . force the monopolist to produce with maximal efficiency, and to hunt down and utilise fully every opportunity for innovation. Perhaps most surprising of all, it can induce the monopolist to institute . . . Ramsey prices . . . ." Ramsey prices is a concept we have not dealt with before solely because in the preceding discussion on price discrimination it was implicitly assumed that a firm can set prices with limited or no concern that it may have to vie for market share with other contestants (actual or potential). This assumption is possibly too restrictive, given that, as remarked earlier, where the competitive process operates monopoly power is only temporary, i.e., over time it crumbles. Ramsey prices in effect take stock of the restrictions on pricing that rivalry (actual or potential) can impose.

Ramsey Pricing

Ramsey prices are those derived from the Ramsey pricing rule, so named after its developer, Frank Ramsey. The mathematics involving the derivation of this rule is not the subject of exposition here, given it has received detailed treatment in Ramsey (1927), Baumol and Bradford (1970), Boiteux (1971), and Brown and Sibley (1986, pp. 194-197), with possibly the most eloquent proof of this rule to be found in Reekie (1979, pp. 42-43). This omission will not, however, come at the expense of presenting what the rule embodies.

In the case of high fixed (common) costs in the short run, independent market demands and an absolute profit constraint (as rivalry can impose), the rule, as noted by Baumol and Bradford (1970, p. 267) requires that each price be set so that its percentage deviation from marginal cost is inversely proportionate to the item's price elasticity of demand. Accordingly, social welfare will be served most effectively by unequal or disproportionate deviations of price from marginal cost rather than by setting prices equal or proportionate to marginal cost.

This indicates, as stipulated by Brown and Sibley (1986, p. 40), that Ramsey pricing has the firm price in *n* markets in accordance with the following rule:

$$Z_i = \lambda / \varepsilon_i \qquad (9.4)$$

where Z_i = markup in the *i*th market, i.e., $Z_i = [(P_i - MC_i)/P_i]$; ε_i = product's elasticity of demand in the *i*th market; and λ = the constraint (amount of reduction) the firm faces on its profit, which does not vary between markets. This is so in order to ensure that the difference in the markup over MC in each market is solely governed by the responsiveness of demand to price.

In Equation 9.4, the low-elasticity markets get high markups and the highly priced elastic markets get low markups. This inverse characteristic of the Ramsey pricing rule is why it is also often called the inverse elasticity rule: prices are raised in inverse relation to the elasticity of demand in each market. Employing this rule and reverting to our example from third-degree price discrimination of a firm supplying a single (technically similar) product to two different markets, Ramsey pricing has the firm price between them in accordance with the markup expression:

$$Z_1/Z_2 = \varepsilon_2/\varepsilon_1 \qquad (9.5)$$

It can be seen that Equation 9.5 is not too dissimilar to Equation 9.2. It shows us that, like third-degree price discrimination, in Ramsey pricing the more inelastic the demand for the firm's product, the greater should be the percentage deviation from MC. Here too, the market with relatively inelastic demand faces a higher price compared to its elastic counterpart. This pricing method has already been demonstrated and, as Baumol and Bradford have pointed out, Ramsey pricing, where significant fixed (common) costs exist, would serve social welfare, in the short run, more effectively than uniform pricing designed to take account of these costs.

In contrast to uniform pricing, Ramsey pricing would tend to alter markets as little as possible from the P = MC equilibrium, since it would result in prices under which consumption in the strong market would depart little from that point and in the weak market consumption would move closer to it. If instead it is decided by decree to set all prices in the short run equal to MC(s) where significant fixed (common) costs exist, then the resulting deficits (the losses the firms would take) would have to be made up by subsidies (funding the firms) out of the government treasury. This creates a public policy dilemma, or call it a social one if you will, aptly sketched by Baumol and Bradford (1970, p. 265) where:

> If these funds are derived by excise taxes this is obviously a decision to make some prices depart from marginal costs after all. Or if it is obtained by an income tax, it is the price of labour that is forced away from its marginal cost. Any tax . . . will unavoidably affect some price. . . . Any level of tax revenue which the government is determined to collect . . . as a means to make up a deficit resulting from a marginal cost pricing arrangement . . . must in practice produce some price distortion.

It is worth noting explicitly the closeness between third-degree price discrimination and Ramsey pricing, such that the latter may in fact be construed as representing a milder form of third-degree price discrimination, i.e., third-degree price discrimination under a profit constraint.[3] In view of this closeness nothing, in terms of the principles presented in this work on the topic of third-degree price discrimination, conflicts with what would be found if Ramsey pricing were to be considered instead. Nonetheless, we must be mindful of a similarity and a distinction here. The similarity relates to thinking of Ramsey pricing and third-degree price discrimination as producing efficient prices, i.e., those that minimize DWL, in the short run. Thus, both Ramsey prices and third-degree prices provide greater total consumer surplus than does a regimen of uniform pricing, which seems more likely to be the consequence of a state interventionist policy than market forces. The distinction relates to seeing that, although third-degree prices and Ramsey prices are those which raise overall consumer surplus in the short run, they do so differently. In third-degree price discrimination this is achieved by the firm's (provider) unconstrained maximization of profits. This requires unrivalled market power and brings us full circle to our conclusion that acquiring such power where government support is absent requires innovations of lasting distinctiveness in their technological, organizational, or product sense. However, the longevity of such power is questionable. It tends to be the case that, where the competitive process is not encroached upon statutorily, acceptable or readily available substitutes to what a firm with monopoly power has or makes will be found or made. This brings us to Ramsey pricing, where the increase in overall consumer surplus is achieved by the firm (provider) maximizing profits by practicing third-degree price discrimination, subject to constraints that business activities as mundane as the vying for market share, in all their variations and manifestations, seem certain to impose.

From the difference in the way price discrimination is practiced between third-degree and Ramsey pricing, i.e., with and without constraints on firm profit and what this carries with it, it can be said that it seems, on the whole, that the innovation mechanism gives rise to price discrimination. Combining this with the innovation rationale referred to earlier, it appears that price discrimination and innovation are inseparable, i.e., the existence of one secures the other and vice versa. A gentler means of price discrimination comes into existence as the transfer mechanism gains ground or becomes more operative than the innovation mechanism. Then third-degree price discrimination moves toward Ramsey pricing.

What, then, does the theory on price discrimination predicate quantitatively, as a general principle, about the impact price discrimination has on consumers, output, and the number of firms in contestable markets where fixed costs exist, compared to if it were prohibited by a uniform price allowing for the coverage of fixed costs? This is an abstract exercise on which little research exists. Nonetheless, Borenstein (1985) has sought to remedy this by hypothetically constructing the consequences of third-degree price discrimination in free-entry markets.[4] Borenstein's work is based on a number of underlying assumptions that Borenstein specified in statistical and mathematical parlance, which amount to the same assumptions specified earlier regarding price discrimination.

In a nutshell, Borenstein (1985, pp. 382-385, 389) assumed that each firm practices Pigouvian third-degree price discrimination under conditions of perfect substitutability, supplying to two independent markets with linear demand schedules, one for a market with an elastic demand, and the other for a market with an inelastic demand. It was furthermore assumed that each firm has the same cost of production for its product, made up of the same MC and a large fixed cost between the markets, i.e., this depicts a short-run situation. Building on these assumptions by means of numerical simulation, Borenstein's hypothetical construction furnished the results presented in Table 9.1. Commenting on these findings, Borenstein (1985, pp. 391, 392) notes:

> Price discrimination . . . results in more firms than when the practice is prohibited. . . . The profits from discrimination, however, attract entry . . . and thus increase variety and put downward pressure on prices. Therefore, discrimination would be more likely to increase the quantity sold in these instances than in . . . any . . . in which the number of firms is fixed. . . . The increase in N and decrease in price for the low-price group imply that the sum of consumers' surplus in the low-price group always increases with discrimination. In a few cases discrimination also lowered the price charged to the high-price group. When this happened, the lower price and greater variety necessarily increased total surplus in that group as well.

TABLE 9.1. The impact of price discrimination (average change from the discrimination-prohibited case).

Factor	Percentage
Discount to low-price buyers	26.8
Total number of firms (N)	6.22
Total quantity produced	7.86
Overall consumer surplus	2.48

Source: Adapted from Borenstein, 1985, p. 392.

Nothing in the findings or their interpretation is unexpected. Both conform with the theory of (third-degree) price discrimination presented in here and, most important, with its maxim that price discrimination is preferred to all those cases of nondiscrimination if it increases output and consumer welfare in total. It is difficult to picture where those instances might not occur, except of course if the competitive process is stifled in some way, which seems something more likely to result not from competition but from government regulation of the rights and ways by which firms may compete. The results contained in Table 9.1 also serve as a means of substantiating the exposition on price discrimination rendered earlier. Their appeal is that they provide recourse to theory, as in what theory predicates quantitatively regarding the possible consequences of prohibiting price discrimination when certain conditions hold.

These conditions include having a firm supply, in competition, to independent (elastic and inelastic demand) markets whose demands may be described linearly, a product for which large fixed (common) costs exist exceeding its constant (across the markets) MC. When these conditions apply, as they do in the short run wherever innovation is involved, theory suggests that price discrimination ought not to be prohibited by law or anything of like manner for a uniform price allowing for the coverage of these large fixed (common) costs. If this were to happen, the theory suggests, using the results in Table 9.1, then on the average this is likely to see the elastic market experience an increase in its price level of 27 percent. In addition, on the average this is also likely to see the total number of firms, total quantity produced, and overall consumer surplus drop by 6, 8, and 2.5 percent respectively. No breakdown for this last figure is given between the elastic and the inelastic markets. If it existed, it would be seen that its composition would be made up of a large decrease in consumer surplus for the price-sensitive consumers (buyers) and a much smaller one for the price-insensitive ones.

Having addressed the first issue, we now move to the second one. This is intended to offer, as a matter of reflection on the work that has been presented on price discrimination thus far, a number of conclusions regarding what the implication of regulatory polices prohibiting price discrimination is likely to be. By analogy, this would also serve to answer the question posed earlier, which asked whether price discrimination should be seen as an anticompetitive business practice, i.e., one that potentially or actually halts competition.

It has been the aim of everything that has been presented thus far to instill the conception that cogent reasons exist to doubt that price discrimination halts rivalry or that it works to the detriment of consumers. Since monopoly generally implies lower outputs and higher prices, and since economic welfare is unlikely to be adversely affected where the firm's profit-maximizing output with discriminatory pricing is greater than that with nondiscriminatory pricing, then price discrimination should qualify as a competitive activity. This is borne out by the appearance of the practice of raising access to products that may otherwise not even be supplied or would be supplied in minimal quantity only, and of increasing overall the volumes sold at prices consumers are prepared to pay. All this in turn suggests that the reasons, whatever they might be, as to why price discrimination is outright prohibited in the South African competition statute and other statutes, are ill-bred. Our exposition on price discrimination offers three conclusions in this regard.

First, the grounds for state regulation of prices, as in the imposition of uniform prices, are weak, whilst the consequences of such regulation injure the very people that the state usually undertakes to serve, i.e., the indigent or poor. Second, the grounds for abolishing price discrimination are weak and the consequences of actually doing it appear in all likelihood to be equally ill-founded. A public-policy decision such as this is very likely to lead to no choice (i.e., lack of product variety), retarded or halted innovation, the imposition of unduly high prices on the poor or indigent, and the deprivation of consumers, especially those with low-income, from what they could have otherwise consumed.

Third, a state-interventionist policy of uniform price regulation can lead to fewer firms in a market compared to where price discrimination is allowed to exist. Thus, such a policy itself may end up stifling competition, since the price it brings about has the property of guaranteeing the long-lasting absence of price flexibility. This is something more reminiscent of monopoly power than that vested in firms by the competitive process. The policy precludes the reduction in price for the price-sensitive buyers that competition in the form of price discrimination, most likely to reveal itself here in demand creation, can bring about. It is likely that the policy can do the same for the less-price-sensitive buyers by precluding competition in the form of price discrimination, most likely to reveal itself here through demand diversion.

Reflecting on the U.S. experience with the Robinson-Patman Act (enacted in 1936), Carlton and Perloff (2000, p. 642) observe that the "consequence of the . . . Act . . . is higher prices to consumers. . . . The . . . Act has led to substantial litigation (although government litigation has waned recently) and has also distorted pricing in many markets. . . . This law has harmed consumers."

This summary is not an isolated incident. Reflecting on similar consequences of the Act, the U.S. Department of Justice observed that

> the Act has not shown itself to be capable of promoting the antitrust goals of continued competitive vigour and low prices. In fact, the Act is regulatory in nature and its enforcement is based on a series of faulty presumptions. (U.S. Department of Justice, 1977, p. 250)

The Department consequently came to the conclusion that "serious consideration should be given to repealing the Robinson-Patman Act" (U.S. Department of Justice, 1977, p. 261). All this, in conjunction with our presentation on price discrimination and the consequences of its prohibition, justifies skepticism toward all those instances where the practice is prohibited or encroached upon by state regulation. In the context of South Africa, given the incorporation of the Robinson-Patman Act into the country's competition law, it provides clear enough evidence in support of not having this provision in the country's competition books at all.

Apart from the strong theoretical grounds for questioning the assumption that prohibiting price discrimination is likely to be of benefit to consumers, the exceptions under the law, in the South African case contained under §9(2), illustrate further problems with the prohibition itself. The case in point is to be found in the phrases *good-faith, price differences,* and *equivalent transactions* that the exceptions contain, all of which, it must be stressed, only add to the shortcomings of the prohibition, specifically of the way it was conceived. This may not be outright obvious, and so to shed light on the matter we shall make two remarks, borrowing from Reekie (1998, 2000) to do so. Regarding good-faith and price differences, Reekie (1998, p. 19) noted,

> The difficulty . . . with the law is illustrated by the "good-faith" price matching defence. To succeed, the seller must show that the matched price is itself lawful. This necessitates knowledge of the competitor's own price and cost structure—but in a classic Catch-22 if he shows he has such knowledge he may be prosecuted for conspiring to restrain trade. . . . Further confusion is caused by the phrase "price differences" which is used in the legislation, not "price discrimination", which is a technical term indicating disproportional price:marginal cost ratios. Thus identical prices with different costs (uniform price discrimination) can not be touched by the legislation.

We should delve a little more here, and note that under the catch-22 situation the firm, in addition to likely being prosecuted for conspiring to restrain trade, may alternatively find itself the subject of prosecution for entering into a prohibited horizontal agreement for (allegedly) colluding.

On "equivalent transactions" Reekie (2000, p. 59) asked,

> What is equivalent? A manufacturer may wish to raise his share of the market. Should he price at the same level today to two different distribution channels if he anticipates one channel has a much higher growth potential tomorrow? If he believes the one channel has a more efficient (lower cost) method of reaching the consumer and can expand more rapidly tomorrow than the other

channel, how can he encourage that for his own (but also the final consumer's) benefit? The answer is to price ahead of demand by lowering price to the channel with high potential—a common business practice but one with *prima facie* evidence of unjustifiable price discrimination.

Taking stock of these remarks and combining them with the earlier presentation on prohibiting price discrimination, it appears that it is socially undesirable, in terms of production and consumption, to have state regulation pronounce on matters as fundamental to the functioning of the competitive prices as pricing freedom. From the grandiose failures of the Communist era, such interventionism has little to recommend for itself.

By analogy, so should anything of a similar guise, which is what a price discrimination ban is, for it either allows the state to decide what the market price should be or may do the same by creating an environment conducive to rent-seeking where less-efficient firms come to seek defense from their more-efficient rivals. The possibility of such an action should not be dismissed, given that its prize, as our treatment on the prohibition of price discrimination suggests, is a monopoly price. This may also explain why, as reported by Carlton and Perloff (2000), there is a substantial amount of private litigation is taking place under the Robinson-Patman Act.

Before moving to the following chapter to discuss the topic of measuring concentration, which is long overdue by now, we must discuss one other point. The point is subtle and concerns an activity that usually does not have an apparent intimate affiliation with price discrimination.

MARKETING

As emphasized earlier, if price discrimination is to be practiced by a firm at all this requires that the firm seals off the markets it sells to from one another. This sealing off involves keeping the demands of the different markets the firm sells to independent, which in turn requires that consumers be kept in separate groups (segments). Further, it was noted that in practice consumers are frequently divided by firms according to time, that is, impatience (cinema versus video movies), geographical location (foreign versus domestic), income (luxury versus standard option), ability to shift to other products (industrial versus home use), and quality (first versus second grade).

The practical tool by which a firm achieves this division is by marketing, and specifically by marketing differently to the different markets in a manner that ensures that no arbitrage takes place, i.e., each market has little or no chance of buying the product meant for the other market. Hence, we can consider marketing and everything it involves (e.g., promotion, advertising, tie-in-sales, and so on) to move hand-in-hand with price discrimination. Marketing activities, with all their corresponding costs (whatever they might be), are all for the purpose of informing consumers (buyers) in the different markets what the firm offers them in relation to its rivals or lack thereof. This involves communicating to them that the product they want is available at a price they are willing to pay. In this way, marketing ought to be pictured as an activity a firm engages in to open up markets or give consumers greater access and variety to the products they demand. Encroaching upon an activity such as this, for instance, by having state regulation control what amount of marketing may take place, seems likely to stifle competition and undermine the ability of a seller to price discriminate effectively. The firm cannot encourage greater use of what it offers through the demand-creation and demand-diversion components of price discrimination if it has limited ability to tell consumers what they stand to benefit from buying the product. This seems likely to produce uninformed buyers and disinterested sellers, which would very likely lead to prices congealing, i.e., becoming monopoly-like. Consumers have no information about where in the market a better deal or price is to be exacted. Producers have none to offer, as they know they cannot inform consumers to their advantage. With all sellers compelled to behave alike, competition at the supply level is effectively choked and we have a market price identical to that of a collective monopoly. This outcome, which a regulation tampering with the amount of marketing a firm may undertake can produce, is the same as what we examined previously on the ban of price discrimination in favor of a uniform price (recall price P^* in Figure 9.2).

An extreme example of showing the effects of what we have described in this chapter can possibly arise if legislation prohibited firms (sellers) from advertising altogether or, alternatively, instructed that they cease at once incurring any marketing costs. Such prohibitions in practice would probably not be as extreme as what we have described here, but then the resulting effects we have described would still exist, with the only difference that the·adversity of their impact might not be as pronounced. The crux of the matter, as identified by Lachmann (1978b, p. 28), is that a market in the true economic sense means a process of exchange; an allocation reflecting the transmission of knowledge. Advertising, whereby firms disseminate market information, provides consumers with knowledge that promotes competitive results, such as product variety, lower prices, and a check on profit-taking. Some examples of this are empirically demonstrated and confirmed in, among others, Benham (1972), Boyer (1974), and Comanor and Wilson (1979).

To summarize, this chapter began by stating what were seen, inter alia, as key per se prohibitions in the (South African) Competition Act of practices that dominance (monopoly power) is considered to give rise to. Of all the prohibitions examined, namely monopoly pricing, predatory pricing, and price discrimination, the aim was to demonstrate that these activities should not be viewed as anticompetitive outright just because a dominant firm (one with market power) may produce them. Strong (theoretical) reasons exist to see each of these activities as symptomatic of rivalry and not as something that works against competition. In the case of monopoly pricing, if it prevailed without government support this would reflect competition of the Schumpeterian-Littlechild sort, where the innovation mechanism is temporarily overpowering the transfer mechanism, resulting in price skimming. Over time the transfer mechanism comes to gain ground and this price skimming becomes subject to the Reekie product filter, which leads to marginal cost being approached in the long run.

In the case of predatory pricing it was found that if it existed on the assumed premise that it requires the sacrifice of short-run profits, then this itself renders the practice unviable. Assuming that predation is successful, then every costly period of predatory pricing would have to be followed by a period of recoupment—high prices to recover the losses experienced in the predatory price war. This in itself illustrates why predation is an improbable strategy for the deterrence of entrants and for the elimination of existing rivals. If the predator raises prices after the predation an entrant will come, lured by the profits. For the predator the decision then is either to follow predation and incur short-run losses that could turn into long-run losses, given the high chance of entry, or allow entry outright. This last option appears plausible for the incumbent (the predator) to adopt, given that the "victim" of predation (the entrant) can in all likelihood foresee the gain to come after predation, i.e., monopoly prices, which will give it all the incentive to stay in the market so as to be able to benefit from them in due course. Thus, entry takes place, rendering predation ineffective.

In the case of price discrimination we observed that the practice is highly unlikely to work to the detriment of consumers in the short run. The opposite seems likely to apply. It was shown that equity and consumption rationales exist for allowing firms to practice price discrimination. In addition, price discrimination was demonstrated to move hand in hand with product variety and consumer choice. Furthermore, it was shown that discrimination results in more firms than when the practice is prohibited. The profits from discrimination attract entry and thus increase variety and put downward pressure on prices. This in turn means that discrimination is likely to increase, not decrease, output.

Following price discrimination, the increase in the number of firms and the decrease in price for the market with price-sensitive buyers implies that the sum of consumers' surplus in this market always increases with discrimination. Spontaneous price discrimination is also likely to lower the price charged to the market with price-insensitive buyers. When this happens, the lower price and greater variety necessarily increase total surplus in that market as well.

Finally, we pointed out that the ability of a firm to price discriminate is intimately affiliated with marketing. When legislative restrictions on marketing are imposed it is possible for this to produce an outcome, i.e., price inflexibility, identical to that of banning price discrimination.

The following chapter deals with a topic intimately affiliated with our coverage of competition.

Chapter 10

Measuring Market Concentration

What follows concerns the measurement of a market's competitiveness with the use of measures that describe market structure and/or serve as a prima facie indicator of market power or competition among firms. These measures, referred to as concentration indices, numerically determine a market's competitiveness, namely whether a market is characterized by firms lacking market power (as in perfect competition), dominant firms (as in oligopoly), or a monopoly.

In the case of the South African competition regulator and others that abide by similar competition legislation, concentration indices serve the purpose of revealing whether dominance in the market or industry is being investigated and whether in turn this gives rise to all those (in conventional interpretation) restrictions on competition that monopoly power brings with it, whether proposed horizontal mergers or acquisitions stand to produce something of like manner, or whether all in all dominance could give rise to the practices discussed previously.

Several measures of concentration have been devised to determine how the proportions of firms are spread in a market, amongst which are the concentration ratio, the Herfindahl-Hirschman index (HHI), the rank correlation coefficient (for its application see Downie, 1958, p. 147; Reekie, 1981; and Scott and Reekie, 1985), and the Hymer-Pashigian index (HPI) (Hymer and Pashigian, 1962; see also Reekie, 1989, p. 49). To these can also be added the comprehensive concentration index, also referred to as the Horvath index (HI) (Horvath, 1970). To gain an understanding of how each index is calculated and what each one involves, we now turn to discussing them individually.

The concentration ratio measures the percentage of a market (usually expressed in turnover terms) accounted for by the market's n largest firms, where n is an arbitrary selected number that is taken to

doi:10.1300/5505_10

be 3, 4, 8, or 10. However, a preference exists to take n as 3 or 4, since it enables one to clearly delineate a market into dominant and fringe firms. Mathematically:

$$CR_n = \sum_1^n s_i \qquad (10.1)$$

where n refers to the n largest firms in a market, and s_i is the market share (expressed as a proportion) of the ith firm. The larger the CR_n the more monopolistic the industry is. Evidently, two problems are encountered when using this measure to judge competitiveness in the market.

First, it excludes the remaining $1-n$ firms; in other words, the measure takes no cognizance of the industrial behavior of the remaining firms in the industry and does not indicate whether the tail of firms is composed of a few medium-sized or large firms or many small ones. Likewise, the CR_n does not indicate whether the group of top firms it looks at is composed of giant and/or small firms.

Second, under CR_n no account is taken of the inequality in firm sizes. One should expect that, with the decline in market share as one moves down the ranks, smaller firms contribute proportionately less to market concentration by an extent related to their control of the market.

To deal with the shortcomings of the CR_n, the HHI is used. This measure takes account of the total number of firms in an industry and focuses on the inequality in firm sizes. It is accordingly a measure of relative concentration in contrast to the CR_n, which is a measure of absolute concentration. The HHI is obtained by summing the squares of the firms' market shares (expressed as proportions). Mathematically:

$$HHI = \sum_1^n s_i^2 \qquad (10.2)$$

The squaring of the shares means that smaller firms contribute proportionately less to the value of the index. The HHI rises as the inequality in shares among market participants increases (i.e., as a few firms come to dominate a market). The shortcoming of the HHI is that it gives large firms heavy weighting, which may make it reflective of their level of concentration. For instance, the square of the market share of a firm with a 20 percent share of the market is 0.04 and that of a firm with a 1 percent share of the market is 0.0001. During the summation, the presence or lack of this last number makes no difference to the HHI value. This shortcoming of the HHI should not be viewed negatively. Rather, it indicates that the index may have useful properties where there are data limitations.

Falling between the CR_n and the HHI is the Horvath Index, proposed by Horvath (1970). The HI looks at the actual proportions of firms participating in the market and at the inequality in firm sizes so it is a combined measure of absolute and relative concentration. The HI is given by:

$$HI = s_1 + \sum_{i=2}^{n} s_i^2 \times \left[1 + (1 - s_i)\right] \qquad (10.3)$$

where s_1 is the market share of the first firm.

Under the HI, after the first firm the remaining ones, jointly, contribute proportionately less to market concentration. In the case of the remaining firms, smaller firms contribute proportionately much less, compared to the larger ones, to market concentration. This stems from the weighting scheme of the HI where the proportion of a market a firm has is contrasted against the proportion of the market it does not have.

In this sense, the HI also acts as a measure of potential rivalry. A low HI value would indicate that competition is in its infancy, where superior product advantages or productive efficiency by some firms relative to others are yet to emerge, whereas a high value would communicate their presence. The HI shares the same shortcoming as the HHI in that it weights larger firms heavier, which may make it reflective of their concentrations. This should not be viewed negatively, and as with the HHI it indicates that this index may have useful properties where data limitations exist.

The indices we have just described relate to one another as follows. In a nutshell, the CR_n has a value above 0 and a maximum of 1 that could reflect a monopoly or cartel-like market. Values that depart from 1 but are near it are reflective of oligopolistic or monopolistic markets. Values that are not close to 1 are reflective of perfectly competitive, i.e., atomistic markets. The HHI and HI range between 0 and 1, which could reflect a monopoly or cartel-like market. Values in between that are close to 1 are indicative of oligopolistic or monopolistic markets, and values near 0 are indicative of atomistic markets. Given that the HI is a combined measure of absolute and relative concentration compared to the CR_n, which is an absolute measure and the HHI, which is a relative one, numerically the order of the indices would be as follows:

$$CR_n > HI > HHI \qquad (10.4)$$

It ought to be apparent, but if not, it should be recognized that only if recorded at some particular instant the CR_n, HHI, and HI would represent static measures of rivalry, which in turn would render them inadequate for the very purpose for which they were employed, i.e., to ascertain if a market is competitive. A way out of this would be to examine the indices regularly over time. Alternatively, one could use the rank correlation coefficient (used, for instance, by Downie, 1958, p. 147, and Reekie, 1981, p. 51) or the Hymer-Pashigian Index (Hymer and Pashigian, 1962; for its use see Reekie, 1989, p. 49, and Scott and Reekie, 1985, p. 46). To shed light on what the last two of these indices involve we examine them independently in terms of the rank correlation coefficient and the Hymer-Pashigian Index.

As has been stated already, the indices described in the previous sections are static in the sense that if not monitored over time they simply record the characteristics of the market-share distribution of firms for a given industry (market) at some particular instant. If, however, the rankings of (dominant) firms in an industry were to change over time, then even persistently high levels of concentration would not imply the absence of competitive forces. This is what the rank correlation coefficient attempts to determine by examining the changes over time in the rank positions of firms in an industry. The rank correlation coefficient derives its formulation from statistics, and technically it may either be computed via Spearman's rank correlation coefficient, ρ, or via Kendall's correlation coefficient, τ. Statistically, it is common knowledge that significance tests (for the association between the variables correlated) based on either of the coefficients yield almost identical results. Empirically (see for instance Downie, 1958, p. 147; Reekie, 1981; and Scott and Reekie, 1985), greater use seems to be made of Spearman's ρ, although there is no reason why Kendall's τ should not also be used. Nonetheless, given the popularity of the former measure, we confine this discussion to the rank correlation coefficient by Spearman's formulation (Ott, 1993, p. 467), which is given by:

$$\rho = 1 - 6\sum d_i^2 \Big/ \left[n\left(n^2 - 1\right) \right] \qquad (10.5)$$

where d_i = differences in firms' ranks between any two time periods; and n = number of firms.

Although by construction the rank correlation coefficient, ρ, ranges in values between plus 1 and minus 1, in interpreting the changes in firms' ranks for a given industry over time we are interested in the coefficient's absolute value. If ρ turns out to be very high, i.e., either 1 or near 1 in absolute terms, then the ranking positions of firms are either unchanged or have changed very little, implying that the studied industry is uncompetitive. The reverse would apply for values of ρ near to or at 0 (in absolute terms). Put differently, the more movement that occurs in the positioning of firms, the lower is the calculated coefficient and the more competitive a market or an industry is deemed to be. It must be stressed here that a low ρ must not be equated with the presence of atomistic firms only. A low ρ is also possible for a market made up of dominant firms. This would happen if between any two periods the cardinality of the market shares of firms is such that it leads to a superficial ordinality in their ranking. This would occur where, irrespective of actual changes in rank, numerically the market shares between the few rivals remain very close to one another. This would be an example of competition among equally capable rivals all inclined to live and let live.

It should be noted that the rank correlation coefficient says little of the inequality in market size between the firms in an industry other than to reveal, over time, the difference (or lack thereof) in market positioning of each firm and thereby for the industry overall. The result is that the index, although giving information on the vigor of rivalry in a market, gives no information on the structure of a market, i.e., it does not reveal whether a market is characterized by dominant or atomistic firms. It may be argued here that the more competitive a market is, the more change in firm rank there is and the lower ρ is. However, a market can undergo fundamental economic changes and experience no corresponding change in firm ranking. For example, an industry composed of two firms, firm A with a 55 percent market share and firm B with a 45 percent market share, would produce a rank correlation coefficient of unity even if A's share increased to 90 percent, say, in response to the company developing a new product, and B's share declined to 10 percent of the market in response to its inability to provide an alternative to A's offer.

To redress the deficiency of the (Spearman) rank correlation coefficient, use can be made of the HPI, which takes account of all firms but is only affected by them (large and small firms alike) if they grow substantially, that is, if they experience significant change in market size. The initial formulation of the index (Hymer and Pashigian, 1962, p. 85) is based on totaling the changes (by taking differences) between two distinct points in time of the market shares of the firms in an industry. Reekie (1981, p. 52) has proposed a modification to the HPI requiring the summing up of the absolute differences of each firm's market share between two distinct points in time (t_1 and t_2). Mathematically:

$$\text{HPI} = \sum_{i=1}^{n} \left| s_i^{t_1} - s_i^{t_2} \right| \tag{10.6}$$

The higher the value of the index, the more unstable and hence the more competitive the market is. For example, assume that for a market in Period 1 two firms had market shares of 51 percent and 49 percent and that in Period 2 the market shares of the same firms swapped in the reverse order. The HPI in this instance would be 4. However, had the market shares changed from 51 and 49 percent to 99 and 1 percent, the HPI would have a value of 96, implying a high degree of economic change.

It should be noted that the HPI says little of the inequality in market size between the firms in an industry other than to reveal, over time, the difference (or lack thereof) in market size of each firm and thereby for the industry overall. The result is that the index, although giving information on the vigor of rivalry in a market, gives no information on the structure of a market, i.e., it does not reveal if a market is characterized by dominant or atomistic firms. It may be argued here that the more competitive a market is (or the less monopoly-like it is) the greater the degree of economic change will be revealed by the HPI.

This, however, would ignore that in innovation-based markets such as pharmaceuticals a monopoly (or a dominant firm) enlarges the spectrum of product offerings by creating product variety, thereby leading to market expansion. In such a case, even though a firm may dominate others over time, its market share may remain unchanged because through the expansion of the market the firm's sales have increased commensurately and rivals have kept pace. The HPI would miss all that. Its value would be 0, implying lack of vigor in competition.

In using all the concentration measures examined up until now it was assumed that they act as full-information indices in that the data necessary for their calculation were considered to be readily available. In practice, however, this may not happen because whatever data are available may be incomplete. In those instances where markets are comprised of firms with market power, the situation could be remedied with the use of partial-information indices, so named as they require only part of the necessary data for a market's concentration to be calculated. In the section that follows it is proposed that (either of) two such indices be used. They build on the data shortages/advantages we stressed the HHI and HI could possess. We refer to these proposed indices as the modified HHI (m-HHI) and the modified HI (m-HI). To sketch the concept behind these indices we now move to the following section.

CALCULATING CONCENTRATION UNDER DATA SHORTAGES

This section proposes modifications to the HHI and HI to deal with cases where few data are available other than the largest market shares. Whether the HI and HHI require full use of data depends on whether the market shares are symmetrically distributed. If not, equivalent results would be produced if the HHI and HI are calculated on the basis of the *n*-largest market shares. The resulting indices so computed can be called the (m-HHI) and m-HI.

The reason why the modified indices would produce identical results as their actual counterparts in the case of skewed data is because the actual counterparts require that the assumption of data be fulfilled symmetrically (pertaining to the firms' market shares). If not, then the large market shares pool the indices toward them. In the case where the market-share data has low levels of skewedness or meets the symmetric assumption, using all observations to compute the indices becomes important because as many market shares are above the mean market-share level as are below it.

The cutoff point for the number of firms or products to consider for the m-HHI and m-HI should depend on the severity of the skewedness. The smaller this is, the larger n should be, and the larger it is, the smaller n should be. Suppose that one is confronted with the hypothetical market-share distribution in Table 10.1. Market 1 follows a more symmetrical market-share distribution compared to Market 2. Accordingly one can expect that for Market 2 the partial-information indices, m-HHI and m-HI, would yield identical results to the full-information ones, HHI and HI. The higher the degree of skewedness of the market shares, the closer the modified indices would be to their actual counterparts. For Market 2, n was taken to be 4. The results are presented in Table 10.2. The m-HHI and m-HI have the same values (to the second decimal) as the HHI and HI. For Market 1, where the distribution of market shares is more balanced, the m-HHI and m-HI are not desirable proxies for the HHI and HI. The use of the m-HHI and m-HI is advocated where data limitations exist and it can be justly assumed or verified that for the market as a whole the market-share distribution is highly skewed.

TABLE 10.1. Hypothetical market share distribution (percent).

Market 1	Market 2
22	50
20	20
18	15
16	9
14	4
10	2

TABLE 10.2. Concentration indices of Market 1 and Market 2.

Index	Market 1	Market 2
CR4	0.7600	0.9400
HHI	0.1760	0.3226
HI	0.4535	0.6330
m–HHI ($n = 4$)	0.1464	0.3206
m–HI ($n = 4$)	0.3981	0.6291

Everything on the discussion of concentration until now has operated on the implicit assumption that we have a market for which the concentration can be calculated. This should automatically tell us that whatever the concentration measure used, its value is affected by the way a market is defined. To shed more light on this topic let us turn to the following section.

MARKET DEFINITION AND CONCENTRATION

As already stated, whatever the concentration measure used, its value is affected by the way a market is defined. Once markets are defined, as our concentration formulae reveal, concentration is relatively easy to calculate. However, the fact still remains that market definition and concentration are inseparable. Different market definitions lead to potentially different market shares and "as a practical matter, the broader the market definition, the lower market concentration will tend to be" (Salop, 1987, p. 10).

If markets are defined tightly, market shares are inflated and high concentration results. It is for this reason that any narrow market definition employed by competition authorities must be treated with caution, not least because in such an instance it may not require much to "prove" that an industry or its incumbents are acting anticompetitively. By defining a market tightly, firms would be assigned larger market shares than is otherwise the case and in turn concentration measures, such as the CR_n, HHI, and the HI, would be pushed into reflecting high concentration where actions by antitrust authorities are legally but not economically warranted. It appears, as presented by Salop (1987, p. 7), that a way by which competition authorities may resolve this and verify the appropriateness of the market definition, is to determine whether the market power to which the definition gives rise creates a potential for buyers to substitute other products (demand substitution) and sellers of other products to execute capacity switchovers (supply substitution). In the former instance the inspection would require assessing the industry (market) on the basis of its consumption stance, whereas in the latter instance it would require assessing it on the basis of its technological perspective. Assessing the consumption stance is done with the use of the cross-elasticity of demand, and assessing the technological perspective is done with the use of the cross-elasticity of supply. In both cases the interest is in cross-elasticities that are positive.

The meaning of a positive cross-elasticity of demand between two goods is that they are substitutes, so that increasing the price of the one increases the quantity demand for the other. Hence, a positive cross-elasticity of demand is a sign of a competitive market, indicating that the more acceptable substitutes are to consumers, the more certain it is that they would switch from one to another product if the price of any one of them increased relative to the other(s)—say, as a result of market power coming into effect. Such power can then be viewed as insignificant in that the existence (actual or potential) of alternatives dilutes it.

The meaning of a positive cross-elasticity of supply is akin to that of a positive elasticity of demand, except that the reference is on supply. A positive cross-elasticity of supply between two firms signifies that the one's factors of production (capital plus labor) could be readily transferred to producing the products of the other should any one firm raise the price for its product(s) relative to the other. Hence, a positive cross-elasticity of supply is a sign of a competitive market indicating that firms are closely competing with one another, making it improbable that market power will bear fruit.

However, as Reekie (2000, p. 50) warns us, care must be taken when relying on the cross-elasticities of demand and supply to verify the way a market is defined. Competition can still exist between (any) two products falling in the same market even though their cross-elasticity of demand is not positive, i.e., it is negative. This is very likely to occur where rivalry between the firms for the products they make leads consumers to see products as not quite the same, making consumers that buy more or all of the one or the other product regard either as a "necessity." Then, if the price of either product was to increase, this may not mean that the quantity demanded for the other would increase. On the contrary it could well decrease, especially if the price increase rests on Dean's price skimming, where consumers see a quality advantage, however defined, to exist. By analogy, in such an instance, the cross-elasticity of supply between the producers making the products would also be negative, given that what they make is not completely compatible with the other. This in turn seems likely to mean that the modi operandi between firms in terms of their production would differ, otherwise the firms would reproduce each other's offerings. Thus, the cross-elasticity of supply between two rivals that sell what to some extent are substitutable products may end up being negative.

The point of this discussion is that no fast and easy rules exist to define a market. The situation could be partially offset with the use of the cross-elasticity of demand and supply to verify whether the selected market definition makes room for competition. Although the conventional norm for competitive markets here is a positive value for each of these elasticities, any negative values should not be automatically interpreted as indicative of lack of competition. Negative values would seem certain to happen where the innovation mechanism of the competitive process is at play, with the transfer mechanism being either outpaced or having yet to come into force. Simply put, competition is taking place mainly on Schumpeterian as opposed to imitative terms, inviting in its precincts both promotional and R&D activities, jointly forming part of the rivalry arsenal of firms to produce product differentiation between them. Where the reverse holds we should anticipate the cross-elasticities to have the expected positive sign.

This chapter serves as an extension of all the work done on monopoly power in the previous chapters, in that it explicates the computational tools by which a market's competitiveness can be measured. Some of these measures were discussed in greater detail, both in the case where complete data for the firms' market shares exist and where this is not the case. It was noted that if the measures are to correspond to what they are attempting to record, i.e., the competitive process, they should be analyzed over time.

If not, we are confined to static measures of competition that are utterly inconclusive, in that they cannot tell something about a process that is continuous and hence does not occur in strictly demarcated periods. As a matter of discourse to Lachmann (1976, p. 55), we can simply condense this by saying that the competitive process is not fixed in time. If so, we must then express a reservation but not a condemnation of studying the competitive process over well-demarcated periods of time. Although such an approach is from a tabulation stance desirable to all static measures of competition, as it would draw us somewhat closer to observing the process ex-post, we must not mistake this to mean that we have learned all there is to know about it. This is so because the competitive process is continuous and not continual.

It was emphasized that the values of the concentration indices move hand in hand with the definition awarded to a market in that an inverse association exists between the two. Very tight market definitions assume away rivalry and inflate concentration, with the reverse applying where the market definition is very wide. A way by which the suitability of the market definition can be tested is to examine if it allows for a positive cross-elasticity of demand and supply. If these are found, then the market is competitive on imitative grounds and the transfer mechanism of the competitive process dominates. If the opposite applies, that is, the elasticities are negative, then the market is competitive on innovative grounds and the innovation mechanism of the competitive process dominates.

Probably it is imperative that we make an important appeal at this point regarding our numerical interpretation of the cross-elasticities previously referred to and to no lesser extent of the measures of competition discussed. This appeal concerns the use of these numerical devices in that they must not become the exclusive means by which the competitiveness of a market is to be determined by a regulator, whether an economist or bureaucrat. It is all too easy with their use, assuming that anthropomorphism applies in the science of human action—economics—as well as it does in the natural sciences, to slip into what Mittermaier (1986, pp. 236-249), in a somewhat little-known work, termed mechanomorphism. The matter we have at hand is eloquently described by Mittermaier (1986, p. 237):

> A scientist engages in anthropomorphism when he ascribes human attributes to what is otherwise recognised as inanimate or at least not human. By analogy we may say that an economist engages in mechanomorphism when he ascribes mechanical properties to what is otherwise recognised as an aspect of human affairs or when he treats an economic system as though it were a mechanical system.

Hence in the sphere of competition or in an examination of the competitive process, as Mittermaier (1986, p. 241) put it, we "may regard mechanomorphisms as mongrel conceptions which refer neither to physical phenomena nor to mental phenomena and their economic derivatives and therefore correspond to nothing that is real." The conclusion we should draw from Mittermaier's mechanomorphism is that great care should be exercised when using the measures proposed to assess competition, in that their failure to comply with what is expected of them in terms of the perfect competition nirvana must not in any way be interpreted to mean the absence of competition.

As an example of this and to clarify the case in point it should be accepted by now from this work that a price not equaling marginal cost need not at all be a sign of the absence of rivalry. On the contrary, in a free market it is what shows that competition of the innovative kind, the one without which the imitative sort cannot bear fruit, is alive and well.

This chapter concludes the theoretical exposition of monopoly power, and we now proceed to an application of the theory. The South African pharmaceutical industry is used to accomplish this task for three simple reasons. First, the industry offers fertile ground to apply what has been said thus far about innovative rivalry being a sine qua non in pharmaceutical markets, where the innovations of today serve as the imitations of tomorrow (Reekie, 1997, pp. 35-47). This innovative feature of the industry stems from the ongoing demand on the part of patients and the medical profession alike for therapeutically advanced offers.

Second, in the industry, as demonstrated by Scott and Reekie (1985), firms compete within therapeutic submarkets under conditions of intense rivalry for their products (i.e., the cross-elasticity of demand is positive).[1] In addition, this rivalry takes place in a virtually complete absence of import (tariff) barriers to trade (IDC, 1998, pp. 15-24). Third, at the supplier (firm) level the market is free in the economic sense of the word, i.e., government rules do not prescribe how firms should price or the price at which they may sell. This pricing freedom also covers the new product introductions firms make. This last feature of the country's industry, which could be deemed as the most important of the lot, makes it unique in the world in that only a few other countries' pharmaceutical markets share it, for instance, the United States (Ballance et al., 1992, p. 149). From a public-policy perspective it appears this is not the norm. A detailed survey by Ballance and colleagues (1992, p. 141) on the price-control policies of pharmaceuticals in fifty-six countries revealed that

> almost all governments regulate product prices, though a few choose to limit profits or to influence prices through more indi-

rect means. Both governments and insurers are usually involved in the price-setting exercise in industrialised countries. In developing countries, however, a majority of the population is not covered by health insurance and price regulations are almost exclusively in the hands of public officials.

Chapter 11

The Market Structure of the SA Pharmaceutical Industry

This examination of the pharmaceutical industry in South Africa is informed, among others, by De Villiers and Scott (1986), Scott and Reekie (1985, 1987), Reekie (1999) and the reports of the various government commissions that at one point or another since the 1960s have examined the industry. In particular, use was made of the following government commissions' reports:

1. Report of the Commission of Inquiry into High Cost of Medical Services and Medicines (1962). This is also known as the Snyman Report, after its chairman H. W. Y. Snyman.
2. Report of the Commission of Inquiry into the Pharmaceutical Industry (1978). This is also known as the Steenkamp Report, after its chairman W. F. J. Steenkamp.
3. Fifth Interim Report of the Commission of Inquiry into Health Services—Interim Report on Pharmaceutical Services (1985). This is also called the Browne Report, after its chairman G. W. G. Browne.
4. Report of the Commission of Inquiry into the Manner of Providing for Medical Expenses (1994). This is also called the Melamet Report, after its chairman D. A. Melamet.

Instead of focusing on each of these sources individually, the discussion that follows synthesizes them to present an overall picture of the South African pharmaceutical industry.

The South African pharmaceutical industry is a microcosm of the world pharmaceutical market in that virtually all major multinational pharmaceutical manufacturers operate and also perform R&D in the country. The R&D is mainly in the field of clinical trials; little other

doi:10.1300/5505_11

research is done. Nonetheless, a similar pattern of R&D expenditure exists, carried out by overseas parents and performed by their more innovative South African subsidiaries, as well as by wholly owned South African firms. The pharmaceutical industry is dualistic in the sense that it operates in two distinct markets or sectors: the private and the state (or public). The former market accounts for 80 percent of industry sales by value and 20 percent by volume, while in the latter market the proportions are in reverse (Competition Board, 1999, p. 11). Most firms operate simultaneously in both sectors.

Whether in the private or public market, the industry is characterized by intense rivalry at the firm level, with firms competing within therapeutic submarkets between which the cross-elasticity of demand is either low or negative. Within these submarkets substitutability of one product for another exists, i.e., the cross-elasticity of demand is positive.

The private and public sectors purchase pharmaceuticals in very different ways. The state does so via competitive tender, while private-sector purchases are generally initiated by individual prescribing doctors, with reimbursement by medical insurers to dispensers (dispensing doctors and retail pharmacists). In the case of the private market, many of the drugs sold by firms are under patent protection (applying as a rule for innovative medicines only) and what generic medicines are sold are usually marketed in the majority of cases under brand names. In the case of the public market, however, tenders are issued for the bulk purchase of predominantly generic, usually nonbranded, drugs. A generic drug is the off-patent (imitative) equivalent in terms of chemical composition of the drug formerly in patent.

For an orderly review of the industry, we focus separately on each of the sectors that make it up, beginning with the private sector.

THE PRIVATE SECTOR

This section provides an overview of the private sector but, most important, shows that at the supplier level this is a sector characterized by highly intense, ongoing rivalry.

The private sector caters predominantly to those with income and medical coverage. Here patients' drug costs are generally covered either out-of-pocket or, as in the majority of cases, via medical insurers. The latter control the consumption expenditure of pharmaceuticals in two ways, which need not be mutually exclusive. One of the ways focuses on changing the incentives on the prescribing physicians and consumers so as to induce them to moderate their consumption and focus it on the most effective products by altering their drug-prescribing practices or consumption patterns. The other way focuses on implementing a set of rules and regulations that directly control the prescribing practices/consumption patterns in the manner desired. In practice, for instance, medical insurers may have preferred formularies or may outsource the construction of formularies to pharmacy benefit managers (PBMs).

Alternatively, some insurers may not use formularies but rather simply advise dispensers that they will reimburse a so-called maximum medical aid price. The objective here is to induce pharmacists and patients to make cost-conscious decisions regarding the choice of treatment and the use of medication. In addition, different medical insurers vary tremendously in their policies on co-payments, cost sharing, limits, deductibles, and the use of medical savings accounts.

In the private sector doctors may be part of health maintenance organizations (HMOs) or independent practice associations (IPAs) linked contractually to one or another medical insurer and hence confined to the formulary approved by the relevant PBM mechanism. Of course in some cases, for prescribing purposes, medical insurers' patients and doctors also operate on an unrestricted fee-for-service basis.

Overall in the private sector general practitioners are reimbursed either via medical insurers following (some variation of) a managed-care method or a fee-for-service basis. Hospital doctors are similarly reimbursed. In addition to all the aforementioned in connection with the private sector, here medical insurers, as part of their exertion of control on the health care spending of the members they cover, could also restrict patients in their choice of hospitals (or hospitalization benefits).

Moving to the general outlook of rivalry at the firm level in the supply of drugs, it is noted that studies that have been done in this area unanimously sketch a picture in which firms vie for market share in a highly intensive manner. In conducting a nine-year study of competition in the private sector at the firm level, Scott and Reekie (1985, pp. 42, 52) found that very few industries exist in which a market can be lost as quickly as in pharmaceuticals, where market share is highly volatile because the industry introduces new products on a continuous basis. Therefore, firms must innovate in order to hold their positions. The evidence showed that while submarkets tended to be dominated by one or a very small number of firms at a given point in time, these seemingly oligopolistic submarkets are often transient, and due to Schumpeterian innovative competition, market dominance is rarely prolonged.

The same picture of competition in the private sector as that witnessed has emerged from a subsequent study by Reekie (1996), who in addition to this sector also looked at the pharmaceutical markets of Denmark, Germany, the Netherlands, the United Kingdom, and the United States. Reekie set about studying how it is that in each of these markets product innovations affect rivalry between firms and consequently on the prices they set. Reekie's work is authoritative in this regard, as it examined 480 submarkets over a six-year period, averaging the price of the five top-selling products (in revenue terms) in each of the submarkets for each of the years in each of the countries studied. Then he compared the prices of the new products entering those submarkets with their averaged price. On analysis of the results from the study, Reekie (1996, pp. 37, 38) found that irrespective of the country, as a maxim:

> Innovations . . . tend to impact downwards on price, either as they themselves move into the top five products or, in reaction to their appearance, existing members of the top five reduce their prices. The majority of the sub-markets, therefore, not unsurprisingly consistently display price falls. . . .
>
> However, prices can not fall everywhere and forever. And they do not. Stable prices in some sub-markets, while others are falling can simply mean that competition has done or is continuing to do its job. Competition tends to push prices down and to hold them to a floor. Commercial "mistakes" . . . are inevitable, and well documented, and the cost of the error in market judgement is borne by the innovating firm. . . . Given these harsh economic and competitive realities, some products must successfully generate premium prices in order to maintain the incentives for pharmaceutical advance in health care. These are the relatively rare, or blockbuster, major innovations, which possess a substantial quality increment over existing therapies and so can both command and maintain realistic price premiums

for reasonable periods. . . . The results from our study show that . . . Schumpeter's competitive gale of innovation, entry, imitation, rivalry and marketplace turbulence is strikingly adequate in its ability to put downward pressure on prices in most markets in most years.

The portrayal of the competitive process that emerges from these findings is complementary to that of preceding chapters in this work. In the private market rivalry is of the Schumpeterian-Littlechild variety. Here the competitive process is guided by the innovation mechanism, which produces a short-run disequilibrium with monopoly profits. A firm may have an offer that is a rare innovation not previously offered and warranting the imposition of a premium. In essence, we have a situation of temporary price skimming tied to "monopoly power" that either reflects the supply of a new offer that no rival can yet mimic or the creation of a new market where none existed before. This monopoly power, with its concomitant monopoly profits and price skimming, in turn invites emulation on the part of rivals (actual or potential) that through the Reekie product filter set the transfer mechanism in motion to work toward imposing an equilibrium in the long run. In time, in the absence of barriers to entry, the working of the transfer mechanism erodes this price skimming and "monopoly power" to bring (in the long run) the familiar "pure" competition outcome of P = MC. However, it is worth backtracking a little here to examine closer how the transfer mechanism alters the structure of the market in which it resides. Starting from our position of a monopoly as soon as the transfer mechanism begins functioning, in its early stages of operation rivalry between the firms would evolve an oligopolistic market structure of the original Stackelberg kind. Here the costs of production of each producer would be widely different to the extent that some firms would find it advantageous to take up the independent (leadership) positions while the others find it most profitable to adopt the dependent (follower) positions.

Given that such a situation embeds differences in profit taking (albeit smaller than those from the original monopoly position), in order to erode them, this time the transfer mechanism would have firms working toward the original Cournot-type oligopolistic rivalry, thereby leading to the equalizing of productive powers between firms. From here on, assuming these powers have a limit and no barriers to entry of the rent-seeking or government-interference variety exist, the working of the transfer mechanism would result in firms entering the market to dissolve whatever residual profits are left. This would lead to marginal cost pricing being approached in the long run. This pricing would be reached if innovation was something firms did once in a while or once only, that is to say if innovation was atypical of the industry in which the firms operate.

However, where innovation is recurrent, surely by far the more likely scenario, and definitely, as the evidence shows, the one typical of the pharmaceutical industry operating in the private sector, this pricing would only be approximated, because the market does not come to a rest. In such a situation, as Lachmann (1976, p. 60) put it,

> the equilibrating forces, operating slowly, especially where much of the capital equipment is durable and specific, are always overtaken by unexpected change before they have done their work, and the results of their operation disrupted before they can bear fruit.

So we expect the transfer and innovative mechanisms to work interchangeably and, upon the transfer mechanism nearing its end, the innovation mechanism to resume working again. Put differently, the transfer mechanism drives firms from Cournot-type oligopolistic rivalry to that of the original Bertrand kind, which effectively precludes a given market from falling into equilibrium. Translated into expectations,[1] the innovation mechanism comes into being through the divergent expectations firms hold about the success of their new products (goods or services) in relation to what known or unknown rivals can offer. Once such offers begin emerging and the intensity of this increases with the progression to the transfer mechanism, convergent expectations set in.

This is an outgrowth of the transfer mechanism not completing itself in full. This, along with the evidence presented, suggests the mechanism retains the oligopolistic structure for a given market, which may end up to be one with an atomistic semblance or one closer to what the word oligopoly denotes. Either way, competition among commensurate-in-size rivals, whether among a few large firms holding similar market shares or a somewhat larger number of firms sharing similar market shares, lends itself suitably to rivalry of the original Bertrand kind. In such an instance, what equilibrium the transfer mechanism approximated would not prevail for long, as the motive to do one better than a rival, which is what Schumpeterian competition boils down to, activates the innovation mechanism, which brings forward something new to compete over. However, we should not and must not expect the cycle to end here. The competitive process is continuous and so the interplay between the innovation and transfer mechanisms is ongoing.

It should be noted that the discussion of the competitive process in the private sector did not elaborate on the oligopolistic models of discussed earlier, to avoid repetition of what has already been said on these models and to avoid detracting from the main topic of the discussion at hand.

THE PUBLIC SECTOR

This section provides an overview of the public sector. It seeks to inform us that, like the private sector, the public sector is characterized by highly-intensive rivalry at the firm level. The state-administered public sector caters to the poor or indigent. Here pharmaceuticals are bought in bulk by the state (through its provincial authorities) for use in hospitals and community clinics, i.e., the state is a monopsony buyer. In the provincial sector, third-party reimbursement is usually not present and it is well-known that government is explicitly concerned with pharmaceutical cost containment, given that it caters to those with little or no income. However, incidences do exist where the public sector dispenses medication to those with medical cover for a fee. In the public market drugs are dispensed to patients on a free or virtually free basis. This is done against a prescription issued by a state medical practitioner working in a provincial hospital or clinic, or in certain circumstances by a nurse.

In the public market firms obtain business by participating and being the winners to a sealed-bid tender process for the right to supply a therapeutic market. The winner to a tender is the firm able to supply the product called for on the tender at the lowest price. Hence, under this tender process we have an *ex ante* bidding competition for the right to supply the market with an ex-post monopoly condition obtaining once the tender is awarded. It is possible that cases may exist where more than one firm wins a tender. This is a consequence of the sealed-bid tender process, i.e., no one firm knows the other one's offer, in response to which firms are prompted to set prices simultaneously and to compete to supply the (homogeneous) product the tender calls for. In such a case it is possible that some tenders may be simultaneously met by more than one firm, each of which is able to honor the tender at the same price.

In the public sector a prescriber (of pharmaceuticals) is either limited to the purchases made through the tender process or by the stock held in the relevant state clinic or hospital. Doctors, and other medical personnel, are primarily salaried employees of the state sector. In addition to all the aforementioned in connection with the public market it should also be noted that here the prescribing and reimbursement of pharmaceuticals takes place in accordance with the South African Essential Drug List (EDL). This list is an adaptation of the model list of essential drugs employed by the World Health Organization (South African Department of Health, 1998, p. iii). The vast majority of the 300 or so drugs on this list are generic (WTO Secretariat, 2002, p. 96). It is worth observing here that what is referred to as a "drug," whether in the case of the South African EDL or its WHO counterpart, is the chemical composition of the drug, e.g., amoxycillin. Once the various versions in which firms can supply this chemical composition are taken into account, e.g., amoxycillin in 250 mg, 500 mg, or 750 mg, it becomes clear that firms produce or have to supply thousands of pharmaceutical products.

Considering the general outlook of rivalry at the firm level regarding the supply of drugs, the only formal study in this regard shows that the public sector's system of tender bidding has firms vying for market share in a highly intensive manner, in the sense that firms face a very transient demand should they fail to win successive tender bids. The evidence shows that the monopoly position a tender confers on the firm that wins it at a point in time does not guarantee it any safety from a sudden sharp demand change on the part of the monopsony buyers, i.e., the state, next time tendering takes place.

In conducting their nine-year study of competition in the public sector at the firm level, Scott and Reekie (1985) found market concentration here to be higher than in the private sector. Given that product variation is relatively less important than price, various supply characteristics become less important than finding a single source willing to supply at an acceptable price level. Although it is easier for firms to maintain a relatively constant market position in the public market providing the firm acts appropriately, i.e., by setting appropriate prices for given products, domination can be short-lived. As Scott and Reekie (1985, pp. 41, 49) caution,

> The imposition of tender pricing, "winner-takes-all" for a given tender price, on top of an innovative market would seem to concentrate the number of companies dominating each sector to a much greater extent than in the private sector, but to lead to a very similar rate of positional change. . . . [The] government's tender system rather than increasing competition and dispelling dominance of markets by a few companies has the precisely opposite effect and increases the oligopolistic character of the markets. These oligopolies are, however, also of a transient nature. . . . The tender system is not increasing market competition as measured by numbers but is placing business in the hands of fewer firms.

The portrayal of the competitive process that emerges from these findings is to be expected. The object of the sealed-bid tender process is to stimulate competition at the producer level in the sense of having firms compete for the right to supply a submarket for which the state invited tenders. Hence we have a competition for the market, which in turn, as we know, should result in the price for the (homogeneous) good being supplied corresponding to its unit cost, i.e., minimum average cost, of production (whether in the case of one or more than one winner to a tender). The occurrence of such a pricing outcome is further underscored by firms not incurring R&D and marketing (advertising) costs in the case of the manufacture of generic drugs and their sale to the state via the tender system. The former is an outgrowth of generic drugs being the imitation of their formerly in-patent innovative counterparts, which is where firms incur R&D cost (for new product development). The latter is an outgrowth of the tenders specifying outright what is being demanded (except for the price of course) and the public sector purchasing only when a tender is awarded to the firm or firms that win it.

To avoid confusion at later stages, cognizance should be taken of a point regarding the public sector consuming mostly generic drugs. This should not be taken to mean that the sector is not barred from receiving new-generation medicaments, for, as has already been established, in time the drug inventions of today turn into the generics of tomorrow. The monopsony buyer, i.e., the state, like any other buyer of medicines, also has an interest in getting new medicines, given that as a rule such products have better pharmacological action than their older counterparts in treating the illness for which they were created. Thus, a generic product that is an offspring of a new drug would be more in demand than the previous therapy, thereby making the producer of the former in relation to the latter the preferred supplier to a tender. We must be careful now not to confuse preference with choice, i.e., which firm actually gets to supply the tender.

When contrasted against the private sector, the public sector is shown to suppress the innovation mechanism in the sense of its functioning being delayed by public-sector purchases focusing mostly on generics. This situation mimics that described in the previous section, in which innovation is something firms do once in a while or once-off only, which is what $P = MC$ requires. In that sense we could say that the sealed-bid tender process in the public sector is designed to bring forward or impose in the short run the long-run outcome of $P = MC$ or something that in practice is indistinguishable from it. However, we must at this time understand how it is that this outcome comes about.

Rivalry at the firm level in the public sector occurs in an environment where the basic knowledge required for the production (process) of the given product is available and it is only gradually improved upon. In the public sector, little or no requisite exists on the part of firms to carry out R&D and promotional activities in new product development. Here the market engages predominantly in price competition for the good in question and the transfer mechanism outweighs the innovation mechanism, resulting in imitative competition. If this good is very much in demand by the buyer (the state), to warrant the cost of its production (as well as yield a normal profit) competing producers will try to imitate the given production process and, if successful, vie to supply on the tender with the same or a slightly modified product. This will encourage price competition at the supplier level, resulting ultimately in the lowest price being attained for the commodity being called for on the tender. Producers will find that in order to be the winner to a tender as well as yield a normal profit they will have to look for ways to reduce the costs of production, usually by making the production process more efficient. Most producers will drop out of the tender bid altogether, and the one or few firms that remain will be the manufacturers who are able to produce most (cost) efficiently and offer the product at the lowest possible price.

In a nutshell, in the public sector the transfer mechanism of the competitive process takes place between firms that vie for the right to supply a given market on the basis of a given production process and a given (new) product. The outcome is either one of monopoly or oligopoly of the Cournot type. The latter is in view of a few firms getting, on account of their similar positions, to supply the same market with the same or practically indistinguishable product from that called for on the tender. It should be noted here that, unlike the original Cournot-type oligopoly rivalry, what makes the resulting pricing outcome of this form of Cournot-type oligopoly rivalry between a few firms conformant to perfect competition is the tender-bidding process. Its purpose is to draw forward a large number of rivals for the supply of a homogeneous product for which knowledge of its production *process* exists but not its *methods*—on the basis of which firms vie for the sole-supplier position of the tender product.

Given that the tender system encourages competition for the market with the purpose of yielding a price outcome that resembles perfect competition, the mistake should not be made that the monopoly position the tender confers denotes a monopoly price outcome. It could be that such outcome may occur, but this would require two things. The first is Tullockian rent-seeking, namely when manipulation of the political apparatus is undertaken to obtain special privileges in the form of the tender contracts to favor and defend otherwise inept producers. Given, as the evidence shows, the instability of a firm to retain a monopoly position in the public sector, this is not something that appears likely to occur.

The second thing is collusion. An argument could be made that the tender system encourages collusion because the costs of not colluding, i.e., loss of an all-or-nothing contract, are much greater than they are in a more normal sales relationship, such as could be found in the private sector. Perhaps such an argument has substance, but the existence of cartels in the public sector should be doubted for four reasons. First, the state acquires a large range of products. Evidence indicates that the public sector buys more than 2,600 different pharmaceutical products (WHO, 1999, p. 6). With such a product range, it is difficult to picture that a cartel would exist given that, theoretically and practically, such an agreement requires low monitoring, policing, and organizational costs, which is usually only possible in the case of a small range of (homogeneous) products. Second, as Stigler (1964, p. 48) has pointed out, it is unlikely that sales to government would be made at collusive prices since "the government is usually not a sufficiently large buyer of a commodity to remunerate the costs of collusion." By value the public sector is small relative to the private sector, accounting for only 20 percent of the total pharmaceutical industry sales. Third, it is a well-established proposition even to cartel members that if any member of the agreement can secretly violate it he or she will gain larger business than by conforming to it. So to preclude members from chiseling or cheating on the agreement it would be safest to price outright at a level that generates only normal profits, i.e., pricing at the unit-cost level of production. Fourth, the evidence shows that firms are unable to retain a permanent monopoly position in the public sector.

The burning question that arises from these enquiries into the private and public sector markets is how have the two sectors come to evolve such distinct natures?

THE EVOLUTION OF THE PUBLIC AND PRIVATE SECTORS

This section seeks to answer the question of how the private and public sectors have evolved differently. The answer is contained in the theory of price discrimination examined earlier. It will be recalled that the private sector caters predominantly to those with income and medical insurance, whereas the state-administered public sector caters to the poor or indigent. The former relative to the latter sector is far more sensitive to price with regard to its demand for pharmaceuticals. In economic terms this translates into a discrepancy in the price elasticities of demand for pharmaceutical products between the sectors, with the private sector representing a relatively less-price-elastic market compared to the public market. In the jargon of price discrimination, the former is the stronger market whilst the latter is the weaker market.

We have already established that in the short run (which is where firms incur the common [fixed] costs of product development, such as R&D) price discrimination is essential for the functioning of the innovation mechanism of the competitive process. The two are in fact inseparable.

Under price discrimination the firm maximizes profits that must simultaneously serve a dual purpose. The first is the coverage of its common costs at present that amount to nearly half of its total costs of launching a new product (recall the Danzon evidence presented on p. 134). The second is the accumulation of funds that would cover these costs at the next round of product innovations.

The concurrent relation between price discrimination and product variety gives rise to the product variety rationale for price discrimination, the mathematical formulation for which is known as the Koutsoyiannis product variety rule. Here, in the case of the firm launching a new product into separate (independent) markets, the recoupment of its expenditure on R&D would require levying a higher price in the stronger market. This would be so since the elasticity of R&D expenditure (namely the relative change in quantity demanded from a change in R&D expenditure) will be positive in the less-price-sensitive market, and this market will thus encourage innovative expenditure. Conversely, the elasticity of R&D expenditure will not be positive in the highly price-elastic market, and this market will therefore not be conducive to innovative expenditure. Simply put, most of the contribution to the firms' spending on R&D will come from the market with the relatively less-elastic demand. By extension, markets whose buyers are not so sensitive to price compared to those whose buyers are would experience more R&D on the part of firms and correspondingly a greater product assortment.

All this takes us back to our illustration of price discrimination in Figure 9.2 (see p. 141) in that it signals that in the short run departures in price from MC for the former market would exceed those of the latter market. In practice, in the context of the South African pharmaceutical market, what this means is that the funding for R&D would be derived predominantly from the private sector, which would as a consequence be the place where firms would opt to make new product introductions first. Put another way, in line with the product-variety rationale for price discrimination in a dualistic market system such as that in South Africa, R&D expenditure will be largely financed by revenue from the less-price-sensitive (private) market. The tender-based, highly price-elastic (public) market will contribute very little to the funding of R&D, since selling prices there will be close to short-run marginal costs represented by manufacturing costs exclusive of R&D and marketing costs. Support for this has been found by De Villiers and Scott (1986, p. 200), who on inspecting the contribution of each sector to total research and development in the industry found that:

> The private market contribution to R and D will be positive and the provincial market contribution to R and D expenditure will be negative, so that R and D funding will arise from the private market only. . . . The effect of the provincial market segment will be to reduce the level of R and D expenditure. Thus a business which can obtain all its sales in the private market segment will contribute more to R and D funding than one which has split its business between both private and provincial segments.

The De Villiers and Scott finding supports the product-variety rationale for price discrimination and also helps explain why this manner of pricing on the part of firms to recoup R&D costs results in the concentration in the public sector being higher than that in the private sector. Simply put, when firms are faced with price-sensitive buyers, the product range offered will be narrower, product differentiation will be of less consequence, and demand will be concentrated on fewer firms; thus, market concentration on the supply side will be higher. This, as illustrated earlier, is the case for the public sector; the reverse applies for the private sector.

A positive spin-off of this price discrimination, which firms use to cover their R&D costs when selling to markets with differing elasticities of demand, is that it produces as a by-product an equity-pricing outcome. That is, the firms price at a substantially lower level in the more price-sensitive sector compared to its less-sensitive counterpart, thereby producing a (nonphysical) shift of income in favor of the poorer classes the state services. All the government commissions are unanimous in this regard. For instance, on inspecting the differences in price between the private and the public sectors, the Steenkamp Report (1978, p. 26) noted that "the prices charged to the public sector are, as a rule, much lower than those charged to the private sector. . . . In medicine, public healthcare is thus subsidised by private healthcare." This finding is not confined to the Steenkamp Report. On the same subject matter, the Browne Commission reached the same conclusion. On inspection of the differences in price between the private and public sectors, the Browne Report (1985, p. 245) noted that "prices to the provincial administrations (the state) are lower and in certain instances substantially lower . . . than prices to . . . the private sector. This confirms conclusions reached by the Steenkamp Report Commission." The Melamet Commission also observed the same picture and its report (1994, p. 40) deduced that

> In a country like South Africa it may well be that the price discrimination between sectors practiced by manufacturers produces an outcome where the relatively well-off employed patients serviced by the medical schemes movement pay more than the indigent population who consume medicine in the state and provincial sectors.

The Snyman Commission did not make a specific statement on the topic. The Commission's report (1962, p. 188) did, however, describe that at the time differences in drug expenditures existed between the private and public sectors, with expenditures for the former sector being greater than for the latter.

The answer to why public and private sectors have come to evolve so distinct a market structure from each other is contained in the theory and practice of price discrimination, on which firms rely to cover their common (R&D) costs of new product development. For a given product-variety elasticity, as price sensitivity increases a firm's R&D to sales ratio will fall and vice versa. In the former instance this is what holds for the public sector, where correspondingly product variety will be less, buyers will be content with a more homogeneous product range or sellers will restrict themselves to offering a narrower range of products, and in turn demand will be concentrated on fewer firms. The gist of this is that market concentration at the supplier level will rise. Exactly the opposite would apply for the private sector.

A final point remains for discussion, relating to the legislative environment in which the industry operates.

THE LEGISLATURE AND THE INDUSTRY

On the one hand, the South African government, through the Department of Health, has come to contend that the prices of pharmaceutical products in South Africa are far higher than those of markets it deems comparable for both the private and public sector (The Public Protector, 1997, p. 2). On the other hand, the country's competition agency has asserted that the pharmaceutical industry exercises significant market power, which enables it to charge monopoly prices (Competition Commission, 2001, pp. 10-11).

The legislature passed the Medicines and Related Substances Control Amendment Act 90 of 1997—which is presumably intended to make drug prices more affordable. In view of this affordability objective, the act makes provisions, specifically those referring to sections 15C, 22C, and 22G, for the use of public policy tools geared to achieving this objective. The relevant excerpts of the sections introducing these tools read as follows:

§15C [p. 10]: The Minister may prescribe conditions for the supply of more affordable medicines in certain circumstances so as to protect the health of the public, and in particular may—

(a) notwithstanding anything to the contrary contained in the Patents Act, 1978 . . . determine that the rights with regard to any medicine under a patent granted in the Republic shall not extend to acts in respect of such medicine which has been put onto the market by the owner of the medicine, or with his or her consent.

(b) prescribe the conditions on which any medicine which is identical in composition, meets the same quality standard and is intended to have the same proprietary name as that of another medicine already registered in the Republic, but which is imported by a person other than the person who is the holder of the registration certificate of the medicine already registered and which originates from any site of manufacture of the original manufacturer as approved by the council in the prescribed manner, may be imported.

(c) prescribe the registration procedure for, as well as the use of, the medicine referred to in paragraph (b).

§22F [p. 26]: . . . A pharmacist shall . . . dispense an interchangeable multi-source medicine instead of the medicine prescribed by a medical practitioner, dentist, practitioner, nurse or other person registered under the Health Professions Act, 1974, unless expressly forbidden by the patient to do so.

§22G [p. 26]:
  (1) The Minister shall appoint such persons as he or she may deem fit to be members of a committee to be known as the pricing committee.
  (2) The Minister may, on the recommendation of the pricing committee, make regulations—
    (a) on the introduction of a transparent pricing system for all medicines and scheduled substances sold in the Republic; . . .
  (3) (a) The transparent pricing system contemplated in subsection (2) (a) shall include a single exit price which shall be published as prescribed, and such price shall be the only price at which manufacturers shall sell medicines and Scheduled substances to any person other than the State.

In the excerpts "The Minister" refers to the Minister of Health and "multi-source medicine" is another word for a generic medicine.

The gist of the legal language is that the act legalizes under section 15C(b) the practice of parallel importation, allowing for the sale of the same products through channels other than those authorized by the producers of these products in the country's pharmaceutical market. The content of section 15C(a) makes for an ambivalent insertion in the act. It conflicts with the South African Patents Act (Act No. 57 of 1978). In contrast to the Patents Act, it legalizes the unauthorized (by the producer or patent holder) use (granting) of compulsory licensing. This can be clarified with reference to the relevant excerpts of section 56 of the South African Patents Act of 1978, which in providing for the grant of a compulsory license in the case of an abuse of patent rights, reads as follows:

  (1) Any interested person who can show that the rights in a patent are being abused may apply to the commissioner in the prescribed manner for a compulsory license under the patent. . . .

  (2) The rights in a patent shall be deemed to be abused if—
    (a) the patented invention is not being worked in the Republic on a commercial scale or to an adequate extent, . . . and there is in the opinion of the commissioner no satisfactory reason for such non-working;

    (b) the demand for the patented article in the Republic is not being met to an adequate extent and on reasonable terms;

    (c) by reason of the refusal of the patentee to grant a license or licenses upon reasonable terms, the trade or industry or agriculture of the Republic or the trade of any person or class of persons trading in the Republic, or the establishment of any new trade or industry in the Republic, is being prejudiced, and it is in the public interest that a license or licenses should be granted; or

    (d) the demand in the Republic for the patented article is being met by importation and the price charged by the patentee, his licensee or agent for the patented article is excessive in relation to the price charged thereof in countries where the patented article is manufactured by or under license from the patentee or his predecessor or successor in title.

(3) The patentee or any other person appearing from the register to be interested in the patent may in the prescribed manner oppose the application.

(4) (a) The commissioner shall consider the application on its merits and may order the grant to the applicant of a license on such conditions as he or she may deem fit, including a condition precluding the licensee from importing into the Republic any patented articles. . . .

    (b) A license granted under this section shall include a provision that, subject to adequate protection of the legitimate interests of the licensee, the license shall, on application by the patentee, be terminated if the circumstances which led to its grant cease to exist and, in the opinion of the commissioner are unlikely to recur. . . .

(7) In determining the conditions on which any license is granted the commissioner shall have regard to any relevant acts, including the risks to be undertaken by the licensee, the research and development undertaken by the patentee and the terms and conditions usually stipulated in license agreements in respect of the subject matter of the invention, between persons who voluntarily enter into such agreements.

In the excerpts "the commissioner" refers to the commissioner of patents. Contrasting section 56 with section 15C(a) two distinctions are evident. First, it can be readily inferred that whereas the former is conditional upon a licit proof of abuse of market (monopoly) power as exercised by the patent holder, the requirement to do so is obviated in the latter. The second, probably the most important from an economic point of view, is that the former, as contained under subsection 4(c), unlike the latter, mitigates the regulator from assuming the role of an abrogate of the right to property to those (firms) to whom it originally belongs. To appreciate the matter at hand, we must pay tribute to Say (1880, reprinted 1964, p. 127):

It is the province of speculative philosophy to trace the origin of the right of property; of legislation to regulate its transfer; and of political science to devise the surest means of protecting that right. Political economy recognises the right of property solely as the most powerful of all encouragements to the multiplication of wealth, and is satisfied with its actual stability, without inquiring about its origin or its safeguards. In fact, the legal inviolability of property is obviously a mere mockery, where the sovereign power is unable to make the laws respected, where it either practices robbery itself, or is impotent to repress it in others; or where possession is rendered perpetually insecure, by the intricacy of legislative enactments, and the subtleties of technical nicety. Nor can property be said to exist, where it is not a matter of reality as well as of right. Then, and then only, can the sources of production, namely, land, capital and industry, attain their utmost degree of fecundity.

There are some truths so completely self-evident, that demonstration is quite superfluous. This is one of that number. For who will attempt to deny, that the certainty of enjoying the fruits of one's land, capital and labour, is the most powerful inducement to render them productive? Or who is dull enough to doubt, that no one knows so well as the proprietor how to make the best use of his property? Yet how often in practice is that inviolability of property disregarded, which, in theory, is allowed by all to be so immensely advantageous? How often is it broken in upon for the most insignificant purposes; and its violation, that should naturally excite indignation, justified upon the most flimsy pretexts? . . . There is no security of property, where a

despotic authority can possess itself of the property of the subject against his consent. Neither is there such security, where the
consent is merely nominal and delusive. . . .

It is to be observed that the right of property is equally invaded, by obstructing the free employment of the means of production, as by violently depriving the proprietor of the product
of his land, capital, or industry: for the right of property, as defined by jurists, is the right of use or even abuse. Thus . . . the
property of the capitalist is violated, by prohibiting particular
ways of employing it. . . . It is a further violation of the capitalist's property to prohibit any kind of industry, or to load it with
duties amounting to prohibition, after he has once embarked his
capital in that way.[2]

That said, we should now also observe that the Medicines and Related Substances Control Amendment Act of 1997 also legalizes the
practice of generic substitution (under section 22F) and the use (under section 22G) of price controls (single-exit pricing to be set by a
pricing committee).

On the face of it, it could be argued that what the South African
legislature proposes does not appear any different from what the Secretariat of the World Trade Organization and the World Health Organization have conjectured as acceptable means to making drug prices
affordable. In their 2002 joint report titled *WTO Agreements and
Public Health,* these organizations contended that

> several measures exist for making drug prices more affordable:
>
> (a) price controls to restrict manufacturers' selling prices; . . .
> (b) promoting competition through generic products . . . ;
> (c) use of . . . parallel imports and compulsory licensing, for
>   patented drugs . . .

Recommendation (a) is the South African equivalent of single-exit
pricing, with that under (c) corresponding directly to the same provisions contained in the South African Medicines and Related Substances Control Amendment Act of 1997. Recommendation (b) may
be seen as complementary to the generic substitution provision the
act contains.

Let us now examine how sound these proposals or public-policy tools are meeting their objectives. For the sake of coherency, the examination would be conducted in pairs, the one will be made up of parallel importation and single-exit pricing, the other will be made up of unauthorized compulsory licensing and generic substitution. As set out in the order in which the pairs were constructed, we now focus our attention on the first pair.

PARALLEL IMPORTATION AND SINGLE-EXIT PRICING

Single-exit pricing is the policy of direct price controls for which purpose a pricing committee determines a uniform price at which manufacturers may sell their products. Two things may be said of this. First, an assessment of this policy tool on the aggregate, in terms of its impact on the aggregate supply and demand on pharmaceuticals, immediately tells us that it would inhibit the market from clearing. What would be had under single-exit pricing is the well-known price-ceiling case of price controls. In practice, this form of price control would be instigated by the regulator as the maximum uniform price a firm can charge for its product, meaning that a higher price cannot be charged. What this in turn would produce, on the aggregate, is the suboptimal outcome of supply shortage and excess demand. There would be both frustrated buyers and sellers, since total supply cannot be increased and total demand cannot be met, precisely what we know the competitive process would not give us.

Second, it will be recalled from our treatment of price discrimination that where the regulator has to make a provision for allowing firms to cover their large common (fixed) costs, such as R&D, in the short run, the resulting uniform price is very certain to work to the detriment of consumers. Whether in the case of the market with elastic or inelastic demand, such price would act as a monopoly price guarded by legislation from being toppled over, which once again is precisely what we do not expect the competitive process to give us. In the presence of such uniform price it seems very probable that hardest hit by the uniform price would be the consumers with low income, leading them to experience considerable and unnecessary contraction in consumption. Also, it is likely that the market comprised of high-income individuals, which would otherwise have been competitive, would be exposed to a higher price than would prevail if firms were allowed to price freely.

In addition to all this, and perhaps most important, product variety, which is synonymous with consumer choice, would be jeopardized in the long run. Uniform price in the short run would permit only the firms' coverage of their common costs at present. They would not be able to price in a way that allows them to do not only this but also to accumulate the funds necessary to pay for these costs at the next round of product introductions.

All told, it would be justifiable to exercise pessimism toward the single-exit price provision in the statutory books. This can also be extended to apply to the case of parallel imports, which is simply a disguised form of uniform price controls.

Whereas single-exit pricing by its name signifies uniform price controls, it is usually not recognized that this is also what parallel importation means. Parallel importation is the policy of permitting the importation of the same drug to be sold independent of the producer of the product selling it in the country's pharmaceutical market if this product can be obtained cheaper from another market. Parallel importation has an equivalent, namely reference pricing (NERA, 1997, p. 164). Both parallel importation and reference pricing are in common use across EU member countries. Reference pricing is the policy whereby the price the regulator sets for a drug in a given country is the average of the lowest prices of the same drug in other countries.

When read jointly with the parallel importation provision, the single-exit pricing provision, in terms of which a pricing committee is to establish market prices, may amount to legislating for reference pricing if the committee were to engage in international price comparisons to decide what constitutes a maximum uniform price.

It should be easy to deduce from the definitions of these public policy tools that they restrict the firm from meeting the no arbitrage condition of price discrimination. Put another way, the policies have as their goal the narrowing of price differentials for the product the firm sells across different markets (countries). Granted, the existence of considerable common (fixed) costs in the short run the firm would have to cover these from the countries to which it sells, if, as argued by Baumol and Bradford, deficits (firm's losses) and tax subsidies are to be avoided. Then the policy of parallel importation would compel firms in order to permit for the coverage of these costs to set a uniform price akin to the P^* price examined under Figure 9.2 (see p. 141). It has already been made clear that such price is not efficient, i.e., it fails to minimize the DWL to consumers in the short run. By analogy, we may deduce the same to hold for both the case of parallel importation and reference pricing, and to further assert that both these policy tools will have deleterious effects on consumers if they come to upstage price discrimination in the short run. It must also be made clear here that if political pressure in the pursuit of affordable prices is very strong, not only in the parallel importing but also in the parallel exporting country (which itself may allow for parallel importation), then the firm may be significantly impeded in saving for future R&D work. In such an instance the resulting uniform price, although permitting for the recoupment of the common costs at present, would allow for little latitude in that area when it comes to new product development in the future (i.e., the long run).

It seems this is not all there is to the perversity of parallel importation. Reekie (1996, p. 3) and Minford (1992, p. 4), in commenting on the practice of this policy tool, have observed that it attains lower prices through artificial, government-induced means. Specifically, Reekie (1996, p. 3) described the matter as follows:

> in an unregulated situation, where different prices exist between two national markets, international trade or arbitrage tends to remove or correct the differentials. Goods move from low-cost to high-cost countries, lowering prices in the higher priced nation. But where there is regulation-induced parallel trade, as in pharmaceuticals, goods move out of the countries with the lowest (regulation induced) prices to the countries with the higher prices (which tend to be less controlled). Countries with stiff price controls tend also to be those without a strong indigenous pharmaceutical industry, and vice versa.

Thus, as Minford (1992, p. 4) put it,

> unlike normal trade in which the country with the low cost producers exports to the country with the high cost producers, in this government-distorted world the "parallel trade" goes from the high-cost country where prices are forced to be low to the low-cost country where the prices are allowed to be at economic

levels. It is more contorted still: the product so traded comes from the low-cost producers for the most part, since they are the major source for it. Hence we have the strange picture of low-cost products being sold to a high-cost country for unnaturally low prices and then being re-exported back to the low-cost country to take advantage of its higher prices. The net effect of all this is that the low-cost producer sells part of its output to itself at uneconomic prices and wastes resources in two-way transport and distribution in the process.

Incidentally, both Danzon (1997a, p. 138) and the OECD Directorate for Financial, Fiscal and Enterprise Affairs, on conducting separate investigations on the consumer gains from practicing parallel trade for public policy purposes, have observed the same picture. For instance, Danzon (1997a, p. 138) remarked that consumer well-being may be increased by trade if lower prices in the exporting countries reflect either lower input costs or better efficiency, and the importing country's consumers benefit from the lower prices. He further remarked that,

> In the case of parallel trade in medicines, countries that become parallel exporters generally achieve low prices through aggressive regulation or weak intellectual property protection. . . . Although some low price countries have relatively low labor costs, this labor component of . . . production is too small as a fraction of total costs to account for significant price differences. Thus there is no production efficiency gain from exporting from these countries.
>
> Because parallel trade arbitrages price differences that do not reflect real cost differences, it can . . . increase . . . social costs because of additional transportation and other administrative costs, but still be profitable for the trader. . . . In the short run, the saving . . . accrues . . . to the intermediaries—parallel traders, wholesalers and retail pharmacists—not to consumers or payers who . . . still pay the higher regulated price in the importing country.

When it came to its investigation the OECD Directorate noted in its report *Competition and Regulation Issues in the Pharmaceutical Industry* (2001, p. 53) that the primary effect of parallel trade is that it increases the profitability of pharmaceutical wholesalers and retailers. . . . Overall . . . the . . . effect of parallel trade in lowering prices in high-price countries is muted. The primary beneficiaries, in the first instance, are the traders. . . . Parallel trade limits the ability of drug manufacturers to discriminate in their prices across different countries. This raises prices in poorer countries, limiting their access to medicines.

All in all, we should be skeptical as to the proposed price-control measures achieving their goal of lower prices for consumers. Clearly this is something which is neither here nor there and most certainly would seem to lead to decreased product variety and consumer choice (whether measured in terms of consumption or product assortment). The evidence shows that the policy goal of low prices by the proposed price controls is elusive. The outcome is usually one of monopoly price by decree. As was shown in our treatment of price discrimination, this may apply more so in the case of the market with elastic than the one with inelastic demand, but the possibility that this may also come to include the latter must not be excluded. The remedy for such a monopoly price (whether for the elastic or inelastic market or both) would obviously be to remove the price controls that brought it. However, it could be that for a social engineer that price becomes, even though falsely so by reason, the source of inflationary price increases.[3] Then as Schumpeter (1950, p. 455) puts it, "perennial inflationary pressure can play an important role in the eventual conquest of the private-enterprise system by the bureaucracy—the resulting frictions and deadlocks being attributed to private enterprise and used as arguments for further restrictions and regulations." Quite simply, regulation can easily become entangled, carrying a backlash of government controls of unprecedented scale.

We have demonstrated that the practice of price controls (whether in the case of single-exit pricing, parallel importation, or its variant reference pricing) yields a uniform price. In the presence of such uniform price it seems certain that hardest hit would be the consumers with low income, with the uniform price leading them to experience considerable and unnecessary contraction in consumption. The market comprised of high-income individuals, which would otherwise have been competitive, would also likely be exposed to a higher price than would prevail if firms were allowed to price freely.

COMPULSORY LICENSING
AND GENERIC SUBSTITUTION

The legal formulation of the definition of generic substitution can be disentangled with reference to Scott and Reekie (1987, p. 315), who note that in basic terms it

> means the replacement by a pharmacist of a drug or medicine prescribed by a doctor with an alternative drug or medicine of the same active chemical composition. It is very different from the normal use of generic drugs or to the prescription of such drugs by a doctor (generic prescribing), since it empowers a person not actively involved in diagnosis and treatment to change the treatment from one product to another.

What would happen in practice is that a doctor would write a prescription using the original (brand-name) product, yet a pharmacist would have the freedom to dispense any generic version of the product instead. Whereas understanding how generic substitution would operate in practice might be straightforward, the legal language on how compulsory licensing would operate in practice may not be so clear-cut. Nonetheless what is envisaged in this regard can be traced to the OECD Directorate for Financial, Fiscal and Enterprise Affairs. The directorate expressed in its report, *Competition and Regulation Issues in the Pharmaceutical Industry* (2001, p. 48), that

> competition in drug production could be introduced, consistent with ensuring a return to the patent holder and consistent with a system of price controls through a system of compulsory licensing. Under a system of compulsory licensing a patent holder would be required to sub-license the right to manufacture and market a drug to any requesting firm. The requesting firm would pay the patent holder a royalty fee determined by regulation. The level of that fee would be chosen in such a way that the royalty plus direct production costs is equal to the desired (regulated) market price, ensuring the patent holder enjoys the same profit before and after compulsory licensing. This point is worth emphasising. Compulsory licensing, as it is proposed here, does not constrain the profits of the patent holder to a greater or lesser

extent than the price controls, which it replaces. The requirement to pay a royalty would terminate on the date that patent terminates.

However we interpret the goals of the legislator when it comes to the use of generic substitution and compulsory licensing, two things are clear from an economic standing: the former policy has as its goal the imposition of $P = MC$ in the short run, whereas compulsory licensing is intended to be analogous to setting a uniform price under common cost recovery in the short run.

How it would come about that the policy of generic substitution would induce $P = MC$ in the short run has everything to do with convergent expectations. This is why it is imperative that we understand that, in those cases where significant common costs are involved, as in the short run, the policy would not result soon after it falls into practice in deficits and tax subsidies, as was explained in our treatment of price discrimination.

When used over a period of time, the mandated practice of generic substitution would, on the one hand, have consumers conditioned, in the Pavlovian sense, to purchase generic medicines only. As has already been established in our coverage of the public sector, the price of such medicines would be in line with their MC of production, as these medicines do not embody the costs of R&D and promotion (marketing) of innovations. On the other hand, from the mandated practice of generic substitution the producers of innovative products will be conditioned in a way not very different from their consumers. They would know that in the long run their original products would not be procured. Should they then desire to make a sale in the short run, whatever expenditure they have dedicated to R&D and the promotion of their original product would have to correspond to the equivalent for the generic product. This is of course very little or nothing, and so as part of their decision making firms involved in new product development would disengage from the activity altogether, thereby retarding innovation in the long run. This would apply to those firms that are about to enter a new cycle of product innovations. For the firms that are already in such a cycle, their course of action would be to build planned obsolescence into their new-product-development activities. From here there would come a point in time when in the short run firms would price for all practical purposes indistinguishable from MC. However, we must not delude ourselves that this would bring us a lower price. The price for what is now produced, although priced at MC, will end up being higher from the MC level at the time the policy was first put in place.

To understand this we need to recall few things from our section on price discrimination (Chapter 9). First, product variety is synonymous with rivalry, so encroaching upon one or the other amounts to the stifling of both. Second, product variety is inseparable from price discrimination. Third, the profits from discrimination attract entry, thereby increasing variety and putting downward pressure on prices (refer for instance to Borenstein's [1985] findings). Fourth, recall that in Figure 9.2 (see p. 141) it was explicitly assumed that the MC (level) is fixed (constant). In fact, the MC level vacillates depending on the existence (or lack) of rivalry. It is the purpose of competition to lower this level as much as it is the outcome of its absence to raise it. In Figure 9.2, the former instance would be reflected by a downward shift in the MC schedule, whereas the latter would be reflected by an upward one. Combining this with the previous three recollection points, we have the picture of generic substitution raising the overall price level to consumers. By inference from elementary theory we must therefore also deduce that on the aggregate the quantity consumers demand will fall.

In a nutshell, with generic substitution we should expect to have the socially undesired outcomes of high price and less consumption. These, for the sake of reminder, are the very outcomes we do not expect from competition.

Let us now focus our attention on the policy of compulsory licensing. It is envisaged, in terms of the OECD quote previously presented (2001, p. 48), that this policy is to be analogous to setting a uniform price under common cost recovery in the short run. The relevant portion of the text that hints at this: "The requesting firm would pay the patent holder a royalty fee determined by regulation. The level of that fee would be chosen in such a way that the royalty plus direct production costs is equal to the desired (regulated) market price, ensuring the patent holder enjoys the same profit before and after compulsory licensing." Observe that the policy of compulsory licensing would operate differently in the short run, i.e., the immediate term, and the long run. As will be observed later, it is the operation of this policy in the long run that precisely defines what it is that makes it an anticompetitive public policy tool.

In the short run, i.e., the immediate term, some firms will have just come out from a new cycle of product innovations. In this instance, given that the policy intends to be complementary to setting a uniform price under common cost recovery in the short run, its impact would be just the same as that which applied to parallel imports, single-exit pricing, and the uniform P* price case of price discrimination.

In the short run, compulsory licensing would seem to lead to the detriment of increased product variety and consumer choice (whether measured in terms of consumption or product assortment). The outcome would be one of monopoly price by decree. As was shown in our treatment of price discrimination, this may apply more so in the case of the market with elastic demand than it would in one with inelastic demand, but the possibility that this may also come to include the latter must not be excluded. We would thus have a situation not different from the practice of price controls, whether in the case of single-exit pricing, parallel importation, or its variant reference pricing. This is just as the social engineer has it planned, since compulsory licensing is intended to be another addition to the repertoire of price controls. Thus, a uniform price will be yielded, permitting the firm to recoup its short-run common (fixed) costs. As has already been shown in our section on price discrimination, in the presence of such a price it seems certain that hardest hit would be the consumers with low income with the uniform price leading them to experience considerable and unnecessary contraction in consumption. There would also be the likelihood that the market comprised of the high-income individuals, which would otherwise have been competitive, would also be exposed to a higher price than would prevail if firms were allowed to price freely.

In so far as the impact of the policy in the long run is concerned, it should be recognized that in terms of its consequences it would completely correspond to those observed under generic substitution. This is what reveals the policy for what it is, namely something that halts or hinders firms from entering a new cycle of product innovations. Things here aptly fit Say's ([1880] 1964, pp. 128-129) coverage of the subject matter on property rights. It, in so enlightening a manner, reminds us that from a public-policy perspective not weakening "the certainty of enjoying the fruits of one's land, capital and labour, is the most powerful inducement to render them productive." Thus, firms that develop new products knowing that their right of property over what they produce is invaded or diluted to begin with, is not different in any meaningful way from the generic substitution case of firms knowing that in the long run their original products will be substituted. What flows from this congruency is that the socially undesired consequences of generic substitution can be expected to replicate themselves in the case of compulsory licensing if the proposed scheme were to be enforced.

Given that the short and long run alternate, beginning from a point in the long run and with the proposed compulsory licensing scheme being common practice, firms would know that in the long run their right of property over the new products they produce is invaded or diluted. Should they then desire to make a sale in the short run, they would have to confine themselves to products void of the expenditure they would have otherwise dedicated on R&D and on the promotion of new-generation products. This can only be achieved by the firms resorting to their existing (old) product stock. This of course offers limited possibility for innovation, which would mean that firms would have to resort to supplying homogeneous goods only, where the prospect of demand creation and demand diversion that product variety carries with it is muted. From here on in, the short-run firms would for all practical purposes price their products indistinguishable from marginal cost. However, just as in the case of generic substitution, we must not delude ourselves that this would bring us a lower price. The price for what is now produced, although priced at MC, will end up being higher from the MC level at the time the policy was first put in place. To understand this, recall the following. First, product variety is synonymous with rivalry, so encroaching upon one or the other amounts to the stifling of both. Second, product variety is inseparable from price discrimination. Third, the profits from discrimination attract entry, thereby increasing variety and putting downward pressure on prices (see Borenstein, 1985).

Fourth, recall that in Figure 9.2 it is explicitly assumed that the MC (level) is fixed (constant). In fact, the MC level vacillates depending on whether rivalry does or does not exist. It is the purpose of competition to lower this level as much as it is the outcome of its absence to raise it. In Figure 9.2 the former instance would be reflected by a downward shift in the MC schedule, whereas the latter by an upward one. Combining this with the previous three recollection points, we have the picture of unauthorized or universal compulsory licensing raising the overall price level to consumers. By inference from elementary theory, we must therefore also deduce that on the aggregate the quantity consumers demand will fall. Thus, under unauthorized compulsory licensing (the South African case) or its universal variant (the OECD case), which likewise renders the right of property over what is developed perpetually insecure, we should expect to have the socially undesired outcomes of high price and less consumption. This is just the same as in the case of generic substitution and once again, for the sake of reminder, is not what we expect from competition.

In concluding this section we must stress one other point. Both of the public-policy tools we have inspected in this section ultimately represent an indirect form of price control, which penalizes new product development and favors imitative as opposed to innovative competition. Each tool is based on the premise that price competition in the presence of imitation (i.e., perfect competition) is all there is, leading to the observation that price controls must therefore be imposed on innovation. This would be a valid statement if it could be shown that there is no competition under innovation, which has already been shown is by no means the case. As a matter of principle, we know it to be so from the axiom that competition is created by innovation. In so far as the pharmaceutical industry is concerned we have demonstrated that it is defined by rigorous competition.

To summarize, this chapter examined the market structure of the pharmaceutical industry in South Africa and the legal environment in which it operates. We demonstrated that the industry is dualistic in the sense that it operates in two distinct markets or sectors. One is the private (medical insurers) sector and the other is the state-administered public sector.

The private and public sectors purchase pharmaceuticals in very different ways. The state does so via competitive tender, while private sector purchases are generally initiated by individual prescribing doctors, with reimbursement by medical insurers to dispensers (dispensing doctors plus retail pharmacists). In the case of the private market, many of the drugs sold by firms are under patent protection (applying as a rule for innovative medicines only) and the generic medicines sold are usually marketed under brand names. In the case of the public market, however, tenders are issued for the bulk purchase of predominantly generic, usually nonbranded, drugs. A generic drug is the off-patent (imitative) equivalent in terms of chemical composition of the drug formerly in patent.

This discrepancy in the product mix between the sectors was also found to account for why R&D and promotional activities in the private sector outpace those in the public sector, i.e., in the former they exist whereas in the latter they are virtually absent.

Whether in the private or public market, the industry was shown to be characterized by intense rivalry at the firm level with firms competing with one another within therapeutic submarkets—within which substitutability of one product for another exists, i.e., the cross-elasticity of demand is positive. Competition in the private sector is of the Schumpeterian-Littlechild kind, whereas in the public sector it is driven by competition for the market induced by a sealed-bid, tender-based process. Whether in the private or public sector congealing of the firms as well as their products' market shares or positions usually does not occur. In spite of all this it was demonstrated that the industry is embroiled by a legal environment that operates on the premise, contrary to fact, that competition is somehow not present in the industry. In line with this, the regulator has made provisions in the statutory books for both direct and indirect price controls for the purpose of providing consumers with affordable medicine prices. A careful inspection of these controls of single-exit pricing, parallel importation, generic substitution, and unauthorized or universal compulsory licensing revealed that the polices would bestow upon consumers, by virtue of choking rivalry at the supplier or firm level, an outcome directly opposite to what they set out to achieve. All of them would retard or eliminate consumer choice by halting or hindering firms from producing product variety, but most important they would suppress innovation in pharmaceuticals, thereby also stifling rivalry among firms in the long run.

The assumption on the part of the regulator that drug prices need to be made more affordable or the assertion that the industry possesses monopoly power are of the same vintage, in that they imply a conviction that the industry is not competitive and that perfect competition is all that there is. This raises questions as to whether we should subscribe to such a conviction or whether such a conviction is even warranted. We devote the next three chapters to answering these questions. Chapters 12 and 13 are macroeconomic studies of the industry in that they look at the industry as a whole. The first of these addresses the question of whether the industry on the aggregate should be viewed as competitive or monopoly-like. The next examines whether horizontal mergers and acquisition are in any way anticompetitive and, if so, whether they distort rivalry between firms resulting in a monopoly-like industry structure. The final chapter seeks to verify these findings by conducting a microeconomic examining firm rivalry and its resulting product rivalry within the therapeutic submarkets in which firms compete.

Chapter 12

The Pharmaceutical Industry and Monopoly Power

This chapter examines the pharmaceutical industry's monopoly power, in particular researching whether such power exists. Monopoly power is generally considered to bring the firms who possess it supernormal profits. In the pharmaceutical industry, the conception that such profits exist is not new. On account of it Smith ([1812] 1937, p. 101) had this to say:

> Apothecaries' profit is become a bye-word, denoting something uncommonly extravagant. This great apparent profit, however, is frequently no more than the reasonable wages of labour. The skill of an apothecary is a much nicer and more delicate matter than that of an artificer whatever; and the trust which is reposed in him is of much greater importance. He is the physician of the poor in all cases, and of the rich when the distress or danger is not very great. His reward, therefore, ought to be suitable to his skill and his trust, and it arises generally from the price at which he sells his drugs. But the whole drugs which the best employed apothecary, in a large market town, will sell in a year, may not perhaps cost him above thirty or forty pounds. Though he should sell them, therefore, for three or four hundred, or at a thousand per cent profit, this may frequently be no more than the reasonable wages of his labour charged, in the only way in which he can charge them, upon the price of his drugs. The greater part of the apparent profit is wages disguised in the garb of profit.

Remarkably, it would not take much to bring Smith's text to modern times. Few substitutes are required in this regard, such as

doi:10.1300/5505_12

supplanting the word apothecary with the firm doing R&D, i.e., engaged entirely in new product development. The same would have to be done for the wages of labor, i.e., the return to the proprietor of the apothecary, which will now have to denote the rate of return of the firm engaged in new product development conditional upon the risk this activity assumes.

That said, we are still faced with the situation that by conventional, perfectly competitive terms it may appear that the pharmaceutical industry does not confine itself to making the normal (perfectly competitive) rate of return.

As we saw in the previous chapter, the underlying assumption on the part of the regulator is that the industry has monopoly power on the premise that perfect competition is not the norm here. Along such lines, the government is advocating direct or indirect price controls through the imposition of single-exit pricing, parallel importation, generic substitution, and unauthorized or universal compulsory licensing, and the antitrust agency is asserting that the industry has monopoly power.

What we have here can be described in terms of Figure 3.3 (see p. 21). The regulator envisages that the industry prices at level P^M where the corresponding output is Q^M. By pricing in this manner, the industry earns supernormal profit π and induces allocative inefficiency (i.e., potential consumers, whom it would not cost extra to satisfy, refrain from buying because P^M is above their willingness to pay). The DWL triangle measures this allocative inefficiency. The combination of allocative inefficiency and profit making results in the reduction of consumer surplus and so the aim of the regulator is to drive P^M to P^C, thereby adding to the existing consumer surplus (CS) area $\pi + DWL$.

So far so good, but given that competition is created by innovation, and that rivalry on the basis of innovative or new-generation products in both the private and public sector is the standard by which firms vie for market share in the industry, how plausible is this account of the industry on the part of the regulator? This is what we set about to answer in this chapter.

If an industry is deemed to be uncompetitive, the charge must be based on the presence of monopoly power on either or both of the supply and demand sides of the market. In the former, monopoly can be measured by the number of firms in a market, by concentration ratios, or by the persistency of profit taking. However, each of the measures just listed are mere proxies for monopoly power. Ease of industry entry is more important. If an industry is earning profits above the accepted norm as judged by the profit taking, on the average, across all existing branches of industry, and if entry barriers are absent, then new firms will enter that industry. In order to gain sales, they will either price at levels below the ruling rate or introduce superior products. In the long run, this will tend to reduce profits to normal competitive levels either by exerting downward pressure on prices or upward pressure on innovative costs. This gives rise to three propositions:

1. *Proposition 1:* If product innovation in the industry is ongoing (which presupposes the continuous existence of common costs such as R&D) then, in the short run, profit taking within the industry would be moderated by innovative competition. If an industry earns in the short run profits above the accepted norm taken, on the average, to be the profit taking across all existing branches of industry, and if entry barriers (as defined in this work) are absent, then new firms will enter that industry. In order to gain sales they will either price at levels below the ruling rate or introduce superior products. In the long run, this will tend to reduce profits to normal competitive levels either by exerting downward pressure on prices or upward pressure on innovative costs. This would bring about a tendency for the industry's long-run rate of return to correspond to the average for all existing branches of industry, this being what other firms in the industry deem as the competitive (minimum) rate of return they should derive if they are to be in business.

2. *Proposition 2:* Since innovation is recurrent, the industry does not come to rest. Accordingly, any equality, in the short run, with the competitive rate of return will be very short-lived. Profit taking in the industry complies with the Von Misian view of profits (Von Mises, 1949, p. 295) quoted earlier, which states that profits can never be "normal" and that "equlilibrium" can never exist with regard to them; they are always "a phenomenon of deviation from normalcy." As will be recalled, the entrepreneur is the originator of economic development and may be a person, a group, or an institution, such as a firm.

3. *Proposition 3:* If Propositions 1 and 2 hold, then in the short run systematic departures from MC would occur. Put another way, there would be no tendency, in the long run, for DWL to disappear.

Assuming Propositions 1 and 2 hold, then in the short run the DWL in a given period would differ from that of another period. This would be so, since product innovation is recurrent. In the short run, each period would have a DWL referring to a different constellation of supply and demand. Where the product mix of firms in the industry acquires greater but not perfect homogeneity, the resulting DWL in the short run would come close to zero. In turn, exactly the opposite would apply where the product mix of firms in the industry acquires greater heterogeneity in a given period.

We can sum up Proposition 3 with the assertion that it conforms to Say's ([1880] 1964) view of the profit behavior of the manufacturing concern involved with new product development. As Say ([1880] 1964, p. 329) put it:

> Sometimes a manufacturer discovers a process, calculated either to introduce a new product, to increase the beauty of an old one, or to produce with greater economy; and, by observance of strict secrecy, may make for many years . . . profits exceeding the ordinary ratio of his calling. In this particular case the manufacturer combines two different operations of industry: that of the man of science, whose profit he engrosses himself, and that of the adventurer too. But few such discoveries can long remain secret; which is a fortunate circumstance for the public, because this secrecy keeps the price of the particular product it applies to above, and the number of consumers enabled to enjoy it below, the natural level.

This text is self-explanatory and we have to make only four points to bring it in line with modern times. First, the "ordinary ratio of calling" is quite obviously the competitive, namely average profit or rate of return for all existing branches of industry taken as a whole. Second, the "man of science" these days constitutes the R&D function the pharmaceutical manufacturer undertakes. Third, the "adventurer" is none other than the manufacturer (or entrepreneur) who sets in motion the rivalry in the industry by introducing a new product. Fourth, "the natural level" refers to the perfectly competitive point, which we know would not be attained if Proposition 1 and 2 hold. By extension, a DWL would occur in every period, i.e., Say's view of the profit behavior of the manufacturing concern involved in new product development takes place all the time.

That which is stipulated in terms of these propositions would be observed only when pricing freedom existed at the supplier level.

To prove these propositions a measure of profit taking is required, which will also allow us to compute the DWL for Proposition 3. The measure of profit taking adopted here is derived from the price-cost margin referred to earlier. The data used are for the period 1980 to 1998 and are census data, also referred to as manufacturing data. These data give us the aggregated industry figures to enable the computation of the profit measure. Their use is justified on several grounds in the case of this study.

As Liebowitz (1982, p. 231) reminds us, census data are "generally acknowledged to be the data set least tainted by the muddying influence of firms that are diversified across industry lines." Also, many of the firms operating in South Africa are subsidiaries of multinational firms with the reporting of their financial results falling in the aggregated financial statements of their parent companies. These statements provide the consolidated financial performance of these firms' subsidiaries around the world, which despite their breakdown by broad geographic areas (e.g., Africa, Asia, Latin America, and so on) do not go down to specific country level. This makes it practically impossible to tease out the financial results for the South African operations. In spite of this if the South African subsidiary is engaged in the manufacture of pharmaceutical products in South Africa, this activity would usually be recorded under the manufacturing (census) data. This does not apply only to the subsidiaries of multinational pharmaceutical firms. It also includes the domestic (nonforeign) firms. Only a few of the latter firms are listed on the Johannesburg Stock Exchange. Information for those that are not is not readily available. For those that are, teasing out the necessary financial results to derive the measure of profit can be tricky. On the one hand, some of the pharmaceutical firms in question form part of pyramid groups, which report group financial statements in their annual reports. This does not permit for directly discerning the proportion that is occupied in these groups' operations by their pharmaceutical and pharmaceutical-related businesses. On the other hand, those firms on the stock exchange whose financial results of their pharmaceutical operations can be discerned directly are too few in number to use their financial data confidently as being typical of the industry. For instance, at the time of preparing this study it was observed that only one firm is formally recorded by the Johannesburg Stock Exchange under its pharmaceuticals sector. Each of the aforementioned limitations can be overcome with the use of the census data set. Irrespective of whether a firm is listed or not, if it produces, its revenues and costs (more on which will be mentioned later) from production would more than likely be picked up in this data set.

Fourth, given that we are conducting a time-series analysis, it would become cumbersome to account year-on-year for all the mergers and acquisitions that have taken place in the industry in order to determine the necessary adjustments to profit for the single entities that are to emerge out of these transactions. However, irrespective of the merger or acquisition (whether involving multinational or domestic firms) if the single firm so formed manufactures, its revenue and costs would usually appear in the manufacturing data series.

Finally, the propositions refer to unregulated ex-factory (producer) prices as well as being formulated in terms of firms involved in the production of goods. Hence, the proper data for the study are those at the producer level, which is what the census data covers.

The measure of profit selected for the study is determined from the Lerner index (L).

It is commonly accepted that in using the census data information is not on MC, but on average variable costs. This means that to compute this measure of monopoly power, MC would have to be assumed to be equal to average variable costs. This modification of the Lerner measure along with multiplying and dividing it by output reduces it to the following expression:

$$\text{L-profit} = (\text{Value of Sales} - \text{Payroll} - \text{Cost of Materials})/(\text{Value of Sales}) \qquad (12.1)$$

Equation 12.1 is none other than the ratio of gross-trading profit to sales for the manufacturing concern. For ease of reference we would call this ratio the profit margin. It should be noted here that all profit figures we are furnished with by this measure would be biased upward, that is, they would be overestimated. This is because, as pointed out by Liebowitz (1982, p. 235) and Leach (1994, p. 271), many possible variable costs such as advertising, central office expenses, and R&D are not included in the categories of payroll or cost of materials. Other important costs such as the cost of capital (including risk premium), corporate taxes, and depreciation are also excluded from these categories. Despite all this, the impact that these nonenumerated costs, most notably capital (e.g., machinery), advertising, and R&D, would have on generating revenue for the firms in the industry would be reflected in its value of sales (being the sum of the value of sales for the individual firms). Incidentally, it should be noted with respect to the nonenumerated costs that no adequate data could be found on them to cover fully the period of this study. Taking this into account, along with the five reasons for confining to the use of the manufacturing data series, the profit measure for the industry is calculated as per the L-profit notation.

Having calculated the measure of profit, this measure can be deployed to ascertain the industry's DWL. The customary method is the Harberger procedure (1954, pp. 78-82), which involves calculating the area of the DWL triangle of Figure 3.3 (see pp. 21). Once the Lerner measure of monopoly power for an industry and its elasticity of demand are factored in the calculation of this area (which is half base times perpendicular height) the resulting expression from which the DWL can be determined becomes

$$DWL = \tfrac{1}{2} \times \varepsilon \times P^M \times Q^M \times L^2 \qquad (12.2)$$

Harberger (1954, pp. 79-82) used this formulation to compute the welfare loss of monopoly power in the American manufacturing industry, assuming that the point elasticity of demand for each industry's product (output) was unity, i.e., $\varepsilon = 1$.

Both Posner (1975) and Cowling and Mueller (1978) have cast considerable doubt over whether Equation 12.2 goes far enough in calculating the social costs of monopoly power. Things change if it is acknowledged that it is the possession of market power that allows a monopolist to set a monopoly price. From this premise, retaining the assumptions under which Figure 3.3 is constructed, namely a linear demand and a constant marginal cost, Posner (1975, p. 815) has demonstrated that in the special case where each firm is able to charge the optimum monopoly price, the DWL for an industry is given by

$$DWL = \tfrac{1}{2} \times \pi. \qquad (12.3)$$

This same expression has also been seconded by Cowling and Mueller (1978, p. 729) on the assumption that each firm in a given industry does possess some monopoly power, as implied by the price cost margin it chooses and uses.

It should not be difficult to see how allowing for each firm in a given industry to be a monopolist would cause the DWL figures of Equation 12.3 to exceed those of Equation 12.2. The Posner (1975) and Cowling and Mueller (1978) approaches to measuring the social losses from monopoly are clearly going to increase the estimates. This, as Reekie (1989, p. 63) alerts us, would be due to three things. First, dropping Harberger's arbitrary assumption of ε being equal to unity will raise the value. Second, the increase in the relevant geometric area, which now becomes a rectangle as opposed to a triangle, is substantial. Third, by dropping the decimal fraction L^2, the estimates must increase.

It could be contended that the assumption that each firm in an industry is a monopolist is extreme. This may or may not be void of merit, but it is hoped that enough material has been provided in this work to support it. In practice firms tend to compete in ways that enable them to erect downward-sloping demand curves for their products, i.e., firms create monopoly power. Firms achieve this by making themselves the only producer or supplier of their product(s).

This encompasses elements of branding, quality, and some unique factor that no rival can match. All of these require promotional and R&D activities, and jointly form part of the rivalry arsenal of firms that produces product differentiation between them. Simply put, the Posner-Cowling-Mueller measure of DWL may be seen to epitomize innovative competition. Taking this into account, in this study the pharmaceutical industry's dead weight loss would be calculated from Equation 12.3, where π would be taken to equal the industry's L-profit.

TESTING FOR PROPOSITION 1

To prove Proposition 1 it would have to be shown empirically that the pharmaceutical industry's L-profit is no different, statistically speaking, from that of the country's manufacturing sector as a whole. This is done by applying the fairly routine two-sample t-test analysis to the following hypothesis:

Ho: On the average, no difference exists between the pharmaceutical industry's profit margin (GPp) and the profit margin of the manufacturing sector (GPm) as a whole. Mathematically GPp = GPm.

Ha: On the average, a difference exists between the pharmaceutical industry's profit margin and the profit margin of the manufacturing sector as a whole. Mathematically GPp ≠ GPm.

If the alternative hypothesis holds, it would thereafter have to be determined from the t-tests whether this difference is one in which the pharmaceutical industry's profit margin exceeds that of the overall manufacturing sector, i.e., GPp > GPm, or vice versa, GPp < GPm. The results of the two-sample t-test procedure are summarized in Table 12.1.[1] The results are self-explanatory. Empirical support for proposition 1 emerges from looking early on at the mean of the pharmaceutical industry's profit margin in conjunction with its standard deviation and how this corresponds to the manufacturing sector. On the average, over the period of the study, the industry's profit margin has fluctuated little around 11.9 percent (0.119 × 100) of its sales. The Development Bank of Southern Africa reported similar average manufacturing profit margins for the pharmaceutical industry in Pharmaceutical Investment Scoping Analysis (2001, p. 14).

The section of interest in the table that establishes the formal proof of Proposition 1 is that of the Aspin-Welch unequal variance test. The p-value for the t-test of the no-difference (null) hypothesis, when rounded off, is 0.98, which exceeds the chosen level of significance of 0.05. Thus the null hypothesis cannot be rejected. The conclusion that can be drawn from this main result is that no difference exists between the pharmaceutical industry's profit margin and that of the overall manufacturing sector.

This finding is expected. It joins a list of other studies that have failed to show that the pharmaceutical industry has profit margins excessively above those of the manufacturing sector combined. For instance on inspection of the profitability of the industry the Snyman Commission (Snyman Report, 1962, p. 191) reported that it failed to find excessive profit margins or profits at the production level of pharmaceuticals. The subsequent Steenkamp Commission (Steenkamp Report, 1978, p. 27), on its own examination of the level of profits in the pharmaceutical industry against those of the various

TABLE 12.1. Comparing the rate of profit between the pharmaceutical industry and the overall manufacturing sector (1980-1998).

Two-Sample Test Report

Descriptive Statistics Section

Variable	Count	Mean	Standard deviation	Standard error	95% LCL of mean	95% UCL of mean
GPm	16	0.1195082	1.117559E-02	2.793896E-03	0.1135532	0.1254633
GPp	16	0.1193506	1.883403E-02	4.708508E-03	0.1093147	0.1293866

Note: T-alpha (GPm) = 2.1314; T-alpha (GPp) = 2.1314.

Confidence-Limits of Difference Section

Variance assumption	DF	Mean difference	Standard deviation	Standard error	95% LCL of mean	95% UCL of mean
Equal	30	1.57577E-04	1.548571E-02	5.47502E-03	-1.102392E-02	1.133907E-02
Unequal	24.40	1.57577E-04	0.0219001	5.475025E-03	-1.113258E-02	1.144773E-02

Note: T-alpha (Equal) = 2.0423, T-alpha (Unequal) = 2.0621.

Tests of Assumptions Section

Assumption	Value	Probability	Decision (5 percent)
Omnibus normality (GPm)	2.3605	0.307199	Cannot reject normality
Omnibus normality (GPp)	2.7262	0.255862	Cannot reject normality
Modified-Levene equal-variance test	5.3663	0.027544	Reject equal variances

Aspin-Welch Unequal-Variance Test Section

Alternative hypothesis	T-value	Prob. level	Decision (5 percent)
Difference < > 0	0.0288	0.977273	Accept Ho
Difference < 0	0.0288	0.511363	Accept Ho
Difference > 0	0.0288	0.48637	Accept Ho
Difference: (GPm) − (GPp)			

Sources: Bulletin of Statistics 1980-1999 and *South African Statistics* 1980-2001, Statistics South Africa; *Sectoral Data Series* 1995, Industrial Development Corporation; *Foreign Trade Statistics* 1980-1998 and *Monthly Abstract of Trade Statistics* 1980-1999, government printers on behalf of the commissioner for South African Revenue Services.
Note: Due to lack of available data it was not possible to calculate the profit margin for the pharmaceutical industry for 1994, 1995, and 1997. Thus, the two-sample t-test analysis was confined to sixteen rather than nineteen observations.

manufacturing sectors stated that "the figures revealed by the . . . investigation do not support the view that the pharmaceutical industry in South Africa is, as a whole earning excessive profits, particularly if its risks are borne in mind." The Browne Commission struck a conclusion not dissimilar to that of the Steenkamp Commission. On conducting its own investigation on the profitability of the industry the Commission (Browne Report, 1985, p. 16) remarked that

> it is necessary to point out that the total profits in the pharmaceutical industry in South Africa are less than the profits of individual mining houses and the bigger industrial companies. This indicates that the total profits made on pharmaceuticals are not exorbitant.

Finally, on inspecting the cost of medicines in South Africa, the Melamet Commission (Melamet Report, 1994, pp. 37-41) found no evidence of it encompassing monopolistic markups by pharmaceutical manufacturers.

TESTING FOR PROPOSITION 2

If Proposition 2 holds, then over time we should observe the pharmaceutical industry's profit, as expressed by its expected profit margin (GPp), to be cyclical around the perfectly competitive or normal profit level taken as the average profit margin for the manufacturing sector as a whole. To observe whether this profit behavior on the part of the industry exists the fairly regular, locally weighted, regression smoothing scatterplots procedure was used, abbreviated as lowess. Lowess was applied to the industry profit margin in order to ascertain its expected profit margin. In our case the smoothed values from lowess were obtained by running a weighted regression of the industry's profit margin on time. Here the central point in the data gets the highest weight and points farther away based on the distance of the absolute difference between the central time point and each of the other time points in the data set receive less. The estimated regression is then used to predict the smoothed (expected) value for the profit margin at the central point only. The procedure is repeated to obtain the remaining smoothed values, which means a separate weighted regression is estimated for every point in the data. Recall that there

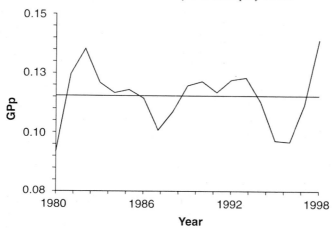

FIGURE 12.1. Pharmaceutical industry profit behavior. *Note:* Three missing values generated.

were three missing observations at the time the t-test analysis was carried out. The lowess procedure generated values for these missing observations, presented in Figure 12.1.

The horizontal line in the diagram represents the mean profit margin level for the manufacturing sector. This line is the normal profit line, which may also be referred to as the perfectly competitive line. No distinction is made in this work between these two terms, which are used interchangeably. What is observed in the diagram corresponds to Proposition 2 and is complementary to the work on competitive process. Put another way, for the period of the study, the pharmaceutical industry's expected profit behavior conforms to the Von Misian view of profits. This has several important ramifications in a number of distinct areas, specifically:

1. Support for the Von Misian view of profits in conjunction with the support for Proposition 1, quite simply tells us, in stark contrast to popular belief, that in the long run excesses in profit taking from the perfectly competitive norm do not prevail precisely because of innovation taking place in the short run.
2. The evidence conforms with ease of entry into the pharmaceutical industry. Put another away, it appears that if barriers to entry

exist, they must be insignificant. The evidence suggests that if the industry is earning profits above the accepted norm as judged by the profit taking, on the average, across all existing branches of industry, then new firms will enter the industry. In order to gain sales they will either price at levels below the ruling rate (by offering me-too products or offering inventions of their own that build on or around the existing products) or introducing superior products. In the long run this will tend to reduce profits to normal competitive levels, either by exerting downward pressure on prices or upward pressure on innovative costs. Because the competitive process is continuous, this would keep on recurring with each new cycle of the competitive process.

3. It follows that any assertions that the industry has monopoly power or behaves like a collective monopoly (i.e., a cartel) do not stand up to scrutiny. In some public circles the assertion of monopoly power comes under the garb of the patent system granting new pharmaceutical products a monopoly position, correspondingly leading to the industry's overall profit rate being consistently above the perfectly competitive norm. By virtue of the previous points, applying this garbed assertion also does not stand up to scrutiny.

4. In relation to the cyclical profit behavior of the pharmaceutical industry, the perfectly competitive line is stationary. Put another way, it appears the perfectly competitive line is void of any economic activity. For instance, the line misses out on informing us of all innovative activity, in the short run, that the innovation mechanism of the competitive process initiates at the time of its operation. This is what the moves from trough to peak in the cycles in the diagram depict. By the same token, the line misses out on informing us of all imitative activity, in the short run, that the transfer mechanism of the competitive process harbors at the time of its operation. This is what the moves from peak to trough in the cycles in the diagram depict. All this raises considerable doubt as to whether perfect competition should be held as the appropriate competitive yardstick by which we should judge rivalry among firms in the pharmaceutical industry. On the contrary, the support for the Von Misian view of profits renders the evidence complementary to Schumpeter's (1949, p. 106) view of

perfect competition, namely as a competitive yardstick measure that "has no title to being set up as a model of ideal efficiency."

5. It follows that clear economic advantages exist in having a free pricing system that allows manufacturers' products to enter markets at the risk and at prices of their choosing. If firms were compelled to price in a way that keeps them at the perfectly competitive level in the short run, quite clearly, as the diagram of the pharmaceutical industry profit behavior illustrates, two consequences would seem imminent. The impact of the innovation mechanism, namely increasing product variety and ultimately culminating in product breakthroughs (reflected in the peak of the industry's profit rate) will never be experienced (whether in the short or long run). So too will there be no experience (whether in the short or long run) of the impact of the transfer mechanism, namely aggressive price competition below the price level that secures normal profits and ultimately culminates in firm rivalry yielding the lowest possible market price (reflected in the trough of the industry's profit rate).

6. It is regularly argued by the funders of health care, i.e., the medical insurers in the private sector and the state in the public sector, that patented or innovative pharmaceutical products absorb much of their budgets for long periods of time. On the basis of the previous points, these arguments appear rather unfounded. If the profit behavior diagram is examined closely, and if the peak profit rates for the industry are taken as reflective of such products being offered by firms, it can be seen that these supernormal profits persist for an extremely short time. It appears this time is no longer than a year. Thereafter prices move toward levels that either support normal profits in the long run or go a step further in the sense of developing into fiercer price rivalry between firms until the lowest possible price level from competition is identified.

Note that research by Grabowski and Vernon (1994, pp. 398-399) indicates that it seems to be the norm for pharmaceutical firms to depend for their sales on only a few of the innovative products they make. Only three out of every ten new products firms develop cover the average R&D cost for developing a new product, while only two out of every ten products developed provide returns above that level.

TESTING FOR PROPOSITION 3

Here, the fairly routine one-sample t-test analysis is applied to the pharmaceutical industry's DWL, expressed here as a percentage of total industry sales (DWLPTSALES), testing for the following hypothesis:

Ho: On the average, the pharmaceutical industry's DWL is not different from zero. Mathematically put, DWLPTSALES = 0.
Ha: On the average, the pharmaceutical industry's DWL is positive. Mathematically put, DWLPTSALES > 0.

From Proposition 3 we expect a positive DWL, i.e., support for Ha. This would be evidence of the industry leaning toward innovative rather than imitative competition in the long run. In this sense the DWL would not be a measure of the size of allocative inefficiency but of the price society would pay for having product variety instead of product homogeneity in the long run.

Recall that the industry's DWL is calculated from Equation 12.2 using the industry's profit margin figures for the period 1980-1998, comprising the sixteen observations used to prove Proposition 1 and the three profit-margin figures obtained from the lowess procedure in proving Proposition 2. The results of the one-sample t-test analysis are presented in Table 12.2.

Given that product innovation is recurrent, we can see how the results in Table 12.2 show that in the short run each period has a DWL referring to a different constellation of supply and demand. Where the product mix of firms in the industry acquires greater but not perfect homogeneity, the resulting DWL in the short run almost disappears (which is what the minimum DWL value of 4.4 percent in the study period reflects). In turn, exactly the opposite would apply where the product mix of firms in the industry acquires greater heterogeneity in a given period (which is what the maximum DWL value of 7.3 percent in the study period reflects).

The section of interest in the table that establishes the formal proof of Proposition 3 is that of the t-test for difference between mean and value. The p-value for the t-test of the no difference (null) hypothesis is 0, which is below the chosen level of significance of 0.05. Thus, the

TABLE 12.2. Pharmaceutical industry dead-weight loss as a percentage of total industry sales (1980-1998).

Summary Section of DWLPTSALES

Count	Mean	Standard deviation	Standard error	Minimum	Maximum	Range
19	5.880527	0.8932368	0.2049226	4.395	7.33	2.935

Tests of Assumptions Section

Assumption	Value	Probability	Decision (5%)
Omnibus normality	2.5746	0.276013	Cannot reject normality

T-Test for Difference Between Mean and Value Section

Alternative hypothesis	T-value	Prob. level	Decision (5%)
DWLPTSALES < > 0	28.6963	0.000000	Reject Ho
DWLPTSALES > 0	28.6963	0.000000	Reject Ho

Means Section of DWLPTSALES

Parameter	Mean
Value	5.880527
Std error	0.2049226
95 percent LCL	5.45
95 percent UCL	6.311053
T-value	28.6963
Prob. level	0.000000

null hypothesis can be rejected. The conclusion that can be drawn from this main result is that a DWL of significance can be expected from the pharmaceutical industry in the long run. Put another way, for the period of the study, the pharmaceutical industry's profit behavior conforms to Say's view of the profit behavior of the manufacturing concern affiliated with new product development. We can see from the results of Table 12.2 that 95 percent of the time the pharmaceutical industry's DWL may be expected to range between 5.45 percent and 6.31 percent of total industry sales in the short run. Its expected value in that range is 5.88 percent.

It should be noted that in the case of the pharmaceutical industry the DWL has an interesting interpretation. Given that in the pharmaceutical industry innovation is an indispensable condition of rivalry between the firms and, if it is recognized that this innovation is supported by the patent system, then the industry's DWL can be interpreted as the cost of the patent system to society. Such a supposition is not far-fetched. On the one hand, its theoretical underpinnings can be traced to the discussion on pp. 210-213 in this chapter. On the other hand, the study has been carried out against the background of a strong patent system for pharmaceutical products, as enforced by the Patents Act No. 57 of 1978, granting pharmaceutical inventions a nominal patent life of twenty years.

By extension, from the expected value of the DWL the cost of the patent system to society in the short run is expected to be 5.88 percent of total pharmaceutical industry sales. On its own accord this number appears small, but it would be appropriate to determine how small it is in relation to what it amounts to for the public at large. To illustrate the case in point, we focus on the last year of our study. The South African population numbered 42,131,000 in 1998 (Statistics South Africa, 2000). In the same year South Africa's GDP per capita at producer prices was R15,650.39 (South African Reserve Bank, 2000) while the ex-factory value of sales for the pharmaceutical industry, as taken at the time of compiling Table 12.1, amounted to R8,646 million. Applying to this last number the expected value of the DWL and thereafter dividing the resulting figure by the population number, the cost of the patent system in the short run to the South African public is found to be R12.07 per capita.

This last number represents 0.08 percent ($=100 \times 12.07/15650.39$) of the per capita income of the average South African. A minuscule price to pay, given that it grants access to the advances in medicinal treatment and is what society voluntarily gives up (assuming a free-pricing system at the manufacturer level) for the choice of innovative rather than imitative competition.

It is, however, imperative to keep in mind that the evidence in support of Propositions 1, 2, and 3 do not support, to put it mildly, assumptions or beliefs that the pharmaceutical industry possesses monopoly power or anything that would assist it to acquire such power.

If the industry lacks monopoly power in the long run, should we expect mergers and acquisitions to have a long-run impact that reverses this? Perhaps we may say in advance that the answer to this question is no. This answer is informed by the studies carried out by Leach (1992, 1997). At the very, least these studies invalidate any presumptions of a relationship between the concentration of the pharmaceutical industry and monopoly power. Nonetheless, to provide a detailed answer strictly with reference to the pharmaceutical industry, we now turn to the next chapter.

Chapter 13

The Impact of Mergers and Acquisitions

The aim here is to identify whether mergers and acquisitions in the pharmaceutical industry in any way produce results mimicking those of monopoly or collusion. Evidence from previous chapters suggests that this is not likely to be the case. On the contrary, it supports the likelihood that mergers and acquisitions indicate not the decline of competition but its undoubted vigor. Here it will be recalled that a number of reasons were offered for firms merging or acquiring one another, which, broadly speaking, fell into two categories: for efficiency and for avoiding business failures. An instance involving the merger or acquisition for efficiency would see the announcement of a merger or takeover at one firm in an industry accompanied by a positive revaluation of other industry members. This stems from the production technologies of close competitors being by definition closely related. Thus, the news of a proposed efficient merger can also signal opportunities for the rivals to increase their productivity. For example, the proposal announcement may disseminate information that enables the rivals to imitate the technological innovation motivating the acquisition. If such innovation activity requires merger, then the stock prices of the rivals will be bid up in anticipation of the expected gains from the future merger activity. The proposal announcement by the merging firms or the firm doing the acquiring is not the only channel of information spillover.

For instance, publications (media or press releases), meetings (industry gatherings, conferences, and technical workshops), hiring employees from the merged firms, public disclosure laws (e.g., patent laws and any disclosure provisions contained in competition statutes), conversations with employees of the merging firms, judicial decisions (legal precedents), and so on. Each of the aforementioned channels informs competitors about the way their merging rivals intend to

doi:10.1300/5505_13

operate and works toward spelling out the productive operations of the joint firm. The result of the productive-efficiency view of mergers and acquisitions is to demonstrate that it is unlikely for mergers and acquisitions to produce a significant expansion of the merging firm's share of the market compared to their rivals. If there is evidence of this, it contradicts the argument that the merging firms initiate a (monopolistic) "predatory" price war after the consummation of the merger. If horizontal mergers and acquisitions fulfilled the predatory pricing theory, then nonmerging rivals would have been subjected by such mergers or acquisitions to a negative (abnormal) performance in terms of their rates of return, market share, or rank.

In as far as the instance involving the merger or acquisition for avoiding business failures is concerned, Dewey (1961, p. 257) summarized it thus:

> Most mergers, of course, have virtually nothing to do with either the creation of market power or the realisation of scale economies. They are merely a civilised alternative to bankruptcy or the voluntary liquidation that transfers assets from falling to rising firms. "Civilised" is perhaps an inadequate word. As a method of transferring capital from one management to another, the merger is superior to bankruptcy or voluntary liquidation since it avoids the loss that inheres in the destruction of any going concern.

To establish, empirically, whether in the long run mergers and acquisitions in the pharmaceutical industry have increased the market power of the merging firms in relation to their nonmerging, the overall difference in market share of the group of firms involved in mergers and acquisitions between 1989 and 1999 is examined, measured by value, vis-à-vis that of the group of their nonmerging rivals. The overall market share difference (between 1989 and 1999) for each group was taken to be the mean of the differences in the market shares of the firms making up each of them. Beginning from 1999, the classification of whether a firm fell in the merged or nonmerged group of firms was done retrospectively. The corresponding market share of the merged firm in 1989 was obtained at that time by summing the market shares of the firms that had already formed a single entity by 1999. By analogy, this same summation principle was applied to the cases involving acquisitions.

A separate study was conducted for the private and the public sector using data from Intercontinental Medical Statistics (IMS). IMS is a market research house and the principal collector of firm and product sales information in the pharmaceutical industry. In the case of the private sector, the data applied to the ethical market. This is the market for drugs dispensed on prescription. In the case of the public sector, the data applied to the provincial hospital market. The investigation for each sector was confined to the top twenty companies by value. These firms are typical of their respective sectors. Since 1989 they have consistently accounted for around 80 percent of the private and public market by value. In the private sector, of the top twenty firms examined, 55 percent fell in the merged group, whereas the remaining 45 percent fell in the nonmerged group. The proportions for the public sector were 60 percent and 40 percent, respectively.

To ascertain whether mergers and acquisitions in the pharmaceutical industry give rise to monopoly power or collusion, or put another way, whether they increase its concentration in the long run, use was made of the fairly routine one-way analysis of variance (ANOVA) procedure. The procedure was used to test the following hypotheses in respect of both the private and the public sectors:

> Ho: On the average, no discrepancy exists between the market share difference of the merged (M) and nonmerged (NM) groups of firms. Mathematically put, M = NM.
>
> Ha: On the average, no equality exists between the market share difference of the merged (M) and nonmerged (NM) groups of firms. Mathematically put M ≠ NM.

Obviously, evidence in support of the null hypothesis would be indicative of mergers and acquisitions having no impact on the pharmaceutical industry's concentration in the long run. To preserve order in our presentation of the results from this hypothesis test, the findings for the private sector and the public sector are given in separate sections.

THE PRIVATE SECTOR

In the case of the private sector, if the monopoly view holds we should here expect an increase in the overall market share of the merged group of firms, which should on the average be greater than the decrease in the overall market share of the nonmerged group of firms. Simply put, on the average, merged firms come to acquire a greater proportion of the market than their nonmerged counterparts. In the context of the Ha hypothesis, this would mathematically be expressed as follows: M > NM. However, if the collusion view were true, mergers and acquisitions would create a price umbrella that nonmerged firms would undercut for a relatively greater profit and a higher proportion of the market. Thus, if collusion was the motive for mergers and acquisitions, we should expect an increase in the overall market share of the nonmerged group of firms that should on the average be greater than the decrease in the overall market share of the merged group of firms. On average, nonmerged firms come to acquire a greater proportion of the market than their merged counterparts. In the context of the Ha hypothesis this would mathematically be expressed as follows: M < NM.

The first doubt of the collusion hypothesis comes from the split between merged and nonmerged firms. Collusion promises increases in market share for the nonmerged (tacitly colluding) firms as much as it does for the merged (explicitly colluding) ones. Thus, if the collusion view were true, one ought to have found most if not all firms residing in either group. This, as we know, is not the case. That mergers and acquisitions fail to give rise to monopoly power or collusion and thereby to increased concentration in the pharmaceutical industry in the long run is formally confirmed by the results of the one-way ANOVA procedure presented in Exhibit 13.1. The relevant section in the table is the Kruskal-Wallis nonparametric, one-way ANOVA, in view of its parametric counterpart having violated the assumption of the normality of the residuals (p-value = 0.0009 is lower than α) but having satisfied their equal-variance assumption (p-value = 0.6264 is above α). The relevant p-value is this for the not-corrected-for-ties Kruskal-Wallis test. This value is 0.1598, which is greater than the chosen 5 percent level of significance, in turn meaning that the null hypothesis that the overall (median) market share differences between the merged and nonmerged group of firms are equal cannot be rejected. The conclusion that may be drawn from this main result is that in the long run, mergers and acquisitions should have no influence on the level of concentration in the private sector of the pharmaceutical industry.

EXHIBIT 13.1.
One-way ANOVA for differences in market share for the period 1989-1999 between merged and nonmerged firms (private sector).

Descriptive Statistics for Market Share Difference

	Mean	Median
Merged	−0.38	−0.28
Nonmerged	0.24	0.23

Tests of Assumptions

Assumption	Test value	Probability level	Decision (0.05)
Skewedness normality of residuals	−2.7772	0.005483	Reject
Kurtosis normality of residuals	2.4759	0.013289	Reject
Omnibus normality of residuals	13.8430	0.000986	Reject
Modified-levene equal-variance test	1.0832	0.311754	Accept

Box Plot Section

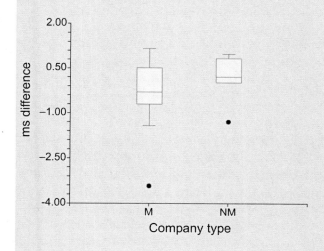

(continued)

(continued)

Expected Mean Squares Section

Source term	DF	Term fixed?	Denominator term	Expected mean square
A: Company type	1	Yes	·S(A)	S+sA
S(A)	18	No		S(A)

Note: Expected mean squares are for the balanced cell-frequency case.

Kruskal-Wallis One-Way ANOVA on Ranks—Hypotheses

> Ho: All medians are equal.
> Ha: At least two medians are different.

Test Results

Method	DF	Chi-square (H)	Probability level	Decision (0.05)
Not corrected for ties	1	1.975469	0.159869	Accept Ho
Corrected for ties	1	1.975469	0.159869	Accept Ho
Number sets of ties	0			
Multiplicity factor	0			

Source: Data from IMS Health.

When the finding that prompted this conclusion is examined along-side the median market share differences for the merged and non-merged groupings, the picture we see is this: Holding all else constant, on the average, the long-run effect of mergers and acquisitions has been a loss of market share for the merged group of firms, in turn met by a corresponding gain in market share from the nonmerged group of firms. In the long run, whatever merged firms have lost, non-merged firms have gained.[1] The following suggests a number of possibilities why this may be.

The first and obvious possibility is that some firms may have entered into mergers or acquisitions that were inefficient (for whatever reason) in the first place. Such assessment is, however, only possible ex post facto, since de facto we have no reason to believe that the firms would have merged if they knew this would have been the wrong decision. Second, the evidence supports Dewey's (1961) afore-mentioned description of why mergers and acquisitions take place. Some mergers and acquisitions are entered into by firms for defensive reasons—because their situation would have been worse without them. In this instance the market share of the joint firm that came out of the merger or acquisition may have failed to increase over time but at least the destruction of an otherwise going concern was avoided. Third, it could be that the mergers and acquisitions delivered on their productive efficiency, which although essential for price competition, given that it involves producing a given product in the least-costly way among rivals, may not have been enough in the context of the private sector. Here the rivalry between firms is not on price alone. It also encompasses two other key elements, namely product variety and promotional activity. Thus, having a merger or acquisition produce a single firm that is competitive in the long run on price alone would not count as much as it also being competitive in product variety and promotion. This would seem to be especially true where these things form part and parcel of the vying for market share between firms.

Accordingly, it seems that mergers and acquisitions may have produced firms that are weak in these areas relative to their nonmerged counterparts, in response to which the latter come to succeed in taking market share away from the former.

The fourth and final possibility is that the merger or acquisition delivered the introduction of new products (product variety)[2] for firms versed in productive efficiency, but in a way that made the non-merging rivals, in the long run, better at handling these activities than their merging counterparts. This is not an unlikely outcome. It will be recalled that through information spillover channels the single entity arising out of the merger or acquisition may find itself unable to profitably exploit its knowledge of productive efficiency, product variety, and marketing without conveying hints to others. These are things that are perhaps impossible to conceal, since the dissemination of superior knowledge means that other firms can judge it by its success, whether actual or potential. Consequently, in the long run, on the aggregate, nonmerged firms more than likely will come to take market share away from their merged counterparts.

All told, what we should remember about mergers and acquisitions in the private sector is that they have no bearing on the level of concentration of this sector in the long run, given that they do not conform with the monopoly or collusion view of why they take place. On the contrary, as stated earlier, it appears mergers and acquisitions should not be taken as a sign of restricting competition but as a reflection of its undoubted vigor. In that sense, any public policy that reduces the incidence of mergers has a cost in the sacrifice of efficiency, whether we choose to measure this in technical, product-variety, marketing (promotional), or organizational terms. It would seem on the grounds of this that from an antitrust or similar perspective, attacking or viewing adversely mergers and acquisitions in the private sector of the pharmaceutical industry appears to be misplaced, both in terms of theory and evidence.

THE PUBLIC SECTOR

The results of the one-way ANOVA procedure for the public sector are presented in Exhibit 13.2. If the monopoly or collusion view is to apply here, the same proofs must be established as for the private sector. This can be inferred with reference to the Kruskal-Wallis nonparametric one-way ANOVA section contained in Exhibit 13.2, which is used instead of its parametric counterpart for the same reasons as those referred to in presenting the findings for the private sector. This number is greater than the chosen 5 percent level of significance, in turn meaning that the Ho hypothesis cannot be rejected.

Testing the same hypothesis as that for the private sector, the p-value in the public sector for the not-corrected-for-ties Kruskal-Wallis test is 0.4874. The conclusion that may be drawn from this main result is that in the long run mergers and acquisitions should have no influence on the level of concentration of the public sector in the pharmaceutical industry.

When the finding that prompted this conclusion is interpreted alongside the median market share differences for the merged and nonmerged groupings what emerges is this: holding all else constant, the long-run effect of mergers and acquisitions has been to increase the market share of the merged group of firms and to have this increase matched, on the average, with a corresponding increase in market share by the nonmerged group of firms.

EXHIBIT 13.2.
One-way ANOVA for differences in market share for the period 1989-1999 between merged and nonmerged firms (public sector).

Descriptive Statistics for Market Share Difference

	Mean	Median
Merged	1.09	0.70
Nonmerged	−1.09	0.57

Tests of Assumptions

Assumption	Test value	Probability level	Decision (0.05)
Skewedness normality of residuals	−2.5332	0.011302	Reject
Kurtosis normality of residuals	2.3419	0.019183	Reject
Omnibus normality of residuals	11.9020	0.002603	Reject
Modified-Levene equal-variance test	0.1705	0.684524	Accept

Box Plot Section

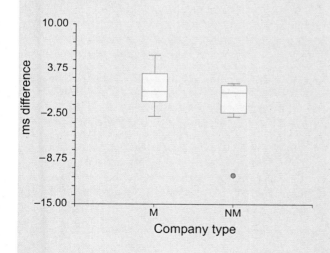

(continued)

(continued)

Expected Mean Squares Section

Source term	DF	Term fixed?	Denominator term	Expected mean square
A: Company type	1	Yes	S(A)	S + sA
S(A)	18	No		S(A)

Note: Expected mean squares are for the balanced cell-frequency case.

Kruskal-Wallis One-Way ANOVA on Ranks—Hypotheses

Ho: All medians are equal.
Ha: At least two medians are different.

Test Results

Method	DF	Chi-square (H)	Probability level	Decision (0.05)
Not corrected for ties	1	0.4821429	0.487453	Accept Ho
Corrected for ties	1	0.4821429	0.487453	Accept Ho
Number sets of ties	0			
Multiplicity factor	0			

Source: Data from IMS Health.

This is than a straightforward proof of our familiar productive efficiency hypothesis.[3] The direct proof of this hypothesis in the context of the public sector is not at all surprising if we are to remind ourselves that competition here is solely on the basis of price, as product variety and promotional activities are not the key means by which firms vie for market share under the sealed-bid tender process.

If mergers and acquisitions do "confer" to the firms that enter into them economies of scale greater than those of their rivals, the evidence shows that these seem on average to be insufficient to make the rivals worse off in the long run.

As a consequence of this, the firm formed from a merger or acquisition does not in the long run experience a significant expansion in its market share in relation to its nonmerging rivals. The latter come to match this increase.

The implication of this finding for the public sector is that (holding all else constant) mergers and acquisitions are crucial if a firm is to produce a given good in the least costly way and if, by reciprocity, this is to allow the sector to benefit from low prices on the tenders it invites.

In examining the merged grouping of firms in the public sector, it was observed that 84 percent of the firms that made it up came from the private sector's merged group of firms. This immediately tells us two things, namely,

1. the explanation for why we get a zero-sum game situation in the private sector resides chiefly with the second and third possibilities furnished in the previous section;
2. it follows that if mergers are defensive in the private sector because of poor pipeline of new products, then merging firms (on the defensive) become even keener to win contracts for the state sector if their existing (old) products are to remain in the business at all.

To summarize, this chapter began by asking whether, if the pharmaceutical industry lacks monopoly power, one should expect mergers and acquisitions to reverse this. According to the findings in this chapter, the answer to this question must be no. They invalidate any presumptions of a relationship between the concentration of the pharmaceutical industry and monopoly power. The evidence before us does not lend itself to suggestions that mergers and acquisitions in the pharmaceutical industry, whether in the private or public sector, produce collective monopoly or similar outcomes. The picture that emerges suggests that mergers and acquisitions in the industry encourage vigorous competition.

Each of these macroeconomic studies looked at the pharmaceutical industry in total. The main message these studies send out is that the pharmaceutical industry is competitive, characterized by intense rivalry at the firm level allied with strong competitive pressure at the product level. In the background of this competitive scene is a free-pricing environment at the manufacturer level, i.e., one void of price controls, particularly on new product introductions, and a strong patent system that seems to grant firms that develop new or breakthrough products a very temporary monopoly. We must, however, acknowledge here that on account of the evidence it seems "monopoly" is just too strong a word.

In order to render our final verdict that what has been observed in this chapter is indeed competition, we now proceed to the microeconomic study of the industry.

Chapter 14

A Microeconomic Inspection of the Industry

A microeconomic study on the industry is aimed at verifying the findings of the two macroeconomic studies previously presented. These studies, broadly speaking, showed two things. One, the pharmaceutical industry is highly competitive, to a degree in excess of perfect competition. This is brought about by innovation. Two, mergers and acquisitions have had no effect on the industry's overall concentration with those firms involved in mergers and acquisitions experiencing no disproportionate increases or decreases in their market share relative to their nonmerging rivals.

All told, the microeconomic study would have to mirror those two broad findings if it is to be in support of the macroeconomic studies that were carried out. To find out if this is the case, we now present the findings of the microeconomic analysis of competition in the pharmaceutical industry. This analysis is broken up into two sections, one dealing with the private and the other with the public sector. We will begin with the private sector and thereafter will focus on the public sector. Before we proceed, we need to remind ourselves of a few things.

Whereas our macroeconomic studies looked at the industry as a whole, it should be recalled from our chapter introducing us to the pharmaceutical industry that in the industry firms compete within therapeutic submarkets, where substitutability of one product for another exists. Cast in economic jargon, we are saying that the cross-elasticity of demand within submarkets is positive.

For both of the sectors an eleven-year study between 1989-1999 was carried out using IMS data. The study for the private sector is confined to the ethical market, i.e., drugs dispensed on prescription, and the study for the public sector is confined to the provincial

doi:10.1300/5505_14

hospital market. In the private sector between 1989 and 1999, a total of 185 comparable therapeutic submarkets were identified at the third level of the anatomical therapeutic classification system, as devised by the World Health Organization. The corresponding figure for the public sector is 166 therapeutic submarkets. Competition in the therapeutic submarkets, whether in the private or public sectors, is examined by looking at these markets' concentration levels over time.

Given that in the pharmaceutical industry product competition affects firm rivalry, it is both the levels of concentration by the firms and their products that are considered in both the private and the public sector. Obtaining the concentration levels of the therapeutic submarkets is accomplished in two ways. One is to study the population, i.e., all the comparable therapeutic submarkets. The alternative is to focus on a sample that would produce results indistinguishable from a study of the population. The latter approach is adopted here.

SAMPLE-SIZE SELECTION

For the sample to produce results identical to the population, it would have to be representative of the population. Some ways this may be achieved include using random, systematic, stratified, or cluster sampling. In each case the sample selected would have to be tested for randomness (i.e., if it is uniformly distributed). The purpose of selecting a random sample is to ensure that no bias occurs in the selection, such as selecting therapeutic submarkets that can prove a given supposition. The way to achieve no bias is to ensure that each therapeutic submarket has an equal chance of being selected from the population of comparable submarkets.

In selecting a sample size four things must be addressed:

1. The size of the effect that the sample size is to detect. As the study looks at changes in concentration over time it was appropriate that the sample size should detect small differences in concentration, as small as 1 percent, since the objective is to pick up changes in the concentrations of therapeutic submarkets (whether increases or decreases) as soon as they take place;

2. The level of significance, α. This indicates the risk one is willing to take of using a sample that picks a difference in concentration

when none actually exists. In this case α was set at 0.10 and 0.20 to examine how this would affect the sample size;
3. The population standard deviation, σ. This refers to the spread of the concentrations encompassing all therapeutic submarkets. It is customary to identify σ from previous studies. The alternative is to use the estimated standard deviation from the sample, but, of course, one cannot draw the sample until one has specified the sample size. Given that no estimates on σ were found in the literature reviewed, two σ's were tried out to investigate their effect on the sample size. The one is three standard deviation units and the other five standard deviation units from the overall (mean) concentration; and
4. The power of the sample size, 1-β. This involves the selection of β, which is the risk one is willing to take of using a sample that picks up no difference in concentration when in fact there is such. By contrast the power of the sample size refers to the probability of the sample to detect differences in concentration that exist. In our case β was chosen at 0.10 and 0.20 to assess how this would affect determining the sample size.

Given that the population standard deviation is not known, the calculation for the sample size is based on the familiar t-distribution using the well-known one-sample (paired) t-test, testing the following two-sided hypothesis:

Ho: No differences in concentrations are detected between 1989 and 1999.

Ha: Differences of 1 percent in concentrations, in either direction, are detected between 1989 and 1999.

The results for this two-sided test are presented in Table 14.1a and Table 14.1b.

Time limitations and practical restrictions lead to sample sizes of forty-four and forty-three therapeutic submarkets being selected for the analyses of rivalry in the private and public sector.

Systematic sampling was used to draw out the submarkets. Here a random start was obtained first, and after that every fourth submarket was sampled until forty-four and forty-three submarkets in each sector were extracted.

TABLE 14.1a. Sample size report for one-sample t-test (Ho: $Mean_0$ = $Mean_1$ versus Ha: $Mean_0 \neq Mean_1$)—private sector.

Power	N	Alpha	Beta	$Mean_0$	$Mean_1$	S	Effect size
0.90410	56	0.10000	0.09590	0.0	1.0	3.0	0.333
0.80170*	44	0.10000	0.19830	0.0	1.0	3.0	0.333
0.90370	46	0.20000	0.09630	0.0	1.0	3.0	0.333
0.80065	34	0.20000	0.19935	0.0	1.0	3.0	0.333
0.90069	100	0.10000	0.09931	0.0	1.0	5.0	0.200
0.80036	85	0.10000	0.19964	0.0	1.0	5.0	0.200
0.90277	88	0.20000	0.09723	0.0	1.0	5.0	0.200
0.80338	71	0.20000	0.19662	0.0	1.0	5.0	0.200
0.90397	19	0.10000	0.09603	0.0	2.0	3.0	0.667
0.81992	15	0.10000	0.18008	0.0	2.0	3.0	0.667
0.90834	15	0.20000	0.09166	0.0	2.0	3.0	0.667
0.81655	11	0.20000	0.18345	0.0	2.0	3.0	0.667
0.90325	43	0.10000	0.09675	0.0	2.0	5.0	0.400
0.81147	34	0.10000	0.18853	0.0	2.0	5.0	0.400
0.90569	35	0.20000	0.09431	0.0	2.0	5.0	0.400
0.81135	26	0.20000	0.18865	0.0	2.0	5.0	0.400

Source: Data from IMS Health.
Note: *refers to the power of the selected sample size.
Randomness test for selected sample size:

(a) Private sector: χ^2 = 1.0000 with df = 9, p-value = 0.999438
(b) Public sector: χ^2 = 0.7209 with df = 7, p-value = 0.998170

$\alpha = 0.05$.
Unknown standard deviation (S). $N = 185$.

It may be argued that each sector's sample size is small. It should nevertheless be noted that the findings to emerge from each sample would be no different if all comparable submarkets were considered. This is so for four reasons.

First, as the histograms of the systematic samples and the corresponding uniform probability plots in Figure 14.1 and Figure 14.2 reveal, each sector's sample is representative of the population. That is

TABLE 14.1b. Sample size report for one-sample t-test (Ho: $Mean_0$ = $Mean_1$ versus Ha: $Mean_0 \neq Mean_1$)—public sector.

Power	N	Alpha	Beta	$Mean_0$	$Mean_1$	S	Effect size
0.90300	54	0.10000	0.09700	0.0	1.0	3.0	0.333
0.80324*	43	0.10000	0.19676	0.0	1.0	3.0	0.333
0.90543	45	0.20000	0.09457	0.0	1.0	3.0	0.333
0.80833	34	0.20000	0.19167	0.0	1.0	3.0	0.333
0.90563	95	0.10000	0.09437	0.0	1.0	5.0	0.200
0.80214	81	0.10000	0.19786	0.0	1.0	5.0	0.200
0.90019	83	0.20000	0.09981	0.0	1.0	5.0	0.200
0.80313	68	0.20000	0.19687	0.0	1.0	5.0	0.200
0.90724	19	0.10000	0.09276	0.0	2.0	3.0	0.667
0.82331	15	0.10000	0.17669	0.0	2.0	3.0	0.667
0.91051	15	0.20000	0.08949	0.0	2.0	3.0	0.667
0.81864	11	0.20000	0.18136	0.0	2.0	3.0	0.667
0.90396	42	0.10000	0.09604	0.0	2.0	5.0	0.400
0.80715	33	0.10000	0.19285	0.0	2.0	5.0	0.400
0.90343	34	0.20000	0.09657	0.0	2.0	5.0	0.400
0.80289	25	0.20000	0.19711	0.0	2.0	5.0	0.400

Source: Data from IMS Health.
Note: *refers to the power of the selected sample size.
Randomness test for selected sample size:

(a) Private Sector: χ^2 = 1.0000 with df = 9, p-value = 0.999438
(b) Public Sector: χ^2 = 0.7209 with df = 7, p-value = 0.998170

α = 0.05.
Unknown standard deviation (S). N = 166.

simply to say that it comes from a uniform distribution. Aside from the visual confirmation, a formal confirmation of this is also provided by each sample's test of randomness. For either of the samples, the p-value of this test is 0.99 (refer to Table 14.1), which is above the chosen 5 percent level of significance, confirming that the samples are random (i.e., coming from a uniform distribution).

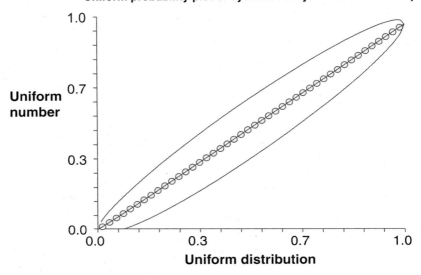

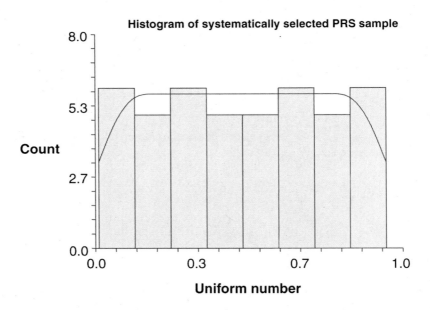

FIGURE 14.1. Probability and histogram plot for private sector (PRS) sample.

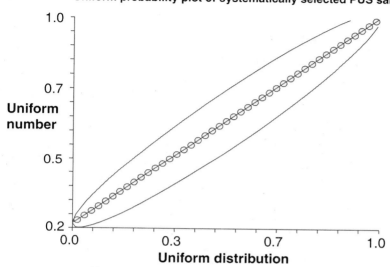

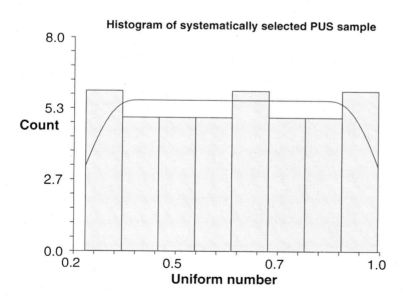

FIGURE 14.2. Probability and histogram plot for public sector (PUS) sample.

Second, each sample carries a 10 percent chance of wrongly picking differences in concentration when such do not actually exist. Third, each sample has an 80 percent chance of detecting differences in concentration if such exist. Fourth, the chosen sample sizes are sensitive to picking differences in concentrations. The smallest effect size or difference (i.e., increase or decrease) in concentrations that each sample would pick up is 0.33 percent.

Once the submarkets were drawn out, their concentration at the firm and product level was computed using the four-firm concentration ratio—CR4, the Herfindahl-Hirschman index—HHI, and the Horvath index—HI. The HHI and HI indices were computed in their normal (not modified) way. Predominant use is made of the HI index, given it is a combined measure of absolute and relative concentration. In the computation of the indices, merged firms were counted as one (i.e., their market share were summed to get the market share for the merged firm) and acquired firms were treated the same way (i.e., their market share was added to the acquirer). In the case of the firms' products, products belonging to firms that had formed a union had their market shares summed. Products that were offered by only one firm also had their market shares summed.

It is of much interest at this time that we learn what the results for each sector reveal. We begin with the private sector.

THE PRIVATE MARKET

In the private market of the top twenty firms in 1999, 70 percent were around in 1989. This, however, conceals the level of rivalry taking place in the market. The eleven-year study in Table 14.2 shows that very few companies have retained their original ranking in the top twenty.

Rank Changes

As an indicator of the level of entry in the marketplace the second top company in 1999 was ranked fifth in 1989, the thirteenth top company in 1999 was ranked twenty-fifth in 1989, the second-ranked firm in 1989 had fallen to eighth by 1999, and so on. In the pharmaceutical industry the top is a very slippery place. The reason is innovation. New products are continuously introduced and if any firm

TABLE 14.2. Rankings of firms by revenue—private sector.

Company	1999 ranking	1989 ranking	1999 market share	1989 market share
A	1	1	9.77	9.02
B	2	5	7.39	6.22
C	3	3	6.48	7.77
D	4	4	5.86	6.56
E	5	7	5.11	4.83
F	6	6	4.94	5.06
G	7	9	4.47	4.24
H	8	2	4.38	7.80
I	9	8	4.08	4.36
J	10	11	2.92	3.35
K	11	13	2.88	2.86
L	12	14	2.86	1.94
M	13	25	2.84	2.20
N	14	12	2.60	2.96
O	15	10	2.48	3.90
P	16	27	2.25	1.26
Q	17	24	1.52	1.35
R	18	23	1.40	1.37
S	19	33	1.38	1.06
T	20	42	1.36	0.85

Source: Data from IMS Health.

wishes to hold a leadership position or outperform its rivals it must innovate. Of the top twenty products in 1989, 40 percent were no longer available in 1999 and only 25 percent had kept their top-twenty status by 1999, as shown by Table 14.3.

In a period of eleven years only five products in the top twenty in 1989 were still in the top twenty in 1999. These are A, C, D, J, and Q. Superior new products had overtaken all the others, which were either no longer offered or their commercial positions had plunged. The 2nd ranked product in 1989 had fallen to 99th in 1999, the 8th ranked

TABLE 14.3. Rankings of products by revenue—private sector.

Product	1989 ranking	1999 ranking	1989 market share
A	1	2	1.74
B	2	99	1.47
C	3	12	1.41
D	4	5	1.35
E	5	32	1.12
F	6	85	1.01
G	7	–	1.00
H	8	185	0.92
I	9	27	0.88
J	10	4	0.83
K	11	–	0.77
L	12	–	0.73
M	13	196	0.71
N	14	–	0.63
O	15	42	0.62
P	16	–	0.61
Q	17	7	0.60
R	18	–	0.59
S	19	–	0.58
T	20	–	0.57

Source: Data from IMS Health.

product in 1989 had fallen to 185th in 1999, the 10th ranked product in 1989 had risen to 4th in 1999, and so on.

The product and firm-ranking tables show how innovation is crucial to competition. No firm can rest on its laurels content with a market lead. It takes a relatively short period of time for a product to gain or lose a position in the market. An inspection of the absolute changes in rank of the top four performers at the firm and product levels across the (sampled) therapeutic submarkets reveals a similar but more detailed picture of rivalry, as shown in Table 14.4.

TABLE 14.4. Absolute changes in rank by first four firms, private sector (percent of therapeutic submarkets), shift in rank from 1989.

Top 4 firms in 1999	np	ns	rs_1	rs_2	rs_3	rsm_3	Total
A	21.4	40.5	21.4	9.5	0.0	7.1	100.0
B	43.6	12.8	23.1	15.4	0.0	5.1	100.0
C	38.7	16.1	16.1	12.9	3.2	12.9	100.0
D	44.8	13.8	13.8	10.3	13.8	3.4	100.0
Total	36.2	22.0	19.1	12.1	3.5	7.1	100.0

Source: Data from IMS Health.
np = Not previously present in a therapeutic market.
ns = No shift in rank.
rs_1 = Shift in rank by one position.
rs_2 = Shift in rank by two positions.
rs_3 = Shift in rank by three positions.
rsm_3 = Shift in rank by more than three positions.

In Table 14.4, the absolute shift in rank of the top four firms in 1999 was examined compared to their positions in 1989. A firm not present in a submarket relative to 1999 was cited as not being previously present in the submarket. This gives us a measure of entry into new markets. In most therapeutic submarkets, their top four firms in 1999 were not around a decade earlier. The evidence shows that on the average 36 percent of therapeutic submarkets did not have their top four firms occupy these positions eleven years earlier. As for the remainder, none of the top four firms experienced a change in rank over the course of eleven years in 22 percent of the submarkets. Over the same period of time, 19 percent of therapeutic submarkets had their present top four firms change rank by one position, and 12, 3.5, and 7 percent of therapeutic submarkets had their present top four firms change rank by two, three, and more than three positions, respectively. From all the submarkets examined, the first-ranked firm did not exist eleven years earlier in 21 percent of the cases, and over the same period of time this firm experienced no change in rank in 41 percent of them. It was, however, displaced by one and two ranks in 21 percent and 10 percent of submarkets, respectively, and by more than three ranks in 7 percent of them. As one moves down Table 14.4, one notes an opposite pattern in the ranking distribution of the second, third, and fourth-ranked firms. For instance, from all the submarkets examined, the second-ranked firm did not exist eleven years earlier in 44 percent of them and over the same period of time it experienced no change in rank in 13 percent of them. It was, however, displaced by one and two ranks in 23 percent and 15 percent of submarkets, respectively, and by more than three ranks in 5 percent of them.

Even though only the top four firms are examined here, market power, which here is measured by the frequency of entry and the ability to retain the first rank or be one or two away from it, differs for each firm. The evidence shows that beginning as early as the top four positions in a market, a clear division is discernible between leaders (the first-ranked firm) and followers (the firms below it). The former display a more stable market position relative to the latter. Overall this points to two things. First, replacing the first-ranked firm in a market is not as regular or as easy as replacing the ones in the remaining ranks. Second, as one goes down the ranks, the volatility in market position increases. This indicates that the ranks of firms are in a transitory state, implying that competition is at work, and in turn that the ability of a firm to provide unique products determines how stable its market position is. The absolute shift in rank within the sampled therapeutic sub-markets of the top four products in 1989 compared to their positions in 1999 exhibits a similar pattern as that for the firms, as shown in Table 14.5.

The results in Table 14.5 show that on the average the top four products in 29 percent of therapeutic submarkets no longer existed eleven years later. Over the course of the same time, none of the initial top four products experienced a change in rank in 19 percent of submarkets over the course of eleven years. As for the rest of the submarkets, 23 percent saw changes in the rank of their top four products by one position, while 10, 4.5, and 14 percent had rank changes of two, three, and more than three positions, respectively. From all the submarkets examined, the first-ranked product was not around eleven years later in 26 percent of the cases, and in the same period it experienced no change in rank in 38 percent of the cases. It was, however, displaced by one, two, and more than three ranks in 26, 2, and 7 percent of submarkets, respectively. As one moves down Table 14.5, one notes an opposite pattern in the ranking distribution of the second-, third-, and fourth-ranked product. For instance, from all the submarkets examined the second-ranked product did not exist eleven years later in 29 percent of the cases, and in the same period it experienced

TABLE 14.5. Absolute changes in rank by first four products, private sector (percent of therapeutic submarkets), shift in rank by 1999.

Top 4 products in 1989	np	ns	rs_1	rs_2	rs_3	rsm_3	Total
A	26.2	38.1	26.2	2.4	0.0	7.1	100.0
B	29.3	19.5	24.4	12.2	2.4	12.2	100.0
C	36.8	7.9	21.1	13.2	7.9	13.2	100.0
D	23.5	5.9	20.6	14.7	8.8	26.5	100.0
Total	29.0	18.7	23.2	10.3	4.5	14.2	100.0

Source: Data from IMS Health.
np = Not previously present in a therapeutic market.
ns = No shift in rank.
rs_1 = Shift in rank by one position.
rs_2 = Shift in rank by two positions.
rs_3 = Shift in rank by three positions.
rsm_3 = Shift in rank by more than three positions.

no change of rank in 19 percent of the cases. It was, however, displaced by one, two, three, and more than three ranks in 24, 12, 2, and 12 percent of submarkets, respectively.

The rank shifts for the products interpreted in conjunction with the rank shifts for the firms indicate that a firm that has worked its way to the top position in a market would be in a lesser state of flux compared to its rivals because of its ability to provide unique offers that gain market lead relative to rivals. As one goes down the ranks, fewer firms are able to make such offers. In such instances, products become easier to reproduce, making their positions and those of the firms who make them less stable. In general, there are few therapeutic sub-markets in the private sector with few products or firms.

In 1999, 66 percent of therapeutic submarkets carried five but less than forty products, whereas 34 percent carried at most four products, with little change occuring in these proportions in 1989 (Table 14.6).

Similarly, in the same year, 67 percent of therapeutic submarkets carried five but less than forty firms and 37 percent carried at most four firms, with little change occuring in these proportions in 1989 (Table 14.7).

According to the CR4 index, only 20 percent of therapeutic submarkets in 1999 had low-to-moderate firm-concentration levels (Table 14.8).

TABLE 14.6. Classification of therapeutic markets at the firm level by number of firms (percent of therapeutic submarkets).

Number of firms in therapeutic markets	Private sector	
	1989	1999
At most four firms	28.6	33.3
Five but less than forty firms	71.4	66.7

Source: Data from IMS Health.

TABLE 14.7. Classification of therapeutic markets at the firm level by number of firms (percent of therapeutic submarkets).

Number of products in therapeutic markets	Private sector	
	1989	1999
At most four products	29.3	34.2
Five but less than forty products	70.7	65.8

Source: Data from IMS Health.

Therapeutic Submarket Concentration

The CR4 measure in Table 14.8 indicates that the majority of submarkets contain dominant firms. The HHI and HI reveal that in 1999, 74 percent and 60 percent of therapeutic submarkets, respectively, had low-to-moderate firm-concentration levels, indicating that the disproportionate allocation of market share between dominant and follower firms is not severe. A breakdown of the CR4 by the number of firms therapeutic submarkets have shows this measure is pooled toward reflecting the concentrations prevalent in the submarkets with few firms (Table 14.9). This suggests the CR4 is not a reliable informant of rivalry.

Whereas for the submarkets with few firms, the CR4 at the firm level resides in the high concentration bands, for the markets with many firms it shows that 32 percent of them have low-to-moderate firm-concentration levels, 18 percent have moderate-to-high firm-

TABLE 14.8. Classification of therapeutic submarkets at the firm level by concentration (percent of therapeutic markets).

| | Private sector | | | | | |
| | CR4 | | HHI | | HI | |
Interval	1989	1999	1989	1999	1989	1999
0.00 to 0.10		2.38	4.76	9.52		
0.10 to 0.20			14.29	9.52		
0.20 to 0.30			9.52	16.67	2.38	7.14
0.30 to 0.40			19.05	11.90	4.76	7.14
0.40 to 0.50		2.38	21.43	9.52	11.90	4.76
0.50 to 0.60	4.76	7.14	11.90	11.90	7.14	14.29
0.60 to 0.70	7.14	4.76	2.38	4.76	23.81	11.90
0.70 to 0.80	4.76	4.76	2.38	9.52	23.81	14.29
0.80 to 0.90	14.29	11.90		4.76	11.90	21.43
0.90 to 1.00	69.05	66.67	14.29	11.90	14.29	19.05
Total	100.00	100.00	100.00	100.00	100.00	100.00

Source: Data from IMS Health.
Multinomial test of HI:

(a) 1989: $\chi^2 = 15.1429$ with df = 7, p-value = 0.034211.
(b) 1999: $\chi^2 = 8.2857$ with df = 7, p-value = 0.308075.

$\alpha = 0.05$.

concentration levels, and the remainder have firm-concentration levels that fall in the high concentration bands. However, a look at the HI index shows that in the submarkets with few firms 7 percent have firm-concentration levels falling in the moderate concentration bands, 43 percent have firm-concentration levels ranging from moderate to high, and the remainder fall in the high concentration bands. This suggests that in the submarkets with few firms competition is taking place amongst equally large rivals, with no pronounced dominance between the firms in half of the instances. The CR4 does not reveal this. By the same token it does not reveal that lack of dominance is a characteristic in the submarkets with many firms.

TABLE 14.9. Firm concentration of therapeutic submarkets in the private sector broken down by number of firms (percent of therapeutic markets in 1999).

Interval	Therapeutic submarkets with at most four firms		Therapeutic submarkets with five but less than forty firms	
	CR4	HI	CR4	HI
0.00 to 0.10			3.57	
0.10 to 0.20				
0.20 to 0.30				10.71
0.30 to 0.40				10.71
0.40 to 0.50			3.57	7.14
0.50 to 0.60			10.71	21.43
0.60 to 0.70			7.14	17.86
0.70 to 0.80		7.14	7.14	17.86
0.80 to 0.90		42.86	17.86	10.71
0.90 to 1.00	100.00	50.00	50.00	3.57
Total	100.00	100.00	100.00	100.00

Source: Data from IMS Health.

The HI index for these submarkets shows that combined, 86 percent of them have firm concentration in the low-to-moderate and moderate-to-high levels, with 14 percent of them having firm concentration residing in the high concentration levels. In short, whereas the CR4 suggests that in general submarkets are monopolistic, the HI or HHI reveal they are oligopolistic. The evidence shows dominant firms whose market share is not substantially larger compared to that of follower firms. This conforms to our discussion of the private sector contained in Chapter 11. Contrasting the HI concentration levels in 1999 against 1989 shows us that with time the tendency has been for the firm concentrations of therapeutic submarkets to fall in the low-to-moderate and moderate concentration bands. Around 48 percent of therapeutic submarkets in 1989 resided in low-to-moderate concentration levels with the corresponding figure for the same levels in 1999 being 26 percent (Table 14.8). In addition, in 1999 the combined proportion of submarkets with firm concentrations in the low and low-to-moderate concentration bands increased by 7.1 percent from 1989. Over the same period of time, the combined proportion of therapeutic submarkets falling in the moderate-to-high and high concentration bands increased by 14.3 percent. What all these changes in concentration indicate is that all therapeutic submarkets were in a transitory state in terms of the market share changes firms underwent.

Some therapeutic markets converted to high concentration levels and others to low concentration levels, signaling that markets are working in accordance with the competitive process. Markets where rivals came to make homogeneous offers moved toward atomistic competition. By contrast, markets in which product heterogeneity between rivals increased moved toward oligopolistic competition or monopoly. The product concentration figures confirm this (Table 14.10).

The transitory nature of the markets at the firm level is echoed by the concentrations of the submarkets at the product level. Whereas

TABLE 14.10. Classification of therapeutic submarkets at the product level by concentration (percent of therapeutic markets)—private sector.

	CR4		HHI		HI	
Interval	1989	1999	1989	1999	1989	1999
0.00 to 0.10			2.44	7.32		
0.10 to 0.20			21.95	9.76		
0.20 to 0.30			14.63	19.51	2.44	7.32
0.30 to 0.40			19.51	4.88	9.76	7.32
0.40 to 0.50	2.44	4.88	12.20	17.07	14.63	2.44
0.50 to 0.60		2.44	7.32	12.20	9.76	19.51
0.60 to 0.70	12.20	4.88	4.88	4.88	26.83	7.32
0.70 to 0.80	9.76	14.63	7.32	9.76	9.76	14.63
0.80 to 0.90	17.07	17.07		2.44	17.07	24.39
0.90 to 1.00	58.54	56.10	9.76	12.20	9.76	17.07
Total	100.00	100.00	100.00	100.00	100.00	100.00

Source: Data from IMS Health.
Multinomial test of HI:

(a) 1989: $\chi^2 = 11.8780$ with df = 7, p-value = 0.104641.
(b) 1999: $\chi^2 = 13.0488$ with df = 7, p-value = 0.070929.

$\alpha = 0.05$.

the proportion of markets with HI product concentration in the moderate concentration bands was 36.6 percent in 1989, by 1999 this proportion had gone down to 21.9 percent. However, whereas the proportion of markets with HI product concentrations falling in the high concentration bands was 26.8 percent in 1989, by 1999 this proportion had gone up to 41 percent. By contrast to these proportions, the combined proportion of markets with HI product concentration in the low and low-to-moderate concentration levels remained unchanged. This suggests that over time product homogeneity has existed in these markets, in contrast to the markets having moderate and high concentrations. The latter two appear to have experienced a decline in product homogeneity, which that has resulted in these markets experiencing increases in concentration.

The submarkets concentration at the product level moves hand in hand with that at the firm level. Increases in the product concentrations of markets sparked by rivalry in product variety between competitors have been met with increases in the firm concentrations of the markets to reflect the ability of the dominant firms to provide unique offers relative to their competitors.

For the markets where product homogeneity has been constant, i.e., no firm has come up with an offer that differs from that of competitors, their product-concentration levels have undergone little or no change. Conversely, these markets have been experiencing decreases in firm concentration, given that because of product homogeneity no firm can gain market lead and whatever advantage in market share exists gets eroded.

The evidence shows that by 1999, the markets at the firm level appear to have reached a transitory equilibrium, i.e., an equilibrium in transition (Table 14.8). Whereas in 1989 the proportions of submarkets at the firm level were not equal across concentration levels, in 1999 the opposite held true. This can be deduced from inspection of the p-value of the multinomial test (for equality in the proportions), which for 1989 was below the chosen level of significance and for 1999 was above it. However, the proportions of the submarkets at the product level stayed equal across concentration levels in both 1999 and 1989 (Table 14.10). This suggests that the observed shifts in the market-concentration levels were prompted at the firm level first, indicating or confirming that product competition is a by-product of firm rivalry. In essence, therapeutic market concentration defined by products would mirror that defined by firms. Firm rivalry in the quest for the introduction of new offers to meet market demand would encourage innovation and R&D. The firms able to meet demand for the new offer earlier than others would become leaders, thereby concentrating the markets at the firm and product levels in their favor. Where the firms, over time, make similar offers, for instance, as in the case of minor therapeutic improvements, two things would take place. One is an increase in the proportion of markets at the firm level, with concentrations falling in the low and low-to-moderate concentration bands. The other is little or no change at the product level in the proportion of markets with concentrations residing in the low and low-to-moderate concentration bands.

To crystallize our discussion of rivalry thus far, we now inspect the (Pearson) correlations between the concentration indices at the firm and product levels (Table 14.11 and Table 14.12). Doing so is warranted by the correlations being statistically significant, keeping in line with economic expectations—as becomes clear from the appraisals that follow—to an interconnectivity between them impelled by a nonequilibrating rivalry at the product level.

In 1999 the CR4 was moderately correlated ($r = 0.69$) with the HI (Table 14.11). Note that the almost perfect correlation ($r = 0.94$) between the HHI and HI should be expected given the HI harbors the HHI in its formulation. The correlation demonstrates that the HI

TABLE 14.11. Pearson correlations and respective p-values for therapeutic markets at the firm level—private sector.

Concentration indices	1999		1989	
	HHI	HI	HHI	HI
CR4	0.602589	0.687408	0.673481	0.864530
	(0.000024)[a]	(0.000000)[a]	(0.000001)[a]	(0.000000)[a]
HHI		0.941024		0.937783
		(0.000000)[a]		(0.000000)[a]
Crombach's alpha	0.889561		0.893945	

Source: Data from IMS Health.
[a]Correlations significant at the 5 percent level of significance for the null hypothesis of no connection in the concentration indices.

TABLE 14.12. Pearson correlations and respective p-values for therapeutic markets at the product level—private sector.

Concentration indices	1999		1989	
	HHI	HI	HHI	HI
CR4	0.797599	0.940502	0.726122	0.890645
	(0.000000)[a]	(0.000000)[a]	(0.000000)[a]	(0.000000)[a]
HHI		0.942563		0.949409
		(0.000000)[a]		(0.000000)[a]
Cronbach's alpha	0.931945		0.915130	

Source: Data from IMS Health.
[a]Correlations significant at the 5 percent level of significance for the null hypothesis of no connection in the concentration indices.

differs little from the HHI and points to both indices giving similar groupings of therapeutic submarkets according to concentration.

In so far as the previously mentioned moderate correlation (of $r = 0.69$) is concerned, its size suggests that a moderate disposition exists on the part of the competitive process to have, in a given market, the top four firms assume a somewhat larger market share than their rivals. What this in turn seems to imply is that, in general, dominant firms do have a greater market share relative to their follower counterparts, but not so great as to grant them long-lasting market power. This is what the decline in the CR4-HI correlation (from $r = 0.86$ to $r = 0.69$) between 1989 and 1999 (in Table 14.11) reflects.

How the discrepancy in market share between dominant and follower firms may have arisen appears in toto to be the outcome of product competition. A near perfect correlation (for instance, $r = 0.94$ in 1999) at the product level exists between the CR4 and HI, indicating that product markets are almost exclusively dominated by the top four selling offers (Table 14.12). This result is complementary to the Grabowski and Vernon (1994) finding presented earlier, namely that firms rely on few successful products for their sales.

The size of the correlation coefficient between the CR4 and the HI is greater at the product than at the firm level, indicating that product markets have a more severe disproportionate allocation of market share than their firm counterparts do. This merely reflects that a difference between products makes a firm a leader or a follower. The evidence shows that gaining high ranking at the firm level goes hand in hand with the ability to have dominant product sellers, and this requires providing mostly new offers or offering existing ones at prices rivals find hard to match. The values for Cronbach's alpha (0.89 for firms—Table 14.11; and 0.93 for products—Table 14.12) show that however many other random samples of comparable therapeutic markets are selected each time, the same correlations as those observed here would be found. Thus, the correlations obtained from the present sample are the same as the ones that would have been obtained if all comparable therapeutic submarkets were considered. The values for Cronbach's alpha also verify that the concentrations from the chosen sample are no different from the ones to be extracted if the population as a whole were to be considered.

It may be argued that the correlations between the CR4 and the HI at the firm and product levels are consistent with the hypotheses falling under the rubric of monopolization, i.e., cartelization or mergers and acquisitions. All things equal, if any of these held, we should have observed most therapeutic markets to fall and persistently occupy the moderate-to-high and high concentration domains. The results contained in Tables 14.8 and 14.10 do not show this to be the case. The evidence suggests that the number of firms has little or no effect on market concentration and that markets that become concentrated do so because of noncollusive considerations. Specifically, the evidence suggests that markets with higher concentration come to acquire their status through dominant firms, which gather greater market share relative to rivals if they are able to innovate and engage in superior productive efficiency. This is a plausible explanation given that it refers to the private sector, a market which over the period of the study has seen the manufacturers of new products having their property rights over these products recognized and protected, as well as an absence of price controls.

Intense vying for market share is taking place at the firm and product levels of the private sector. Let us now see what the picture for the public sector is.

THE PUBLIC SECTOR MARKET

In the public sector 80 percent of the top twenty firms in 1999 were in business in 1989. This, however, conceals the level of rivalry taking place in the sector. The eleven-year study in Table 14.13 shows that very few companies retain their original ranking in the top twenty.

TABLE 14.13. Rankings of firms by revenue—public sector.

Company	1999 ranking	1989 ranking	1999 market share	1989 market share
A	1	3	11.21	5.52
B	2	7	8.20	4.56
C	3	12	8.17	3.02
D	4	8	5.97	4.51
E	5	6	5.64	4.76
F	6	9	4.92	3.81
G	7	1	4.77	15.73
H	8	2	4.51	5.85
I	9	10	3.95	3.57
J	10	11	3.66	3.27
K	11	14	3.21	2.69
L	12	4	2.62	5.47
M	13	58	2.09	0.30
N	14	13	1.99	2.73
O	15	5	1.94	4.77
P	16	43	1.74	0.72
Q	17	16	1.70	2.30
R	18	99	1.69	0.01
S	19	15	1.66	2.45
T	20	36	1.65	0.90

Source: Data from IMS Health.

Rank Changes

As an indicator of the level of entry in the marketplace, the second-ranked company in 1999 was ranked seventh in 1989, the thirteenth-ranked company in 1999 was ranked fifty-eighth in 1989, the second-ranked firm in 1989 had fallen to eighth by 1999, and so on. In the public, as in the private market, the top is a very slippery place. As Table 14.14 shows, in eleven years only four products in the top twenty in 1989 were still in the top twenty in 1999.

TABLE 14.14. Rankings of products by revenue—public sector.

Product	1989 ranking	1999 ranking	1989 market share
A	1	–	2.54
B	2	140	2.23
C	3	–	1.97
D	4	63	1.90
E	5	6	1.83
F	6	37	1.66
G	7	9	1.41
H	8	4	1.37
I	9	–	1.26
J	10	–	1.17
K	11	–	1.01
L	12	33	1.00
M	13	1	0.99
N	14	166	0.98
O	15	–	0.96
P	16	–	0.92
Q	17	124	0.88
R	18	–	0.85
S	19	–	0.84
T	20	115	0.83

Source: Data from IMS Health.

These four products are E, G, H, and M. New products had overtaken all the others, which were either no longer offered or plummeted in position. For instance, the 2nd ranked product in 1989 had fallen to 140th in 1999, the 14th ranked product in 1989 had fallen to 166th in 1999, the 8th ranked product in 1989 had risen to 4th in 1999, and so on.

Just as in the private sector, in the public sector no firm can rest on its laurels, content with a market lead, and it takes a relatively short period of time for a product to gain or lose a position in the market. Tables 14.13 and 14.14 in contrast to their counterparts for the private sector, demonstrate the additional level of risk involved in selling to government on the tender system—where the winner of a tender "takes all."

An inspection of the absolute changes in rank of the top four performers at the firm and product levels across the (sampled) therapeutic submarkets reveals a similar but more detailed picture of rivalry. In the case of firms (Table 14.15), the absolute shift in rank of the top four firms in 1999 was examined and compared to their positions in 1989.

A firm not present in a submarket relative to 1999 was cited as not being previously present in the submarket. This gives us a measure of entry into new markets. On the average, the top four firms were not around in 50 percent of therapeutic submarkets eleven years ago. In

TABLE 14.15. Absolute changes in rank by first four firms, public sector (percent of therapeutic submarkets), shift in rank from 1989.

Top 4 firms in 1999	np	ns	rs_1	rs_2	rs_3	rsm_3	Total
A	39.0	31.7	24.4	0.0	0.0	4.9	100.0
B	60.0	17.1	17.1	0.0	5.7	0.0	100.0
C	44.8	13.8	24.1	17.2	0.0	0.0	100.0
D	58.3	4.2	20.8	4.2	12.5	0.0	100.0
Total	49.6	18.6	21.7	4.7	3.9	1.6	100.0

Source: Data from IMS Health.
np = Not previously present in a therapeutic market.
ns = No shift in rank.
rs_1 = Shift in rank by one position.
rs_2 = Shift in rank by two positions.
rs_3 = Shift in rank by three positions.
rsm_3 = Shift in rank by more than three positions.

19 percent of markets, none of the present top four firms experienced a change in rank over the course of eleven years. In the same span of time, 22 percent of therapeutic submarkets experienced rank changes of their top four firms by one position, while 5, 4, and 1.6 percent of therapeutic submarkets had their top four firms change rank by two, three, and more than three positions, respectively.

From all the submarkets examined, the first-ranked firm was not in business eleven years ago in 39 percent of them, and over the same period of time it experienced no change in rank in 32 percent of them. However, the first-ranked firm was displaced by one and more than three ranks in 24 percent and 5 percent of submarkets, respectively. In the public sector the first-ranked firm has a higher chance of losing its position than does its counterpart in the private sector. This can be attributed to the tender system, where firms must bid annually for the right to supply a given market at the lowest price. In the private sector a firm also has to meet demand constantly, but a failure to meet it at a lower price than rivals need not summarily dismiss it from the market.

As one moves down Table 14.15, one notes an opposite pattern in the ranking distribution of the second-, third-, and fourth-ranked firms. For instance, from all the submarkets examined, the second-ranked firm was not in business eleven years ago in 60 percent of them, and over the same period of time it experienced no change in rank in 17 percent of them. It was, however, displaced by one and three ranks in 17 percent and close to 6 percent of submarkets, respectively.

Even though only the top four firms are looked at, market power, which in this case is measured by the frequency of entry and the ability to retain the first rank or be one or two ranks away from it, differs for each firm. The evidence shows that as early as the top four positions in a market a clear division shows between leaders (the first-ranked firm) and followers (the firms below it). The former displays a more stable market position by contrast to followers.

Because of the tender system, in which contracts are awarded for a specific period of time and companies have to bid against each other each time, when a tender is issued, any of the top four firms in the public market has a higher probability relative to its private-market counterpart of not having been in a given submarket before. This merely reflects the harshness of selling on a tender, where a firm either supplies a submarket or does not. If the tender is lost the firm must settle with reapplying next time. The evidence in the public sector indicates that replacing the first-ranked firm in a market is not as regular or as easy as replacing the ones in the remaining ranks and that volatility in market position increases with a decrease in ranking. These findings show that the ranks of firms are in a transitory state, indicating, just as in the private sector, that the competitive process is at work. The absolute shift in rank, within the sampled therapeutic submarkets, of the top four products in 1989 compared to their positions in 1999 exhibits a similar pattern to the one for the firms (Table 14.16).

On the average, 33 percent of therapeutic submarkets did not have their initial top four products around eleven years later. In 18 percent of those, none experienced a change in rank over this period of time either. As for the remaining markets, in the same span of time, 23 percent of them had their initial top four products change rank by one position, while 14, 5, and 7.7 percent of them had their top four products change rank by two, three, and more than three positions, respectively. From all the submarkets examined, the first-ranked product did not exist eleven years later in 37 percent of them, and in the same period of time it experienced no change in rank in 34 percent of them. It was, however, displaced by one, two, three, and more than three

TABLE 14.16. Absolute changes in rank by first four products, public sector (percent of therapeutic submarkets), shift in rank by 1999.

Top 4 products in 1989	np	ns	rs_1	rs_2	rs_3	rsm_3	Total
A	36.6	34.1	17.1	4.9	2.4	4.9	100.0
B	28.1	15.6	37.5	9.4	3.1	6.3	100.0
C	33.3	8.3	12.5	29.2	8.3	8.3	100.0
D	30.0	0.0	25.0	20.0	10.0	15.0	100.0
Total	32.5	17.9	23.1	13.7	5.1	7.7	100.0

Source: Data from IMS Health.
np = Not previously present in a therapeutic market.
ns = No shift in rank.
rs_1 = Shift in rank by one position.
rs_2 = Shift in rank by two positions.
rs_3 = Shift in rank by three positions.
rsm_3 = Shift in rank by more than three positions.

ranks in 17, 5, 2.4, and 5 percent of submarkets, respectively. As one moves down Table 14.16 one notes an opposite pattern in the ranking distribution of the second-, third-, and fourth-ranked products. For instance, from all the submarkets examined the second-ranked product did not exist eleven years later in 28 percent of them, and in the same period of time it experienced no change in rank in 16 percent of them. It was, however, displaced by one, two, three, and more than three ranks in 38, 9, 3, and 6 percent of submarkets, respectively.

The rank shifts for the products interpreted in conjunction with the rank shifts for the firms indicate that a firm that has worked its way to the top position in a market would be in a lesser state of flux compared to its rivals. In the public sector, this is tied to the ability of the top firm to make available offers whose price advantages are difficult to topple by rivals. As one goes down the ranks, fewer firms are able to make such offers. In such instances, firms have built short-lasting production-cost advantages, making their market positions and those of the products they make less stable. In general, a higher proportion of therapeutic submarkets is in the public relative to the private sector operating with few firms.

In 1999, 51 percent of therapeutic submarkets carried five but less than forty firms and 49 percent of submarkets carried at most four firms—a proportion that was 12 percent higher in 1989 (Table 14.17). This indicates that by 1999 more instances occurred in which more than one supplier was used to deliver on a tender. This points to the submarkets in the public sector becoming less monopolistic or increasingly more oligopolistic.

The increase of oligopolistic markets in the public sector is also reflected by the categorization of submarkets according to their number of products (Table 14.18). In 1999, 54 percent of therapeutic submarkets carried five but less than forty products and 46 percent carried at most four products, whereas the corresponding proportions for 1989 were 44 percent and 56 percent, respectively. According to the CR4, 78 percent of therapeutic submarkets in the public sector have firm-concentration levels that fall in the high concentration band (Table 14.19).

The results presented in Table 14.20 raise the same misgivings here as in the case of the private sector over the appropriateness of the CR4 as a sound informant of concentration relative to the HI index.

TABLE 14.17. Classification of therapeutic markets at the firm level by number of firms (percent of therapeutic submarkets).

	Public sector	
Number of firms in therapeutic markets	**1989**	**1999**
At most four firms	61.0	48.8
Five but less than forty firms	39.0	51.2

Source: Data from IMS Health.

TABLE 14.18. Classification of therapeutic markets at the product level by number of firms (percent of therapeutic submarkets).

	Public sector	
Number of products in therapeutic markets	**1989**	**1999**
At most four products	56.4	46.2
Five but less than forty products	43.6	53.8

Source: Data from IMS Health.

Therapeutic Submarket Concentration

The HI index reveals 56 percent of therapeutic markets have firm concentrations falling in the low-to-moderate concentration bands and combined, 44 percent of markets have concentrations falling in the moderate-to-high and high concentration bands (Table 14.19). The proportion of submarkets with HI firm concentration falling in the low-to-moderate levels decreased from 34 percent in 1989 to 24.4 percent in 1999. The combined proportion of markets with firm concentrations falling in the moderate and moderate-to-high concentration bands increased from 29 percent in 1989 to 49 percent in 1999. However, the proportion of submarkets with HI firm concentrations in the high concentration bands decreased from 37 percent in 1989 to 24 percent in 1999. These changes point to the markets in the public sector being in a state of flux, as well as to indicating an increase in the formation of oligopolistic markets.

TABLE 14.19. Classification of therapeutic submarkets at the firm level by concentration (percent of therapeutic markets)—public sector.

Interval	CR4 1989	CR4 1999	HHI 1989	HHI 1999	HI 1989	HI 1999
0.00 to 0.10						
0.10 to 0.20			2.44	7.32		
0.20 to 0.30			17.07	12.20		
0.30 to 0.40			14.63	19.51		2.44
0.40 to 0.50			12.20	9.76	2.44	4.88
0.50 to 0.60			4.88	14.63	14.63	12.20
0.60 to 0.70			4.88	7.32	17.07	7.32
0.70 to 0.80			4.88	4.88	12.20	29.27
0.80 to 0.90			12.20	4.88	17.07	19.51
0.90 to 1.00			26.83	19.51	36.59	24.39
0.65 to 0.75		2.44				
0.75 to 0.85	9.76	7.32				
0.85 to 0.95	17.07	12.20				
0.95 to 1.00	73.17	78.05				
Total	100.00	100.00	100.00	100.00	100.00	100.00

Source: Data from IMS Health.
Multinomial test of HI:

(a) 1989: $\chi^2 = 15.3415$ with df = 5, p-value = 0.008999.
(b) 1999: $\chi^2 = 18.2439$ with df = 6, p-value = 0.005651.

That these numbers sketch a situation of firm rivalry producing a typical outcome of monopoly or oligopoly is merely symptomatic of the sealed-bid tender process, which essentially outlines what competition amounts to in the public sector. Here, for a given product, in the absence of marketing (promotional) expenditure and little or no expenditure for R&D, the only way left for a firm to acquire greater market share in relation to its rivals is the strength of its productive efficiency. In that sense, the firm that is manifestly stronger either

TABLE 14.20. Firm concentration of therapeutic submarkets in the public sector broken down by number of firms (percent of therapeutic markets in 1999).

Interval	Therapeutic submarkets with at most four firms		Therapeutic submarkets with five but less than forty firms	
	CR4	HI	CR4	HI
0.30 to 0.40				4.76
0.40 to 0.50				9.52
0.50 to 0.60				23.81
0.60 to 0.70				14.29
0.70 to 0.80		25.00		33.33
0.80 to 0.90		25.00		14.29
0.90 to 1.00		50.00		
0.65 to 0.75			4.76	
0.75 to 0.85			14.29	
0.85 to 0.95			23.81	
0.95 to 1.00	100.00		57.14	
Total	100.00	100.00	100.00	100.00

Source: Data from IMS Health.

becomes the sole supplier to a market or is one among few firms equally able to do so.

The evidence suggests that the process of transformation from monopolistic to oligopolistic submarkets in the public sector is not complete. For instance, neither in 1989 nor in 1999 were the proportions of submarkets at the firm and product levels equal across the different concentration levels. This can be discerned by noting that the p-values for the multinomial tests (for equality in the proportions) are below the stipulated significance level, α. For the firm level, the p-value for the test appears in Table 14.19. For the product level the findings from the test appear in Table 14.21.

The lack of equilibrium in the public sector also demonstrates the ephemeral nature of selling on a tender where a firm has to affirm its right to supply a submarket each time a tender is issued. Because of

TABLE 14.21. Classification of therapeutic submarkets at the product level by concentration (percent of therapeutic markets)—public sector.

Interval	CR4		HHI		HI	
	1989	1999	1989	1999	1989	1999
0.00 to 0.10						
0.10 to 0.20			15.38	10.26		
0.20 to 0.30			10.26	10.26		
0.30 to 0.40			10.26	25.64	7.69	5.13
0.40 to 0.50			5.13	5.13	7.69	5.13
0.50 to 0.60		2.56	7.69	10.26	5.13	7.69
0.60 to 0.70	5.13	5.13	10.26	7.69	10.26	23.08
0.70 to 0.80	10.26		5.13	2.56	10.26	17.95
0.80 to 0.90	5.13	10.26	7.69	5.13	23.08	10.26
0.90 to 1.00	79.49	82.05	28.21	23.08	35.90	30.77
Total	100.00	100.00	100.00	100.00	100.00	100.00

Source: Data from IMS Health.
Multinomial test of HI:
(a) 1989: $\chi^2 = 20.4103$ with df = 6, p-value = 0.002340.
(b) 1999: $\chi^2 = 16.1026$ with df = 6, p-value = 0.013214.
$\alpha = 0.05$.

the tender system, greater concentration of submarkets at the firm level is encouraged in the public sector than is the case for the private sector. If more submarkets in the former sector are becoming oligopolistic, then this should lead to a drop in concentration at the product level, given that products from more than one producer would be supplied on a tender. In short, one should expect between 1989 and 1999 the combined proportion of therapeutic submarkets with HI product concentrations falling in the moderate and moderate-to-high bands to move to the lower bands. This is just what we observe.

Whereas the combined proportion of submarkets with HI product concentrations in the moderate and moderate-to-high concentration bands was 33 percent in 1989, this proportion had declined to 28 percent in 1999 (Table 14.21). Conversely, whereas the proportion of submarkets with HI product concentrations in the low-to-moderate concentration bands was 23 percent in 1989, this proportion increased to 36 percent in 1999 (Table 14.21).

To crystallize our discussion of rivalry in the public sector, for consistency—as done in the private sector—we now turn to the (Pearson) correlations between the concentration indices at the firm and product levels for this sector. Here too, the correlations are statistically significant (Table 14.22 and Table 14.23), in conformity to economic expectations of the tender system by which the monopsony buyer— the state—procures drugs.

The CR4 is strongly correlated (for instance $r = 0.79$ in 1999) with the HI at the firm level (Table 14.22).

Note that almost perfect correlation ($r = 0.95$) between the HHI and HI should be expected, given the HI harbors the HHI in its formulation. The correlation demonstrates that the HI differs little from the HHI and points to both indices giving similar groupings of therapeutic submarkets according to concentration.

By and large, the magnitude of the correlations in the public sector exceeds that in the private sector. The joint inspection of the CR4-HI and CR4-HHI correlations attests to this. The pairs are examined jointly to counteract the heavier weighting structure of the HI vis-à-vis the HHI, which would thus not go far enough in accentuating how condensed in market share (the top end of) a market is, where the first firm and its immediate followers do not depart by much in the

TABLE 14.22. Pearson correlations and respective p-values for therapeutic markets at the firm level—public sector.

Concentration indices	1999		1989	
	HHI	HI	HHI	HI
CR4	0.602051	0.796156	0.701701	0.827840
	(0.000031)[a]	(0.000000)[a]	(0.000000)[a]	(0.000000)[a]
HHI		0.951198		0.955077
		(0.000000)[a]		(0.000000)[a]
Cronbach's alpha	0.820411		0.801693	

Source: Data from IMS Health.
[a]Correlations significant at the 5 percent level of significance for the null hypothesis of no connection in the concentration indices.

TABLE 14.23. Pearson correlations and respective p-values for therapeutic markets at the product level—public sector.

Concentration indices	1999		1989	
	HHI	HI	HHI	HI
CR4	0.601638	0.780420	0.723485	0.876647
	(0.000051)a	(0.000000)a	(0.000000)a	(0.000000)a
HHI		0.960985		0.955444
		(0.000000)a		(0.000000)a
Cronbach's alpha	0.845498		0.867699	

Source: Data from IMS Health.
aCorrelations significant at the 5 percent level of significance for the null hypothesis of no connection in the concentration indices.

proportions of the market they occupy. Consequently, the CR4 would not bind strongly enough to the HI in contrast to the HHI, where the market shares of the first firm and the nearby firms come fairly close to one another compared to where they do not. The strength of the CR4-HHI correlation(s) should thus be greater in the former compared to the latter instance. The joint inspection of the numbers in Tables 14.11 and 14.22 ratifies this, confirming that in the public sector, as an artifact of the tender system, therapeutic submarkets end up being more concentrated than their counterparts in the private sector. For the same reason, one observes a strong correlation (for instance, r = 0.78 in 1999) between the CR4 and the HI at the product level (Table 14.23).

Over time, the declines in the correlation coefficients, whether for firms (Table 14.22) or products (Table 14.23), merely reflect what has already been stated, namely that in the public sector the move is away from monopolistic toward oligopolistic markets.

The CR4-HI correlation at the product level in the public sector is smaller to that for the private sector. This in turn reflects that in the public sector firms are not compelled quite as much as they are in the private sector in terms of needing to have products that rank in the top four. This slight ease of pressure translates into little or no requisite to carry out R&D and promotional activities in the public sector. If such activities play little or no role in the way firms vie for market share, then it is not quite as impelling for them to have products that rank within the top four if they are to raise the required revenue for these activities to be performed continuously. Therefore, greater correlation between the CR4 and HI, in the private relative to the public sector, is to be expected.

The values for Cronbach's alpha (0.82 for firms—Table 14.22, and 0.85 for products—Table 14.23) show that however many other random samples of comparable therapeutic markets are selected, each time the same correlations as those found here would be observed. Thus, the correlations obtained from the present sample are the same as the ones that would have been obtained if all comparable therapeutic submarkets were considered. The values for Cronbach's alpha also verify that the concentrations from the chosen sample are no different from the ones that would have been extracted if the population as a whole were to be considered.

Before closing the study for the public sector it is noted, from inspection of the findings in Table 14.17 and Table 14.19, that in the public sector, much like its private counterpart, any suppositions of collusion or mergers and acquisitions for monopoly (inefficiency) reasons are not supported by the evidence. All things equal, the evidence points to therapeutic submarkets, whether at the firm or product level, neither falling nor persistently occupying the moderate-to-high and high concentration domains.

All told, what we should remember from the coverage of the public sector is that it is a market where market shares for both firms and their products are in a state of turbulence.

SYNOPSIS OF THE MICROECONOMIC STUDY

The study was set up to verify the findings of the macroeconomic studies before it. It does that, confirming without a doubt that the pharmaceutical industry, whether examined at the micro or macro level, is highly competitive to a degree in excess of perfect competition. The industry has no monopoly power in the conventional sense. This, however, does not preclude it from approximating the perfectly competitive condition in the long run.

The evidence from the concentration indices at the firm and product levels indicates that therapeutic markets are continuously in a state of flux. This renders no support for any views that the industry may conform to the collusion or collective monopoly (via mergers and acquisitions) hypotheses. If these were true, then over time the majority of markets ought to have remained only in the moderate-to-high and high concentration bands (whether in the case of products or firms). They did not. That mergers and acquisitions have made no impact on the concentration levels of therapeutic submarkets, in the sense of not having increased these levels, is not surprising. Finding this here simply provides more evidence toward Jensen's (1988) summary of findings, which show that mergers and acquisitions have had no bearing on industrial concentration.

In view of the evidence indicating that therapeutic submarkets undergo transition, then, as far as studying the pharmaceutical industry is concerned, here we must dispense with the standard notion that equilibrium represents a stationary point in favor of disequilibrium or equilibrium in transition. In short, over time therapeutic markets migrate from one state to another, with the move being prompted by the presiding equilibrium losing its attractiveness. Such things as the new product, the new method of production, the opening up of a new market, the discovery of a new source of supply of raw materials, and the new form of organizational arrangement all guarantee this.

Our findings of competition in the pharmaceutical industry from the microeconomic study are complementary of, and in fact very much in line with, those of the Scott and Reekie (1985) study referred to in Chapter 11. Both the private and public markets operate under intense rivalry. In the case of the private market rivalry is closely linked to innovative competition, whereas in the public market it is closely linked to imitative competition. In each of the sectors therapeutic markets are contestable, limiting the likelihood of monopoly or monopoly-like pricing. The intermediate correlation between the HI and the CR4 suggests that in the private sector therapeutic submarkets function under oligopolistic competition, in the sense that there are leaders and followers. Although dominant firms have a greater market share relative to followers, this share is not so large as to grant them market power. In the public sector, because of the use of the tender system, markets end up operating under one or a few suppliers, which results in higher concentration at any one point in time compared to the private sector. In the public sector, relative to the private sector, it may be easier to keep a market position, providing the firm meets the required tender prices, but failing which it would be summarily dismissed from commercial leadership.

In the private sector, concentration is not driven by the constraint on the number of firms allowed to operate in a market but by the ability of firms to harness their market power through the product heterogeneity they set in relation to their rivals. The greater the heterogeneity, the greater is the market share gap between leaders and followers.

In a nutshell, what we have to take away with us from this summary, as well as from the three studies performed on the industry, is that its behavior is best depicted by the framework of the competitive process described in this work.

Chapter 15

Conclusion

In the field of economics, particularly microeconomics and, by extension in the orthodox industrial economics (textbook) literature perfect competition has been made into an apotheosis of what competition is and should be.

Why that is, or why we should pass it from one economic generation to the next, is not at all clear, especially when note is taken of what seems to be a self-evident fact, namely that once the perfectly competitive model is taken as the yardstick of competition, the likely outcome seems to be one of mechanomorphism on the part of whoever employs it for this purpose. McNulty (1968, p. 642) pointed out that while all other forms of competition in economic theory represent a mixture of monopoly and competition, perfect competition by contrast is the absence of competition, although for different reasons than pure monopoly, namely that

> Monopoly is a market situation in which intra-industry competition has been defined away by identifying the firm as the industry. Perfect competition, on the other hand, is a market situation which, although itself the result of the free entry of a large number of formerly competing firms, has evolved or progressed to the point of equilibrium where no further competition within the industry is possible.

Thus, when discussing competition we noted that we must think of it not as a datum but as a continuous process, namely the competitive process. In our exposition of this process we noted that it operates by two mechanisms. One is the transfer and the other is the innovation mechanism. The former, as its name reveals, deals with the transfer of market share from one rival to another. Likewise, as the name of the

doi:10.1300/5505_15

latter mechanism suggests, it deals with all those things that bring rivals something new over which to compete, whatever this might be.

The transfer and innovation mechanisms essentially create two distinct markets describing completely different (a) groups of firms and (b) competitive situations. One group works in an environment where the basic knowledge required for the production process is available and it is only gradually improved upon. Here the market engages predominantly in price competition, and the transfer mechanism outweighs the innovation mechanism, resulting in imitative competition.

The other group of firms works in an opposite environment. Here the innovation mechanism outweighs the transfer mechanism, resulting in innovative competition, which covers the following areas:

1. The introduction of a new good—that is, one with which consumers are not yet familiar—or of a new quality of a good
2. The introduction of a new method of production, that is, one not yet tested by experiment in the branch of manufacture concerned, which need by no means be founded upon a discovery scientifically new and can also exist in a new way of handling a product commercially
3. The opening of a new market, that is, a market into which the particular branch of manufacture has not previously entered, whether or not this market has previously existed
4. The conquest of a new source of supply of raw materials, irrespective of whether this source exists or whether it has first to be created
5. The carrying out of the new organization of any industry, such as the creation of a monopoly position (for example, through trustification) or the breaking up of a monopoly position

We expect the transfer and innovative mechanisms of the competitive process to work interchangeably, and with this for markets not to exist permanently in perfect competition (even if that were possible, given that this is a state equivalent to stagnation). Perfect competition is void of innovative activity as well as the rivalry that uncovers the lowest possible market price for products—this in essence being what the sole function of competition is. However, if prices and costs change all the time and so, by correspondence, does the constellation of demand and supply, then holding normal profits as the sign of what is perfect in competition is something we ought to avoid. Our conventional understanding of what normal profit is needs revision to the extent that we should supplant it for the Von Misian view of profit. As Von Mises put it (1949, p. 295),

> Profit and loss are entirely determined by the success or failure of the entrepreneur to adjust production to the demand of the consumers. There is nothing "normal" in profits and there can never be an "equilibrium" with regard to them. Profit and loss are, on the contrary, always a phenomenon of a deviation from "normalcy", of changes unforeseen by the majority, and of a "disequilibrium". They have no place in an imaginary world of normalcy and equilibrium. In a changing economy there prevails always an inherent tendency for profits and losses to disappear. It is only the emergence of new changes which revives them again.

What we are saying thus far is that we have essentially two different ways of analyzing competition in a market. On the one hand, if we are interested in establishing an equilibrium point in studying an industry, we will wish to focus on the familiar state of equilibrium, such as the fulfillment of marginal conditions (e.g., marginal cost = price = marginal utility). In equilibrium competition no longer exists. At this point, the transfer mechanism has ceased to operate. What makes disequilibrium impossible in the long run is competition among entrepreneurs. By definition, these are the originators of economic progress that set the innovation mechanism in motion, which in turn produces short-run disequilibrium. Over time, competitors come to offer marginal improvements over the initial offer and thus by exhausting the potential for such improvements tend to work toward reestablishing an equilibrium in the long run. This process can be impaired when either exchanges are not possible (e.g., for legal reasons) or when resources are owned by a monopoly and entrepreneurs are not successful in proposing arrangements that would induce these owners to relinquish their monopoly.

Although the feasibility of certain prohibited exchanges is limited by the ability of legal authorities to enforce the rules, and although this is a consequence of public intervention in the marketplace, monopolistic resource-ownership as a barrier to competition is often a focus of public concern. It is not quite clear that in many instances such concern should exist, except of course to serve as a precursor of the desire to regulate, thereby taking us into the realm of the regulator knowing what is best, i.e., Hayek's fatal conceit. Two points must be made here in respect of this public concern. First, although the costs of prohibiting certain exchanges will not necessarily be borne by the legal authority, the private resource-owner must bear the opportunity costs of not realizing his or her product onto the market.

When, for example, a producer is the exclusive owner of a commodity, he or she will have no particular advantage over any other producer, since the cost of using this exclusively owned good in the productive process (or of withholding its use) is equal to the opportunity cost of its alternative, i.e., of releasing it onto the market and selling it to other producers.

Also, although prohibition of certain exchanges may often lead to clandestine illicit exchanges that completely escape public attention and control, the reluctance to release exclusively owned resources or, alternatively, charging monopolistic prices for these resources, creates incentives to develop substitutes. Consequently artificial and imposed barriers to competition themselves create incentives to overcome these barriers; such incentives will in due course contribute to an erosion of the positions of either the owner of an exclusive resource or the authority that tries to prohibit the exchanges.

Although the existence of a monopoly creates incentives to develop substitutes for a monopolistically controlled resource, attainment of a monopoly position may serve as an incentive to develop a scarce product in order to enjoy the monopoly thus created. This scenario entails two distinct possibilities. The monopolistic rent may be sought through either genuine innovation, e.g., the development of a product not hitherto known or available, or rent-seeking, when agents try to secure government protection of their economic status. The former is part and parcel of entrepreneurial activity; the latter creates barriers to competition in accordance with Bastiat's economic fable, *A Petition,* quoted earlier.

In the long run, essentially two sources of monopoly exist:

1. Government protection of firms from competition, e.g., legalized monopolies, licensed entries, import duties, quotas, and so on.

2. A permanent advantage enjoyed by the incumbent firm(s) over potential entrants, e.g., sole ownership of some necessary input, access to superior techniques of production, beliefs by customers in the superiority of established products, economies of scale which render new entry uneconomic, and so on.

Of these two, the first is what induces long-lasting monopolies, national champions, and cartels whose exposure to rivalry from others is precluded from bearing the fruit of Schumpeter's perennial gale of creative destruction. The competitive process bestows on firms only temporary monopoly positions, but none to the extent of isolating them from the effects of rivalry altogether. Potential competition tends to force the monopolist to produce with maximal efficiency and to hunt down and utilize fully every opportunity for innovation. Perhaps most surprising of all, it induces the institution of efficient prices, i.e., those that minimize consumer DWL in the short run. These are the well-known third-degree or Ramsey prices.

In the short run, price discrimination affects the equilibrium number of firms in an unsurprising way. Discrimination results in more firms than when the practice is prohibited. The profits from price discrimination attract entry, and thus increase product variety and put downward pressure on prices, in turn making price discrimination something inevitably more likely to increase the quantity sold. The increase in the number of firms and the decrease in price for the low-price group imply that the sum of consumers' surplus in the low-price group always increases with price discrimination. Very likely, cases will occur where price discrimination would also lower the price charged to the high-price group. When this happens, the lower price and greater product variety necessarily would increase total surplus in that group as well.

It is socially undesirable in terms of production and consumption to have state regulation pronounce on matters as fundamental to the functioning of the competitive process as pricing freedom. From the grandiose failures of the Communist era, such interventionism has little to recommend for itself.

By analogy, so should anything of a similar guise, which is what a price-discrimination ban is, for it either allows the state to decide what the market price should be or may do the same by creating an environment conducive to rent-seeking, where less-efficient firms come to seek defense from their more-able rivals. Three things can be said here.

First, the grounds for state regulation of prices, as in the imposition of uniform prices, are weak, whilst its consequences are harmful to the very people that the state usually undertakes to serve, i.e., the indigent or poor. Second, the grounds for abolishing price discrimination are weak, and the consequences of actually doing it appear in all likelihood to be harmful. A public-policy decision such as this is very likely to result in a lack of product variety, to retard or halt innovation, to impose unduly high prices on the poor or indigent, and to deprive consumers, especially those with low-income, of what they could have otherwise consumed. Third, a state-interventionist policy of uniform price regulation can lead to fewer firms in a market compared to when price discrimination is allowed to exist. Thus, such policy itself stifles competition, since the price it brings about has the property of guaranteeing the long-lasting absence of price flexibility. This is something more reminiscent of monopoly power than such vested in firms by the competitive process. The policy precludes the reduction in price for the price-sensitive buyers that competition (in the form of price discrimination most likely to reveal itself through demand creation) can bring about. It is likely that the policy can do the same for the less-price-sensitive buyers by precluding competition (in the form of price discrimination most likely to reveal itself through demand diversion) from coming into effect.

It could be that firms may assemble to form a cartel. If such assembly is convened in a market where the competitive process is not foreclosed, then the arrangement would crumble. It would disintegrate for a number of reasons, but namely the following:

1. The supernormal profits a collusive agreement can produce will act as an incentive to entry and increase the number of entrants (assuming no barriers to entry). This would lead to lower prices (toward MC) and the elimination of monopoly profits.
2. Firms participating in such cartel-based agreements can realize substantial increases in their earnings if they make a small (hard to detect) price reduction in relation to the other cartel members.
3. Some cartel members may be operating at MC levels that allow them to have a larger markup relative to other members. Such members have a greater ability to fluctuate their price, raising

the likelihood that they may price below the cartel price for the same reason as noted in (2).

The danger of cartels persisting for longer than the competitive process will tolerate is in having government create them. The matter here is no different to what Smith ([1812] 1937, p. 116) described, namely that:

> People of the same trade seldom meet together, even for merriment and diversion, but the conversation ends in a conspiracy against the public, or in some contrivance to raise prices. It is impossible indeed to prevent such meetings, by any law which either could be executed, or would be consistent with liberty and justice. But though the law cannot hinder people of the same trade from sometimes assembling together, it ought to do nothing to facilitate such assemblies; much less to render them necessary.

It seems that the evidence regarding mergers and acquisitions shows that they have no bearing on the level of market concentration in the long run. As to why firms enter into mergers and acquisitions, this does not conform with the monopoly or collusion view created by the structure-conduct-performance model. The empirical work suggests that these transactions are entered into by firms to establish product variety and/or productive efficiency, or to avoid business failures (e.g., bankruptcies). In that sense, any public policy that reduces the incidence of mergers has a cost in the sacrifice of efficiency, whether we choose to measure this in technical innovation, product variety, marketing (promotional), or organizational terms.

All things considered, it appears plausible from a public-policy perspective that we steer clear from deploying the SCP paradigm even to judge what is competitive and what not. On the one hand, we have shown that the paradigm's barriers to competition—product differentiation, economies of scale, and absolute cost advantages—have more in common with displaying the vigor of competition than otherwise. On the other hand, the oligopoly models the paradigm relies on were shown not to be what is commonly thought.

The Cournot model was found inappropriate to confirm the SCP conjecture that concentration acquired by collusion or cartelization or by horizontal mergers and acquisitions would produce supernormal profits. In the strict Cournot sense, the possibility of any collusive-type arrangements being likely to occur is rejected on grounds that they would not remain in existence for long. If such arrangements did come about, then bounded rationality (i.e., the limited human capacity to anticipate or solve complex problems) would make it difficult to enforce them, and out of their own accord members would create chiseling opportunities, increasing the odds of crumbling them. The gradual move toward perfect competition with respect to output, consumer surplus, and profit as the number of firms increases can solely be regarded as the result of rivalry (no restrictions on entry) and each firm in the industry having limited productive powers to begin with. This has an important implication for our understanding of horizontal mergers and acquisitions. Given that one of the reasons they take place is to attain productive efficiency, if the Cournot supposition of limited productive capacity were relaxed, then, contrary to popular belief, the Cournot model as it was originally conceived predicts that these transactions would be exerting a downward pressure on price toward the perfectly competitive point.

In as much as the use of the Cournot model is inappropriate to lend support for the SCP paradigm, the same reservations were expressed about the Stackelberg model in that in the strict Stackelberg sense this model does not support any theories that firm dominance retards rivalry. If following a merger or acquisition the joint firm did become a leader, this would chiefly be a result of this firm being economically superior, for instance, by means of product differentiation, economies of scale, or absolute cost advantages, relative to its rivals, who would, in turn, have to settle with being followers. In the original Stackelberg model, such dominance is not the likely result of collusion or cartelization. It is mainly the result of market forces, where the weaker competitor would be unable to successfully keep up the struggle against his or her more powerful adversary. In that context, a possible outcome of firm rivalry under the Stackelberg model is pure (perfect) competition.

Finally when it came to the third oligopoly model, i.e., the Bertrand model, it was shown that it has little to do with being directly in agreement with perfect competition and that it is instead complementary of the competitive process described in this work. The Bertrand model, in the strict Bertrand sense, stipulates that competition does not yield the perfectly competitive point, in the sense that rivalry is something that produces a situation of disequilibrium.

Having dealt with the theory, the two things that should matter most from a public-policy perspective will now be considered. To demonstrate the first of these from a pedagogical perspective, use was made of the pharmaceutical industry. The lesson here is that in markets where pricing freedom is allowed to exist, particularly on new product introductions, and where the right of property is recognized as the most powerful of all encouragements to the multiplication of wealth and investment, competition will keep product prices down.

The second is that the desire to regulate in order to fulfill the role of a dirigiste is socially harmful. As Hayek (1995, p. 10) put it:

> This is simply that if we judge measures of economic policy solely by their immediate and concretely foreseeable effects we shall not only not achieve a viable order but shall be certain progressively to extinguish freedom and thereby prevent more good than our measures will produce. Freedom is important in order that all the different individuals can make full use of the particular circumstances of which only they know. We therefore never know what beneficial outcomes we prevent if we restrict their freedom to serve their fellows in whatever manner they wish. All acts of interference, however, amount to such restrictions. They are, of course, always undertaken to achieve some definite objective. Against the foreseen direct results of such actions of government we shall in each individual case be able to balance only the mere probability that some unknown but beneficial actions by some individuals will be prevented. In consequence, if such decisions are made from case to case and not governed by an attachment to freedom as a general principle, freedom is bound to lose in every case.

Freedom of choice is a general principle that must never be sacrificed to considerations of expediency, because all aspects of freedom would be abolished if they were to be respected only where the concrete damage caused by their abolition can be foreseen.

Notes

Chapter 1

1. Firm profit is total revenue less total costs, while the rate of return for a firm may be defined as profit plus interest divided by the firm's total assets.

2. Total average cost is total cost (fixed plus variable) divided by total output. The rise in total cost from producing an additional unit of output is referred to as marginal cost.

3. Market power is the proportion of the market belonging in the hands of one or few firms. Under such circumstances it is usually considered that market power translates into the ability of firms to set market price(s) above marginal cost. In the short run and in the long run the marginal cost curve crosses the (total) average cost curve at its minimum. Hence, price is also above average cost.

4. When long-run total average costs decrease as output rises there are economies of scale, with the reverse applying in the case of diseconomies of scale. If long-run average costs remain constant as output rises then there are constant returns to scale.

Chapter 2

1. The minimum efficient scale refers to the lowest (or smallest) output level at which long-run average costs are at a minimum.

2. Productive efficiency refers to how close the actual production cost is to the lowest cost achievable. The lowest cost achievable is that of long-run marginal cost of production.

Chapter 3

1. 15 U.S.C §18; see 15 U.S.C §12-21 (1994) for codifications to amendments.

2. Furse (1999, p. 112); it may be tempting to conclude on the basis of the passage that the EU competition legislation does not per se prohibit horizontal mergers, i.e., a rule-of-reason approach is followed. This would be inaccurate. The passage must be read in conjunction with Article 81, §3, ¶3, where it is stated that any concerted practice or category of concerted practices would be exonerated if it can be established that "it contributes to improving the production or distribution of goods or to promoting technical or economic progress. . . ." In short, horizontal mergers are likely to be deemed per se illegal until proved otherwise.

doi:10.1300/5505_16

3. This passage was extracted from the *Government Gazette* (1998, No. 19412, p. 12). The South African Competition Act makes a similar efficiency-defense provision to its EU counterpart, contained in §4, ¶1. It is noted there that the concerted practice or decision would be deemed not to lessen competition if it can be established that "any technological, efficiency, or other pro-competitive gain resulting from it outweighs . . . the effect of preventing or lessening competition."

4. An association of firms in the same line of business that explicitly agrees to coordinate its pricing and production activities is called a cartel.

5. It should be noted here that this refers to monopolistic competition in the Chamberlainian sense: Firms have market power, the ability to raise price profitably above marginal cost, but make zero economic profits. An industry has monopolistic competition if free entry exists and each firm faces a downward-sloping demand curve.

6. The inverse relationship between L and ε stems from the profit-maximizing condition, MR = MC, where MR = $p(1 + 1/\varepsilon)$.

Chapter 4

1. For instance, one may either encounter a case of legalized monopolies (e.g., only a particular firm can supply the market) or subsidies (e.g., import tariffs and quotas).

2. By analogy, as may be evident, this may also be interpreted to mean that Figure 3.3 depicts at a point in time an industry characterized by innovative activity.

3. Asymmetrical firms are the case opposite of symmetrical firms, i.e., firms are not identical with respect to costs, information they hold about the market, and the objectives that they wish to pursue.

Chapter 5

1. A product's life cycle refers to the profit or sales performance of the product over time.

2. An industry is said to be concentrated if a few firms make most or all of its sales.

3. When long-run total average costs decrease as output rises there are economies of scale, with the reverse applying in the case of diseconomies of scale. If long-run average costs remain constant as output rises, then there are constant returns to scale.

Chapter 6

1. OECD is the acronym for the Organisation for Economic Co-Operation and Development.

2. For the definitions on goodwill and reputation, see Stigler (1961a, pp. 218, 224).

3. To gain full appreciation of "On Rent," Chapter 2 of Ricardo's *Principles of Political Economy and Taxation,* it should be read in conjunction with Chapter 6, "On Profits."

4. For the exposition of natural rights, see Locke's second treatise of government in his *Two Treatises of Government* (1698, reprinted 1988), specifically Chapter 4, "Of Slavery," and Chapter 5, "Of Property."

Chapter 8

1. It may be of interest to note here that Cowling and Waterson (1976, pp. 267-268) have demonstrated that for a Cournot-type market of *n* firms (subject to the assumptions stated previously), concentration is directly related to profitability. In particular, they have shown that the industry price-cost margin (L) is the sum of the individual firms' profit margins (L_i), each weighted by the firm's market share (s_i). Mathematically, it is represented as shown here:

$$L = \sum_{i=1}^{n} s_i \times L_i = \sum_{i=1}^{n} s_i^2 \div \varepsilon$$

The expression reveals that, for a given demand, elasticity in an unconcentrated industry, where market shares of firms are small, profits will tend to be low and vice versa.

2. The relevant chapter on oligopoly in Cournot's *Researches into the Mathematical Principles of the Theory of Wealth* is Chapter 7, "Of the Competition of Producers." However, to gain full benefit of the text, one should also read Chapters 5 and 6 (dealing with monopoly), Chapter 8, "Of Unlimited Competition," and Chapter 9, "Of the Mutual Relations of Producers."

3. In the strict Cournot sense, this would apply in those cases where firms produce homogeneous (identical in quality) goods and prior to the merger or acquisition share similar costs of production. By analogy this can be extended to include cases involving heterogeneous goods under the rather restrictive assumption that such goods are like a homogeneous good with different qualities across firms. This assumption is an extension of the theory of uncertainty, which, as Tirole (1998, p. 161) puts it, "considers the same physical good available in two different states of nature as two different economic goods."

4. It may be useful to recall here that average cost equals marginal cost in the long run.

5. It may be worth recalling at this point that some competition authorities view dominance as the inverse of competition.

6. It should be noted that the principles of the theory of monopoly presented in the text also extend to vertical integration. This is the extent to which successive stages in production and distribution are placed under a single enterprise in order to secure sources of supply or markets. Vertical integration is thus an example of natural monopoly in line with the proper definition of the term as laid down by Ropke (1963, p. 157), namely the case where existing sources of economic wealth in the form of input (intermediary) and/or product markets are owned by a single enterprise.

7. Reference is made to Cournot-Nash models. This is actually the same as the conventional Cournot model, where the resulting equilibrium is referred to as a Nash equilibrium, where "each player's strategy is optimal against those of the others" (Nash, 1951, p. 287). The numerical results that the Cournot-Nash model yields are presented in Tables 8.1, 8.2, and 8.3.

Chapter 9

1. Extracted from the European Union *Consolidated Treatise* (1997, p. 71).

2. The terms third-degree price discrimination and price discrimination are used interchangeably. Although it might be contended that second-degree price discrimination—observed as a two-part tariff made up of a fixed (entry-fee) charge and variable charge for each unit actually purchased, which manifests in practice as tie-in sales, bundling, discounting, and such—is not considered, Braeutigam (1989, pp. 1329-1332) has demonstrated that such pricing operates through third-degree price discrimination. Subject to the firm gaining insight into the identity of its customers, which it usually accomplishes by designing and offering self-revealing products that distinguish large from small customers, the fixed charge becomes another price like the variable charge, to be set in accordance with third-degree pricing principles or their gentler variant, Ramsey pricing.

3. A formal proof of this has been presented by Schmalensee (1981, p. 246) and Reekie (1999, p. 286; see Note 4).

4. Borenstein (1985, p. 381) applied Salop's (1979) spatial (monopolistic) competition model to third-degree price discrimination under the assumption that free-entry exists in markets.

Chapter 10

1. This is not solely a hallmark feature of the South African pharmaceutical industry. Reekie's (1978, 1981, 1996) groundbreaking research has established the same to apply for the Danish, Dutch, German, UK, and U.S. pharmaceutical markets.

Chapter 11

1. As pointed out by Shackle (1949, p. 1), forming an expectation is the act of creating imaginary situations, of associating them with named future dates, and of assigning to each the belief that a specified course of action by the firm or entrepreneur will realize the expectation.

2. This quotation from Say's *A Treatise on Political Economy* is extracted from Book I, Chapter XIV, titled "Of the Right of Property." Although the benefit is in reading the whole treatise, it may be of use to read this chapter jointly with Chapter XVII, "Of the Effect of Governments, Intended to Influence Production," and Chapter VII of Book II, "Of the Revenue of Industry."

3. This assumes the conclusion that inflationary price increases are caused by monopoly. However, as Leach (1994, p. 267) informs us, that "idea . . . has been

largely discredited. In fact the idea is easily refuted by standard economic theory. Monopoly implies *high* prices, not *increasing* prices. . . . It is only increasing monopoly power that could bring about *increasing* prices and if it is concentration that is the basis for monopoly power, then increasing prices would require *increasing* concentration." This, as has already been shown, in terms of how permanent it can be, is something more likely to come out of regulation and legislation rather than competition.

Chapter 12

1. Sources: *Bulletin of Statistics* 1980-1999 and *South African Statistics* 1980-2001, *Statistics South Africa; Sectoral Data Series 1995, Industrial Development Corporation; Foreign Trade Statistics* 1980-1998 and *Monthly Abstract of Trade Statistics* 1980-1999, Government Printers on behalf of the Commissioner for South African Revenue Services. Notes: (a) Due to lack of available data it was not possible to calculate the profit margin for the pharmaceutical industry for 1994, 1995, and 1997. Thus, the two-sample t-test analysis was confined to sixteen as opposed to nineteen observations. (b) The data was monitored for any definitional changes with respect to what the pharmaceutical industry and the manufacturing sector encompass. Where these occurred a revised data series (taking into account these changes) was provided by the sources that covered the period of our study. Use was made of the most recent or up-to-date revisions available.

Chapter 13

1. This finding for the private sector is a direct confirmation of the classic zero-sum game from game theory literature, where, as is commonly known, no opportunities of overall gain may be had through the firms (players) colluding. Simply put, our evidence directly refutes the collective monopoly hypothesis as a likely rationale for mergers and acquisitions occurring in the private sector of the pharmaceutical industry.

2. It should be noted, in so far as new product development is concerned, that instances occur in which mergers and acquisitions are the only way to bring the new product to market. These occur where contending firms possess advantages which cannot be duplicated by rivals or exploited in the most profitable manner without the cooperation of rivals. An example of this situation is where a patent standoff occurs between two firms possessing patents which, in the absence of combination or cross-licensing, they cannot exploit without infringing on each other's rights. Then a merger or acquisition becomes the only viable option if a new product is to be produced.

3. In game theory terminology the evidence can be viewed as a confirmation of a non-zero-sum game where the decision of some firms to enter into a merger or acquisition benefits all firms (players) in the industry in terms of having all of their market shares increase by an equivalent amount. This is a result of the productive efficiency rationale for the merger or acquisition taking place. Whatever gains come to accrue from this to the firms of the merger or acquisition, these snowball by means of passing through information spillover channels knowledge to nonmerging

rivals regarding what it is that this productive efficiency entails. If these rivals are very near their merging counterparts in terms of production or reproduction capacity, partial information may be as good as full information, in which case, in the long run, the latter would not succeed in expanding its market share over and above the former.

Bibliography

Act No. 57 of 1978. Patents Act. *Statutes of the Republic of South Africa,* Durban, South Africa: Butterworth Publishers.

Act No. 89 of 1998. Competition Act, 1998. *Government Gazette,* October 30, 1998.

Act No. 90 of 1997. Medicines and Related Substances Control Amendment Act, 1997. *Government Gazette,* December 12, 1997.

Act No. 96 of 1979. Maintenance and Promotion of Competition Act. *Statutes of the Republic of South Africa.* Durban, South Africa: Butterworth Publishers.

Akerlof, G. (1970). The Market for "Lemons": Qualitative Uncertainty and the Market Mechanism. *Quarterly Journal of Economics,* 84: 488-500.

Alchian, A.A. (1950). Uncertainty, Evolution, and Economic Theory. *Journal of Political Economy,* 58: 211-221.

————— (1977). *Economic Forces at Work.* Indianapolis: Liberty Press.

Alchian, A.A. and Demsetz, H. (1972). Production, Information Costs, and Economic Organization. *American Economic Review,* 62: 777-795.

Areeda, P. and Turner, D.F. (1975). Predatory Pricing and Related Practices Under Section 2 of the Sherman Act. *Harvard Law Review,* 88: 697-733.

Armentano, D.T. (1990). *Antitrust and Monopoly: Anatomy of a Policy Failure,* Second Edition. Teaneck, NJ: Holmes & Meier Publishers.

Backhaus, J. (1983). Competition, Innovation and Regulation in the Pharmaceutical Industry. *Managerial and Decision Economics,* 4: 107-121.

Bain, J.S. (1951). Relation of Profit Rate to Industry Concentration: American Manufacturing, 1936-1940. *Quarterly Journal of Economics,* 65: 293-324.

————— (1968). *Industrial Organization,* Second Edition. New York: John Wiley & Sons Publishers.

Baker, J.B. (1999). Policy Watch Developments in Antitrust Economics. *Journal of Economic Perspectives,* 13: 181-192.

Ballance, R., Pogany R., and Forstner, H. (1992). *The World's Pharmaceutical Industries: An International Perspective on Innovation, Competition, and Policy.* Cheltenham, UK: Edward Elgar Publishing.

Balto, D.A. and Mongoven, J.F. (1999). Antitrust Enforcement in Pharmaceutical Industry Mergers. *Food and Drug Law Journal,* 54: 255-278.

Barr, G., Gerson, J., and Kantor, B. (1995). Shareholders As Agents and Principals: The Case for South Africa's Corporate Governance System. *Journal of Applied Corporate Finance,* 8: 18-31.

Barzel, Y. (1968). Optimal Timing of Innovations. *Review of Economics and Statistics,* 50: 348-355.

doi:10.1300/5505_17

Barzel, Y. (1977). Some Fallacies in the Interpretation of Information Costs. *Journal of Law and Economics,* 20: 291-307.

Bastiat, F. ([1845] 1996). *Economic Sophisms.* New York: Foundation for Economic Education Publications.

———— ([1850] 1984). *The Law.* New York: Foundation for Economic Education Publications.

———— ([1851] 1995). *Selected Essays on Political Economy.* New York: Foundation for Economic Education Publications.

Baumol, W.J. (1982). Contestable Markets: An Uprising in the Theory of Industry Structure. *American Economic Review,* 72: 1-15.

Baumol, W.J. and Bradford, D.F. (1970). Optimal Departures from Marginal Cost Pricing. *American Economic Review,* 60: 265-283.

———— (1992). Horizontal Collusion and Innovation. *Economic Journal,* 102: 129-137.

Baumol, W.J., Panzar, J.C., and Willig, R.D. (1982). *Contestable Markets and the Theory of Industry Structure.* New York: Harcourt Brace Jovanovich Publishers.

Benham, L. (1972). The Effect of Advertising on the Price of Eyeglasses. *Journal of Law and Economics,* 15: 337-352.

Berry, S. and Pakes, A. (1993). Some Applications and Limitations of Recent Advances in Empirical Industrial Organization: Merger Analysis. *American Economic Review (AEA) Papers and Proceedings,* 83: 247-258.

Bertrand, J. ([1883] 1992). Review by Joseph Bertrand of Two Books: *The Mathematical Theory of Social Wealth* by Leon Walras and *Researches into the Mathematical Principles of the Theory of Wealth* by Augustine Cournot. *History of Political Economy,* 24: 646-653.

Binmore, K. (1992). *Fun and Games: A Text on Game Theory.* Lexington, MA: D.C. Heath & Company.

Boiteux, M. (1971). On the Management of Public Monopolies Subject to Budgetary Constraints. *Journal of Economic Theory,* 3: 219-240.

Bond, P. (1999). Globalization, Pharmaceutical Pricing, and South African Health Policy: Managing Confrontation with U.S. Firms and Politicians. *International Journal of Health Services,* 29: 765-792.

Booer, T., Edmonds, P., and Oglialoro, C. (1999). Economic Aspects of the Single European Market in Pharmaceuticals. *European Competition Law Review,* 20: 256-264.

Borenstein, S. (1985). Price Discrimination in Free-Entry Markets. *Rand Journal of Economics,* 16: 380-397.

Bork, R.H. (1978). *The Antitrust Paradox: A Policy at War with Itself.* New York: Basic Books Publishers.

Bowley, A.L. (1924). *The Mathematical Groundwork of Economics: an Introductory Treatise.* Oxford: Clarendon Press.

Bowman, W.S. Jr. (1973). *Patent and Antitrust Law: A Legal and Economic Appraisal.* Chicago: University of Chicago Press.

Boyer, K.D. (1974). Informative and Goodwill Advertising. *Review of Economics and Statistics,* 56: 541-548.

Braeutigam, R.R. (1989). Optimal Policies for Natural Monopolies. In Schmalensee, R. and Willig, R.D. (eds.), *Handbook of Industrial Organisation,* Volume 1. (pp. 1289-1346). Amsterdam, the Netherlands: Elsevier Science Publishers BV (North-Holland).

Brown, S.J. and Sibley, D.S. (1986). *The Theory of Public Utility Pricing.* New York: Cambridge University Press.

Browne, G.W.G. (1985). *Fifth Interim Report of the Commission of Inquiry into Health Services: Report on Pharmaceutical Services.* Pretoria, South Africa: The Government Printer.

Brozen, Y. (1970). The Antitrust Task Force Deconcentration Recommendation. *Journal of Law and Economics,* 13: 279-292.

——— (1971a). Bain's Concentration and Rates of Return Revisited. *Journal of Law and Economics,* 14: 351-369.

——— (1971b). The Persistence of High Rates of Return in High-Stable Concentration Industries. *Journal of Law and Economics,* 14: 501-512.

Buchanan, N.S. (1942). Advertising Expenditures: A Suggested Treatment. *Journal of Political Economy,* 50: 537-557.

Burstall, M.C. and Senior, I.S.T. (1992). *Undermining Innovation: Parallel Trade in Prescription Medicines.* London: IEA Health and Welfare Unit.

Cabral, L.M.B. (2000). Introduction to Industrial Organisation. Cambridge, MA: MIT Press.

Canton, E. and Westerhout, E.D. (1999). A Model for the Dutch Pharmaceutical Market. *Health Economics and Econometrics,* 8: 391-402.

Carlton, D.W. and Perloff, J.M. (2000). *Modern Industrial Organization,* Third Edition. Boston: Addison-Wesley Publishers.

Chamberlin, E.H. (1933). *The Theory of Monopolistic Competition.* Cambridge, MA: Harvard University Press.

Church, J. and Ware, R. (2000). *Industrial Organisation: A Strategic Approach.* New York: McGraw-Hill Publishers.

Clemens, E.W. (1951). Price Discrimination and the Multiple-Product Firm. *Review of Economic Studies,* 19: 1-11.

Coase, R.H. (1937). The Nature of the Firm. *Economica,* 4: 386-405.

——— (1946). The Marginal Cost Controversy. *Economica,* 13: 160-182.

——— (1960). The Problem of Social Cost. *Journal of Law and Economics,* 3: 1-44.

——— (1988). The Nature of the Firm: Origin, Meaning, Influence. *Journal of Law, Economics and Organization,* 4: 3-47.

Cocks, D.L. (1975). Product Innovation and the Dynamic Elements of Competition in the Ethical Pharmaceutical Industry. In R.B. Helms (ed.), *Drug Development and Marketing* (pp. 225-254). Washington, DC: American Enterprise Institute Press.

Comanor, W.S. (1986). The Political Economy of the Pharmaceutical Industry. *Journal of Economic Literature,* 26: 1178-1217.

Comanor, W.S. and Wilson, T.A. (1979). The Effect of Advertising on Competition: A Survey. *Journal of Economic Literature,* 27: 453-476.

Competition Board (1981). *Report 4: Investigation into Discrimination in Respect of Prices or Conditions of Sale.* Pretoria, South Africa: Competition Board.

Competition Board (1993). *Report 34: Investigation into the Distribution of Medicine That Is Available to the Public on Prescription by Manufacturers of Pharmaceutical Products*. Pretoria, South Africa: Competition Board.

Competition Board (1999). *Report 73: Investigation into the Transaction Between Fedsure Limited and Adcock Ingram Limited with Regards to the Acquisition by Adcock Ingram Limited of Pharmacare Ltd., a Division of South African Druggists Limited*. Pretoria, South Africa: Competition Board.

Competition Commission (2001). *Competition News*, Fifth Edition. Pretoria: South African Competition Commission.

Competition Commission (2002). *Competition News*, Eighth Edition. Pretoria: South African Competition Commission.

Cournot, A. ([1838] 1927). *Researches into the Mathematical Principles of the Theory of Wealth*. New York: MacMillan Publishers.

Cowling, K. and Mueller, D.C. (1978). The Social Costs of Monopoly Power. *Economic Journal*, 88: 727-748.

Cowling, K. and Waterson, M. (1976). Price-Cost Margins and Market Structure. *Economica*, 43: 267-274.

CSDD (2002). *Outlook 2002*. Boston: Tufts University, Centre for the Study of Drug Development.

Curry, B. and George, K.D. (1983). Industrial Concentration: A Survey. *Journal of Industrial Economics*, 31: 203-255.

Danzon, P.M. (1997a). Price Differentials for Medicines Between and Within Countries. In J.L. Valverde (ed.), *Price Controls for Medicines and the Single Market*, Madrid, Spain: Centro de Estudios de Derecho Europeo Farmaceutico.

——— (1997b). Price Discrimination for Pharmaceuticals: Welfare Effects in the U.S. and the E.U. *International Journal of the Economics of Business*, 4: 301-321.

DBSA (2001). *Pharmaceutical Investment Scoping Analysis*. Johannesburg, South Africa: Development Bank of Southern Africa.

Dean, J. (1951). *Managerial Economics*. Upper Saddle River, NJ: Prentice-Hall Publishers.

De Bornier, J.M. (1992). The "Cournot-Bertrand Debate": A Historical Perspective. *History of Political Economy*, 24: 623-655.

Deman, S. (1994). The Theory of Corporate Takeover Bids: A Subgame Perfect Approach. *Managerial and Decision Economics*, 15: 383-397.

Demsetz, H. (1969). Information and Efficiency: Another Viewpoint. *Journal of Law and Economics*, 12: 1-22.

——— (1973). Industry Structure, Market Rivalry, and Public Policy. *Journal of Law and Economics*, 16: 1-9.

——— (1992). How Many Cheers for Antitrust's 100 years? *Economic Inquiry*, 30: 207-217.

——— (1995). *The Economics of the Business Firm: Seven Critical Commentaries*. New York: Cambridge University Press.

De Vany, A. (1996). Information, Chance, and Evolution: Alchian and the Economics of Self-Organization. *Economic Inquiry*, 34: 427-443.

De Villiers, J.U. and Scott, D.R. (1986). Research and Development Expenditure in Regulated and Unregulated Markets. *Managerial and Decision Economics,* 7: 197-201.

Dewey, D. (1961). Mergers and Cartels: Some Reservations About Policy. *AEA Papers and Proceedings,* 51: 255-262.

——— (1979). Information, Entry and Welfare: The Case for Collusion. *American Economic Review,* 69: 587-594.

——— (1982). Welfare and Collusion: Reply. *American Economic Review,* 72: 276-281.

Dickerson, A.P. Gibson, H.D., and Tsakalotos, E. (1997). The Impact of Acquisitions on Company Performance: Evidence from a Large Panel of UK Firms. *Oxford Economic Papers,* 49: 344-361.

DiMasi, J.A. (1995). Trends in Drug Development Costs, Times and Risks. *Drug Information Journal,* 29: 375-384.

DiMasi, J.A., Hansen, R.W., Grabowski, H.G., and Lasagna, L. (1991). Cost of Innovation in the Pharmaceutical Industry. *Journal of Health Economics,* 10: 107-142.

——— (1995). Research and Development Costs for New Drugs by Therapeutic Category—A Study of the U.S. Pharmaceutical Industry. *PharmacoEconomics,* 7: 152-169.

Domowitz, I., Hubbard, R.G., and Petersen, B.C. (1986). Business Cycles and the Relationship Between Concentration and Price-Cost Margins. *Rand Journal of Economics,* 17: 1-17.

Dorfman, R. and Steiner, P.O. (1954). Optimal Advertising and Optimal Quality. *American Economic Review,* 44: 826-836.

Downie, J. (1958). *The Competitive Process.* London: Gerald Duckworth & Co. Publishers.

Eckbo, B.E. (1983). Horizontal Mergers, Collusion, and Stockholder Wealth. *Journal of Financial Economics,* 11: 241-273.

European Union (1997). *Consolidated Treaties: Treaty on European Union & Treaty Establishing the European Community.* Luxembourg: Office for Official Publications of the European Communities.

Ferrandiz, J.M. (1999). The Impact of Generic Goods in the Pharmaceutical Industry. *Health Economics,* 8: 599-612.

Fisher, F.M. (1987a). Horizontal Mergers: Triage and Treatment. *Economic Perspectives,* 1: 23-39.

——— (1987b). On the Misuse of the Profits-Sales Ratio to Infer Monopoly Power. *Rand Journal of Economics,* 18: 384-396.

Franks, J. and Mayer, C. (1997). Corporate Ownership and Control in the U.K., Germany, and France. *Journal of Applied Corporate Finance,* 9: 30-45.

Furse, M. (1999). *Competition Law of the UK and EC.* London: Blackstone Press Limited.

George, K. and Jacquemin, A. (1992). Dominant Firms and Mergers. *Economic Journal,* 102: 148-157.

Geroski, P.A. (1992). Vertical Relations Between Firms and Industrial Policy. *Economic Journal,* 102: 138-147.

Goldman, M.B., Leland, H., and Sibley, D. (1984). Optimal Nonuniform Prices. *Review of Economic Studies,* 51(2): 305-320.

Grabowski, H.G. and Vernon, J.M. (1994). Returns to R & D on New Drug Introductions in the 1980s. *Journal of Health Economics,* 13: 383-406.

Grossman, S.J. and Hart, O.D. (1980). Takeover Bids, the Free-Rider Problem, and the Theory of the Corporation. *Bell Journal of Economics,* 11: 42-64.

Hall, M. and Tideman, N. (1967). Measures of Concentration. *Journal of the American Statistical Association,* 62: 162-168.

Harberger, A.C. (1954). Monopoly and Resource Allocation. *American Economic Review,* 45: 77-87.

Hay, D.A. and Morris, D.J. (1991). *Industrial Economics and Organisation: Theory and Evidence,* Second Edition. New York: Oxford University Press.

Hay, G.A. and Werden, G.J. (1993). Horizontal Mergers: Law, Policy, and Economics. *AEA Papers and Proceedings,* 83: 173-177.

Hayek, F.A. (1945). The Use of Knowledge in Society. *American Economic Review,* 35: 519-530.

———— (1948). *Individualism and Economic Order.* Chicago: University of Chicago Press.

———— (1978). *New Studies in Philosophy, Politics, Economics and the History of Ideas.* Routledge & Kegan Paul Pulishers.

———— (1994). *The Road to Serfdom.* Chicago: University of Chicago Press.

———— (1995). Introduction. In F. Bastiat (ed.), *Selected Essays on Political Economy* (pp. ix-xii). New York: Foundation for Economic Education Publications.

Hirshleifer, D. and Titman, S. (1990). Share Tendering Strategies and the Success of Hostile Takeover Bids. *Journal of Political Economy,* 98: 295-324.

Holmes, T.J. (1989). The Effects of Third-Degree Price Discrimination in Oligopoly. *American Economic Review,* 79: 244-250.

Horvath, J. (1970). A Suggestion for a Comprehensive Measure of Concentration. *Southern Economic Journal,* 36: 446-452.

Hudson, J. (2000). Generic Take-up in the Pharmaceutical Market Following Patent Expiry—A Multi-Country Study. *International Review of Law and Economics,* 20: 205-221.

Hurwitz, M.A. and Caves, R.E. (1988). Persuasion or Information? Promotion and the Shares of Brand Name and Generic Pharmaceuticals. *Journal of Law and Economics,* 31: 299-320.

Hymer, S. and Pashigian, P. (1962). Turnover of Firms As a Measure of Market Behaviour. *Review of Economics and Statistics,* 44: 82-87.

IDC (1998). *Sectoral Prospects: Growth Guidelines for 80 South African Industries.* Johannesburg, South Africa: Industrial Development Corporation.

Ireland, N.J. (1992). On the Welfare Effects of Regulating Price Discrimination. *Journal of Industrial Economics,* 40: 237-248.

Jarrell, G.A., Brickley, J.A., and Netter, J.M. (1988). The Market for Corporate Control: The Empirical Evidence Since 1980. *Journal of Economic Perspectives,* 2: 49-67.

Jensen, M.C. (1986). Agency Costs of Free Cash Flow, Corporate Finance, and Takeovers. *AEA Papers and Proceedings,* 76: 323-329.

———— (1988). Takeovers: Their Causes and Consequences. *Journal of Economic Perspectives,* 2: 21-47.

Jevons, W.S. (1957). *The Theory of Political Economy,* Fifth Edition. New York: Kelley and Millman Publishers.

Kamien, M.I. and Schwartz, N.L. (1975). Market Structure and Innovation: A Survey. *Journal of Economic Literature,* 13: 1-37.

Kantor, B. (1998). Ownership and Control in South Africa Under Black Rule. *Journal of Applied Corporate Finance,* 10: 69-78.

Kaplan, S.N. (1994a). Top Executive Rewards and Firm Performance: A Comparison of Japan and the U.S. *Journal of Political Economy,* 102: 510-546.

———— (1994b). Top Executives, Turnover, and Firm Performance in Germany. *Journal of Law, Economics, and Organisation,* 10: 142-159.

———— (1997). Corporate Governance and Corporate Performance: A Comparison of Germany, Japan and the U.S. *Journal of Applied Corporate Finance,* 9: 86-93.

Katz, M.L. (1984). Price Discrimination and Monopolistic Competition. *Econometrica,* 52: 1453-1471.

Kawaura, A. and La Croix, S.J. (1995). Japan's Shift from Process to Product Patents in the Pharmaceutical Industry: An Event Study of the Impact on Japanese Firms. *Economic Inquiry,* 33: 88-103.

Kenney, H. (1984). Economic Concentration in South Africa. *Mining Survey* (Chamber of Mines, Johannesburg), pp. 45-50.

———— (1997). Are Financial Markets Different? *Investment Analysts Journal,* 45: 17-24.

Kirzner, I.M. (1986). *Subjectivism, Intelligibility and Economic Understanding: Essays in Honour of Ludwig M. Lachmann on his Eightieth Birthday.* London: Macmillan Press Publishers, UK.

Kitch, E.E. (1977). The Nature and Function of the Patent System. *Journal of Law and Economics,* 20: 265-290.

Koutsoyiannis, A. (1982). *Non-Price Decisions: The Firm in a Modern Context.* London: Macmillan Press Ltd.

Krugman, P.R. (1989). Industrial Organization and International Trade. In Schmalensee, R. and Willig, R.D. (eds.), *Handbook of Industrial Organization,* Volume 2 (pp. 1180-1223). Amsterdam: Elsevier Science Publishers BV (North-Holland).

Lachmann, L.M. (1959). Professor Shackle on the Economic Significance of Time. *Metroeconomica,* 11(1): 64-73.

———— (1976). From Mises to Shackle: An Essay on Austrian Economics and the Kaleidic Society. *Journal of Economic Literature,* 14: 54-62.

———— (1978a). An Austrian Stocktaking: Unsettled Questions and Tentative Answers. In L.M. Spadaro (ed.), *New Directions in Austrian Economics* (pp. 1-8). Kansas City: Sheed Andrews and McMeel Publishers.

———— (1978b). *Capital and Its Structure.* Kansas City: Sheed Andrews and McMeel Publishers.

La Croix, S.J. and Kawaura, A. (1996). Product Patent Reform and Its Impact on Korea's Pharmaceutical Industry. *International Economic Journal,* 10: 109-124.

Leach, D.F. (1992). Concentration and Profits in South Africa: Monopoly or Efficiency? *South African Journal of Economics,* 60: 143-157.

——— (1994). The South African Cement Cartel: A Critique of Fourie and Smith. *South African Journal of Economics,* 62: 254-279.

——— (1997). The Concentration-Profit, Monopoly vs. Efficiency Debate: Some New South African Evidence. *Contemporary Economic Policy,* 15: 12-23.

Leibenstein, H. (1966). Allocative Efficiency vs. "X-Efficiency." *American Economic Review,* 56: 392-415.

Levin, R.C., Klevorick, A.K., Nelson, R.R., and Winter, S.G. (1987). Appropriating the Returns from Industrial Research and Development. *Brookings Papers on Economic Activity,* 3: 783-820.

Liebowitz, S.J. (1982). What Do Census Price-Cost Margins Measure? *Journal of Law and Economics,* 25: 231-246.

Liebowitz, S.J. and Margolis, S.E. (1995). Path Dependence, Lock-In, and History. *Journal of Law, Economics and Organization,* 11: 205-226.

Lindenberg, E.B. and Ross, S.A. (1981). Tobin's q-Ratio and Industrial Organisation. *Journal of Business,* 54: 1-32.

Littlechild, S.C. (1981). Misleading Calculations of the Social Costs of Monopoly Power. *Economic Journal,* 91: 348-363.

Locke, J. ([1698] 1988). *Two Treatises of Government.* Cambridge, UK: Cambridge University Press.

Lu, Z.J. and Comanor, W.S. (1998). Strategic Pricing of New Pharmaceuticals. *Review of Economics and Statistics,* 80: 108-118.

Machlup, F. (1946). Marginal Analysis and Empirical Research. *American Economic Review,* 36: 519-554.

Maloney, M.T. and McCormick, R.E. (1988). Excess Capacity, Cyclical Production, and Merger Motives: Some Evidence from the Capital Markets. *Journal of Law and Economics,* 31: 321-349.

Mandela, N. (1990). Address to South African Business Executives. Speech delivered on 23 May at the Carlton Conference, Business and the ANC, convened by the Consultative Business Movement, Johannesburg.

Mandelbrot, B.B. (1997). *Fractals and Scaling in Finance: Discontinuity, Concentration and Risk.* New York: Springer-Verlag Publishers.

Manne, H.G. (1965). Mergers and the Market for Corporate Control. *Journal of Political Economy,* 73: 110-120.

Mansfield, E. (1985). How Rapidly Does New Industrial Technology Leak Out? *Journal of Industrial Economics,* 34: 217-223.

Mansfield, E., Schwartz, M., and Wagner, S. (1981). Imitation Costs and Patents: An Empirical Study. *Economic Journal,* 91: 907-918.

Mayer, C. (1985). The Assessment: Recent Developments in Industrial Economics and their Implications for Policy. *Oxford Review of Economic Policy,* 1: 1-24.

McManis, C.R. (1998). Intellectual Property and International Mergers and Acquisitions. *University of Cincinnati Law Review,* 66: 1283-1314.

McNulty, P.J. (1967). A Note on the History of Perfect Competition. *Journal of Political Economy,* 75: 395-399.

———— (1968). Economic Theory and the Meaning of Competition. *Quarterly Journal of Economics,* 82: 639-656.

Megna, P. and Mueller, D.C. (1991). Profit Rates and Intangible Capital. *Review of Economics and Statistics,* 73: 632-642.

Melamet, D.A. (1994). *Report of the Commission of Inquiry into the Manner of Providing for Medical Expenses.* Pretoria, South Africa: The Government Printer.

Mill, J.S. ([1871] 1965). *Principles of Political Economy: With Some of Their Applications to Social Philosophy.* Toronto, Canada: University of Toronto Press.

———— ([1859] 1998). *On Liberty and Other Essays.* New York: Oxford University Press.

Minford, P. (1992). Introduction. In M.C. Burstall and I.S.T. Senior (eds.), *Undermining Innovation: Parallel Trade in Prescription Medicines.* London: IEA Health and Welfare Unit.

Mitchell, M.L. and Mulherin, J.H. (1996). The Impact of Industry Shocks on Takeover and Restructuring Activity. *Journal of Financial Economics,* 41: 193-229.

Mittermaier, K. (1986). Mechanomorphism. In I.M. Kirzner (ed.), *Subjectivism, Intelligibility and Economic Understanding: Essays in Honour of Ludwig M. Lachmann on his Eightieth Birthday.* London: Macmillan Press Publishers, UK.

Morgan, E.J. (2001). A Decade of EC Merger Control. *International Journal of the Economics of Business,* 8: 451-473.

Nash, J. (1950). The Bargaining Problem. *Econometrica,* 18: 155-162.

———— (1951). Non-Cooperative Games. *Annals of Mathematics,* 54: 286-295.

———— (1953). Two-Person Cooperative Games. *Econometrica,* 21: 128-140.

NERA (1997). Market Segmentation. In J.L. Valverde (ed.), *Price Controls for Medicines and the Single Market* (147-196). Madrid, Spain: Centro de Estudios de Derecho Europeo Farmaceutico.

Niskanen, W.A. (1971). *Bureaucracy and Representative Government.* Chicago, IL: Aldine-Atherton Publishing.

Obstfeld, M. and Rogoff, K. (1995). Exchange Rate Dynamics Redux. *Journal of Political Economy,* 103(3): 624-660.

OECD (1981). *Multinational Enterprises, Governments and Technology: The Pharmaceutical Industry.* Paris, France: Organization for Economic Co-operation and Development.

———— (1996a). *Abuse of Dominance and Monopolisation.* Paris, France: Organisation for Economic Co-operation and Development.

———— (1996b). *Competition Policy and Efficiency Claims in Horizontal Agreements.* Paris, France: Organisation for Economic Co-operation and Development.

———— (1999). *Oligopoly.* Paris, France: Organisation for Economic Co-operation and Development.

———— (2001). *Competition and Regulation Issues in the Pharmaceutical Industry.* Paris, France: Organisation for Economic Co-operation and Development.

Ott, R.L. (1993). *An Introduction to Statistical Methods and Data Analysis,* Fourth Edition. Boston: PWS-Kent Publishers.

Pashigian, P. (1969). The Effect of Market Size on Concentration. *International Economic Review,* 10: 291-314.

Phlips, L. (1983). *The Economics of Price Discrimination: Four Essays in Applied Price Theory.* New York: Cambridge University Press.

Pigou, A.C. (1960). *The Economics of Welfare,* Fourth Edition. London: Macmillan & Co. Publishers.

Pindyck, R.S. and Rubinfeld, D.L. (1995). *Microeconomics,* Third Edition. Upper Saddle River, NJ: Prentice-Hall Publishers.

Plant, A. (1934). The Economic Theory Concerning Patents for Inventions. *Economica,* 1: 30-51.

Posner, R.A. (1974). Theories of Economic Regulation. *Bell Journal of Economics,* 5: 335-358.

———— (1975). The Social Costs of Monopoly and Regulation. *Journal of Political Economy,* 83: 807-827.

Public Protector, The (1997). *Report 6: Report on the Propriety of the Conduct of Members of the Ministry and Department of Health Relating to Statements in Connection with the Prices of Medicines and Utilisation of Generic Medicines in South Africa.* Pretoria, South Africa: The Public Protector.

Ramsey, F.P. (1927). A Contribution to the Theory of Taxation. *Economic Journal,* 37: 47-61.

Reekie, W.D. (1978). Price and Quality Competition in the United States Drug Industry. *Journal of Industrial Economics,* 26: 223-237.

———— (1979). Industry, Prices & Markets. Oxon, UK: Philip Allan Publishers.

———— (1981). Innovation and Pricing in the Dutch Drug Industry. *Managerial and Decision Economics,* 2: 49-56.

———— (1989). *Industrial Economics: A Critical Introduction to Corporate Enterprise in Europe and America.* Cheltenham, England: Edward Elgar Publishing.

———— (1995). *Prescribing the Price of Pharmaceuticals.* London: IEA Health and Welfare Unit.

———— (1996). *Medicine Prices and Innovations: An International Survey.* London: IEA Health and Welfare Unit.

———— (1997). Cartels, Spontaneous Price Discrimination and International Pharmacy Retailing. *International Journal of the Economics of Business,* 4: 279-285.

———— (1998). A View on the Treatment of Collusive and Restrictive Practices in Competition Policy. *South African Journal of Economic and Managment Sciences,* 1: 8-35.

———— (1999). The Competition Act, 1998: An Economic Perspective. *South African Journal of Economics,* 67: 257-288.

———— (2000). *Monopoly and Competition Policy,* Second Edition. Johannesburg: Free Market Foundation.

Reekie, W.D. and Allen, D.E. (1985). Generic Substitution in the U.K. Pharmaceutical Industry: A Markovian Analysis. *Managerial and Decision Economics,* 6: 93-101.

Reekie, W.D. and Crook, J.N. (1995). *Managerial Economics: A European Text,* Fourth Edition. London: Prentice Hall Publishers.

Ricardo, D. ([1817] 1932). *Principles of Political Economy and Taxation.* London: G. Bell and Sons Ltd.

Robinson, J. (1934). *The Economics of Imperfect Competition.* London: Macmillan Publishers.

Roe, M.J. (1990). Political and Legal Restraints on Ownership and Control of Public Companies. *Journal of Financial Economics,* 27: 7-41.

Ropke, W. (1963). *Economics of the Free Society.* Chicago: Henry Regnery Company.

Ruggles, N. (1950). Recent Developments in the Theory of Marginal Cost Pricing. *Review of Economic Studies,* 17: 107-126.

Salop, S.C. (1979). Monopolistic Competition with Outside Goods. *Bell Journal of Economics,* 10: 141-156.

——— (1987). Symposium on Mergers and Antitrust. *Economic Perspectives,* 1: 3-12.

Say, J.B. ([1880] 1964). *A Treatise on Political Economy or the Production, Distribution & Consumption of Wealth.* New York: Augustus M. Kelley—Sentry Press.

Scherer, F.M. (1965). Firm Size, Market Structure, Opportunity, and the Output of Patented Inventions. *American Economic Review,* 55: 1097-1123.

——— (1980). *Industrial Market Structure and Economic Performance,* Second Edition. Boston: Houghton Mifflin Publishers.

——— (1988). Corporate Takeovers: The Efficiency Arguments. *Journal of Economic Perspectives,* 2: 69-82.

——— (1996). *Industry Structure, Strategy, and Public Policy.* New York: Harper Collins College Publishers.

Schmalensee, R. (1981). Output and Welfare Implications of Monopolistic Third-Degree Price Discrimination. *American Economic Review,* 71: 242-247.

——— (1987). Horizontal Merger Policy: Problems and Changes. *Economic Perspectives,* 1: 41-54.

Schumpeter, J.A. ([1911] 1961). *The Theory of Economic Development: An Inquiry into Profit, Capital, Credit, Interest, and the Business Cycle.* New York: Oxford University Press.

——— (1949). *Capitalism, Socialism, and Democracy.* London: Unwin University Books.

——— (1950). The March into Socialism. *American Economic Review,* 40: 446-456.

Schwert, G.W. (1996). Mark-up Pricing in Mergers and Acquisitions. *Journal of Financial Economics,* 41: 153-192.

Scott, D.R. and Reekie, W.D. (1985). Competition in Atomistic and Oligopsonistic Markets: The South African Pharmaceutical Industry. *South African Journal of Economics,* 53: 39-54.

——— (1987). Savings from Generic Drug Substitution in the RSA—Is It Cost Justified? *South African Medical Journal,* 71: 314-316.

Scott Morton, F.M. (1999). Entry Decisions in the Generic Pharmaceutical Industry. *Rand Journal of Economics,* 30: 421-440.

Shackle, G.L.S. (1949). *Expectation in Economics.* Cambridge, UK: Cambridge University Press.

Sheshinski, E. (1986). Positive Second-Best Theory: A Brief Survey of the Theory of Ramsey Pricing. In K.J. Arrow and M.D. Intriligator (eds.), *Handbook of Mathematical Economics,* Volume 3 (1251-1280). Amsterdam, the Netherlands: Elsevier Science Publishers B.V. (North-Holland).

Shih, M.S.H. (1995). Conglomerate Mergers and Under-performance Risk: A Note. *Quarterly Review of Economics and Finance,* 35: 225-231.

Shleifer, A. and Vishny, R.W. (1988). Value Maximization and the Acquisition Process. *Journal of Economic Perspectives,* 2(1): 7-19.

Smith, A. ([1812] 1937). *An Inquiry into the Nature and Causes of the Wealth of Nations.* London: Ward, Lock & Co. Publishers.

Snyman, H.W.Y. (1962). *Report of the Commission of Inquiry into High Cost of Medical Services and Medicines.* Pretoria, South Africa: The Government Printer.

South African Department of Health (1998). *Essential Drugs Programme: South African Standard Treatment Guidelines and Essential Drug List.* Cape Town, South Africa: CTP Book Printers.

South African Reserve Bank (2000). *Quarterly Bulletin,* Pretoria, South Africa: The Government Printer.

Statistics South Africa (1999). *Census of Manufacturing, 1996,* Pretoria, South Africa: The Government Printer.

——— (2000). *Bulletin of Statistics, 2000,* Pretoria, South Africa: The Government Printer.

——— (2001). *Input-Output Tables, 1998,* Pretoria, South Africa: The Government Printer.

Steenkamp, W.F.J. (1978). *Report of the Commission of Inquiry into the Pharmaceutical Industry.* Pretoria, South Africa: The Government Printer.

Stigler, G.J. (1950). Monopoly and Oligopoly by Merger. *American Economic Association,* 40: 23-34.

——— (1956). The Statistics of Monopoly and Merger. *Journal of Political Economy,* 64: 33-40.

——— (1961a). The Economics of Information. *Journal of Political Economy,* 69: 213-225.

——— (1961b). *The Theory of Price,* Revised Edition. New York: Macmillan Publishers.

——— (1964). A Theory of Oligopoly. *Journal of Political Economy,* 72: 44-61.

——— (1968). *The Organisation of Industry.* Chicago: University of Chicago Press.

——— (1988). *The Theory of Economic Regulation.* Chicago: Chicago Studies in Political Economy, University of Chicago Press.

Stillman, R. (1983). Examining Antitrust Policy Towards Horizontal Mergers. *Journal of Financial Economics,* 11: 225-240.

Suslow, V.Y. (2000). Cartel Contract Duration: Empirical Evidence from International Cartels. Working Paper, University of Michigan Business School.

Tirole, J. (1998). *The Theory of Industrial Organisation.* Cambridge, MA: MIT Press.

Tollman, P., Guy, P., Altshuler, J., Flanagan, A., and Steiner, M. (2001). *A Revolution in R&D: How Genomics and Genetics Are Transforming the Biopharmaceutical Industry.* Boston: Boston Consulting Group.

Train, K.E. (1994). *Optimal Regulation: The Economic Theory of Natural Monopoly.* Cambridge, MA: MIT Press.

Tullock, G. (1967). The Welfare Costs of Tariffs, Monopolies and Theft. *Western Economic Journal,* 5: 224-232.

———— (1993). *Rent Seeking.* Cheltenham, England: Edward Elgar Publishing.

UNIDO (1992). *The World's Pharmaceutical Industries: An International Perspective on Innovation, Competition, and Policy.* Vienna, Austria: United Nations Industrial Development Organization.

U.S. Congress, Office of Technology Assessment (1993). *Pharmaceutical R&D: Costs, Risks and Rewards.* Washington, DC: U.S. Government Printing Office.

U.S. Department of Justice (1977). *Report on the Robinson-Patman Act.* Washington, DC: U.S. Government Printing Office.

Varian, H.R. (1985). Price Discrimination and Social Welfare. *American Economic Review,* 75: 870-875.

———— (1989). Price Discrimination. In R. Schmalensee and R.D. Willig (eds.), *Handbook of Industrial Organisation,* Volume 1. Amsterdam, the Netherlands: Elsevier Science Publishers BV (North-Holland).

Vickers, J. (1985). Strategic Competition Among the Few—Some Recent Developments in the Economics of Industry. *Oxford Review of Economic Policy,* 1: 39-62.

Vickrey, W. (1948). Some Objections to Marginal Cost Pricing. *Journal of Political Economy,* 56: 218-238.

Von Mises, L. (1949). *Human Action—A Treatise on Economics.* London: William Hodge and Company Ltd.

Von Stackelberg, H. ([1934] 1952). *The Theory of the Market Economy.* London: William Hodge and Company Ltd.

Von Weizsäcker, C.C. (1980). A Welfare Analysis of Barriers to Entry. *Bell Journal of Economics,* 11: 399-420.

Weissman, R. (1996). A Long, Strange TRIPS: The Pharmaceutical Industry Drive to Harmonize Global Intellectual Property Rules, and the Remaining WTO Legal Alternatives Available to Third World Countries. *University of Pennsylvania Journal of International Economic Law,* 17: 1069-1125.

Werden, G.J. and Froeb, L.M. (1998). The Entry-Inducing Effects of Horizontal Mergers: An Exploratory Analysis. *Journal of Industrial Economics,* 46: 525-543.

White, L.J. (1987). Antitrust and Merger Policy: A Review and Critique. *Economic Perspectives,* 13-22.

WHO (1999). *Essential Drugs Monitor,* Number 27. Geneva, Switzerland: World Health Organization.

Williamson, O.E. (1968). Economics As an Antitrust Defense: The Welfare Trade-offs. *American Economic Review,* 58: 18-36.

Williamson, O.E. (1979). Transaction-Cost Economics: The Governance of Contractual Relations. *Journal of Law and Economics,* 22: 233-261.

——— (1988). The Logic of Economic Organization. *Journal of Law, Economics, and Organization,* 4: 65-89.

Winter, S.G. (1988). On Coase, Competence, and the Corporation. *Journal of Law, Economics, and Organization,* 4: 163-179.

WTO/WHO (2002). *WTO Agreements and Public Health.* Geneva, Switzerland: World Trade Organization and World Health Organization.

Index

Page numbers followed by the letter "f" indicate figures; those followed by the letter "t" indicate tables.

© 2006 by The Haworth Press, Inc. All rights reserved.
doi:10.1300/5505_18

Concentration ratio
pharmaceutical industry
microeconomic study, private
sector, 248, 253-255,
255t-257t, 259-261, 259t
pharmaceutical industry
microeconomic study, public
sector, 267-274, 269t-273t
purpose of, 161-162
Consumption, in price discrimination,
144
Consumption stance, 169-170
Convergence. *See* Cartels; Collusion
Copies. *See* Imitations
Copyrights, 40. *See also* Patents
Costs
absolute cost advantages. *See*
Absolute cost advantages
agency, 99
average cost changes, 51
average fixed, 134-135
average variable, 16, 17f, 128-131
common costs, 134, 143-144
innovative cost reduction, 51-53
marginal. *See* Marginal costs
opportunity, 80
overhead, 143-144
pharmaceutical patents, 226
pricing below cost, 128-131
recoupment of, 143-144, 146-147,
187-189, 197, 223
research and development, 34-36,
34t, 35t
social. *See* Social costs
sources of lower costs, 85-86
sunk costs, 72-73
Cournot, A., 91-105
Cournot model
assumptions, 91, 94
Bertrand response, 109-111
collusion, 93-94
correctness of assumptions, 97
economic welfare, 93
formulas, 91
horizontal mergers, 116
mergers and acquisitions, 98, 99-101

Cournot model *(continued)*
original text, 94-96
overview, 121, 283-284
perfectly competitive output, 92t
perfectly competitive surplus, 92t,
93t
pharmaceutical industry, private
sector, 179, 180
prevailing monopoly, 97
principal-agent framework, 98-101
profit, 97-98
public sector, 185
quantity control, 96
rivalry in a single period, 96-97
use of algebra, 97
Williamson trade-off conjecture,
101-105, 101f
Cournot's Case, 107
Cowling, K., 215, 216
Cronbach's alpha, 261, 274
Crook, J. N., 23, 23f, 24
Cross-elasticity of demand and supply,
45, 169-172

Danzon, P. M., 134, 198
Data shortages, market concentration
calculations, 167-169, 168t
De Bornier, J. M., 94, 110, 111
De Villiers, J. U., 146, 175, 188
Dean, J., 43, 44, 50, 130
Demand
Clemens-Cocks model of pricing,
44-50, 46f, 47f
conditions in Von Stackelberg
model, 107
creation of, 132-133
diversion, 133
in perfect competition, 15, 16f
product differentiation, 63-64
Demsetz, H., 113, 114, 115
Demsetz hypothesis, 115
Denmark, pharmaceutical markets, 178
Department of Justice, 154
Development Bank of Southern Africa
report, 217

Order a copy of this book with this form or online at:
http://www.haworthpress.com/store/product.asp?sku=5505

THE ECONOMICS OF COMPETITION
The Race to Monopoly

_____in hardbound at $49.95 (ISBN-13: 978-0-7890-2788-7; ISBN-10: 0-7890-2788-7)

_____in softbound at $39.95 (ISBN-13: 978-0-7890-2789-4; ISBN-10: 0-7890-2789-5)

Or order online and use special offer code HEC25 in the shopping cart.

COST OF BOOKS_____

☐ **BILL ME LATER:** (Bill-me option is good on US/Canada/Mexico orders only; not good to jobbers, wholesalers, or subscription agencies.)

☐ Check here if billing address is different from shipping address and attach purchase order and billing address information.

POSTAGE & HANDLING_____
(US: $4.00 for first book & $1.50 for each additional book)
(Outside US: $5.00 for first book & $2.00 for each additional book)

Signature_____

SUBTOTAL_____

☐ **PAYMENT ENCLOSED: $_____**

IN CANADA: ADD 7% GST_____

☐ **PLEASE CHARGE TO MY CREDIT CARD.**

STATE TAX_____
(NJ, NY, OH, MN, CA, IL, IN, PA, & SD residents, add appropriate local sales tax)

☐ Visa ☐ MasterCard ☐ AmEx ☐ Discover
☐ Diner's Club ☐ Eurocard ☐ JCB

Account # _____

FINAL TOTAL_____
(If paying in Canadian funds, convert using the current exchange rate, UNESCO coupons welcome)

Exp. Date_____

Signature_____

Prices in US dollars and subject to change without notice.

NAME_____

INSTITUTION_____

ADDRESS_____

CITY_____

STATE/ZIP_____

COUNTRY_____ COUNTY (NY residents only)_____

TEL_____ FAX_____

E-MAIL_____

May we use your e-mail address for confirmations and other types of information? ☐ Yes ☐ No
We appreciate receiving your e-mail address and fax number. Haworth would like to e-mail or fax special discount offers to you, as a preferred customer. **We will never share, rent, or exchange your e-mail address or fax number.** We regard such actions as an invasion of your privacy.

Order From Your Local Bookstore or Directly From
The Haworth Press, Inc.
10 Alice Street, Binghamton, New York 13904-1580 • USA
TELEPHONE: 1-800-HAWORTH (1-800-429-6784) / Outside US/Canada: (607) 722-5857
FAX: 1-800-895-0582 / Outside US/Canada: (607) 771-0012
E-mail to: orders@haworthpress.com

For orders outside US and Canada, you may wish to order through your local
sales representative, distributor, or bookseller.
For information, see http://haworthpress.com/distributors

(Discounts are available for individual orders in US and Canada only, not booksellers/distributors.)

PLEASE PHOTOCOPY THIS FORM FOR YOUR PERSONAL USE.
http://www.HaworthPress.com   BOF06